Christopher Andersen

MADONNA

unauthorized

SIMON & SCHUSTER
NEW YORK   LONDON
TORONTO   SYDNEY
TOKYO   SINGAPORE

For Kate and Kelly

"Power is a great aphrodisiac,
and I'm a very powerful person."

1

"I'd rather walk through a fire than
around it."

The event had been mapped out with all the secrecy and precision of a preemptive military strike. Invitations, featuring a crude drawing by the groom's brother of the couple in a sort of *American Gothic* pose, asked friends to come to a joint "birthday party" (his twenty-fifth, her twenty-seventh) on August 16, 1985, for actor Sean Penn and Madonna. "The Need for Privacy and a Desire to Keep You Hanging," read the invitations, "Prevents the Los Angeles Location from Being Announced Until One Day Prior."

Even the caterer, Beverly Hills' celebrated Spago restaurant, was kept in the dark until the last minute. Spago owner Wolfgang Puck was given photographs of the wedding site and maps of the layout so he could plan the food service, but only at the final hour was he actually given a specific address.

News operations scrambled frantically to discover the wedding site. The Malibu Colony home of Sean's parents, producer Leo Penn and his wife, Eileen, was staked out—although reporters were stopped at the curb by a guard armed with a .357 magnum handgun. The equally well-guarded Malibu home of Sean's friend and fellow "Brat Pack" member Timothy Hutton was another possibility. Then rumors began to fly that the ceremony was to be held at a church, igniting a flurry of calls to local parishes. When the appointed day arrived, tipped off in advance by guest Andy Warhol to the real location of the secret site, an army of journalists descended on 6970 Wildlife Road, the palatial, $6.5-million clifftop home of real estate developer and Penn family friend Dan Unger.

Fittingly, the scene at the Unger home more closely resembled a war than a wedding. While armed security guards scanned the horizon with infrared binoculars looking for intruders—namely, members of the press—their blazer-clad brethren checked the credentials of each guest who passed through the ten-foot-high steel gates. Reporters dressed as waiters climbed over the walls, picked up silver trays, and began serving sushi and Cristal champagne to the guests. An Italian photographer, his face blackened and wearing full battlefield camouflage, had crouched in the bushes for seventeen hours, only to be summarily kicked off the premises— sans film—forty minutes before the ceremony began.

It would not be so easy to banish the battalion of press helicopters that churned overhead, sending down a swirling backwash and drowning out even the Pacific's roar. The publicity-loathing Penn, enraged at the presence of the helicopters, ran down to the beach and scrawled FUCK OFF in twenty-foot-high letters in the sand. For nearly a half hour, he paced up and down the beach, shaking his fists at the choppers and yelling profanities. "He went," in the words of one guest, "completely nuts." Then he returned to the house, loaded a semiautomatic pistol, and crept out into the bushes commando-style.

On the verge of hysteria, Madonna pleaded with Penn to put the gun away. Instead, he screamed obscenities at her and shoved her out of the way. He then proceeded to empty the gun in the direction of the helicopters. "I'd love to see one of those helicopters burn," he told his stunned bride-to-be, "and the bodies inside melt." All the shots missed their mark. "I think he was basically firing warning shots, trying to scare us off," one of the airborne reporters recalled, "but it's still a miracle that one of the helicopters didn't crash and burn right in front of the wedding party."

However shocking Penn's pistol-waving antics may have been, Madonna was not exactly the model of decorum; on more than one occasion, she took the opportunity to flip her middle finger skyward. Penn, now turning on those around him, demanded to know "who screwed up." His bride-to-be reminded him that, had he followed her suggestion and allowed in one or two photographers, the air assault might have been forestalled. It was not a concession to be expected of a man who routinely attacked photographers and refused to do interviews even to promote his own films.

When a guest asked the couple, who had been house-hunting in Malibu, if they planned to circle their property with a tall fence, Penn answered unhesitatingly. "A fence, nothing," he said with an unsettling grin. "We're going to have gun towers."

At six-thirty P.M., with 220 friends, family members, and some of Madonna's former lovers of both sexes gathered poolside, the couple appeared for the ceremony. He was clad in a $695 double-breasted Gianni Versace tuxedo purchased off the rack at a Rodeo Drive boutique. She wore an off-white gown with a ten-foot train, a pink-and-silver sash covered with dried roses and semiprecious jewels, and a jaunty black bowler hat.

Prophetically, Madonna and Sean Penn stood on the brink of a cliff to exchange wedding vows before Judge John Merrick. "Although there will be times that your moods may falter," he told them, "and you'll question each other's motives, the faith and love that you share will help to show that your inconsistency is only for the moment." Then, to the pulsating strains of "Chariots of Fire," the groom lifted his bride's veil and kissed her. The guests, who had not heard the vows over the din of the invading choppers, leapt to their feet and cheered.

Moments later, the newly married couple materialized on a balcony of the house. He welcomed their guests to "the remaking of *Apocalypse Now*," then toasted "the most beautiful woman in the world" with champagne before ungallantly sticking his head up Madonna's dress in search of her garter (which was dutifully caught by his little brother, actor Chris Penn). After the mandatory bouquet toss (it was snatched by Madonna's look-alike younger sister, Paula), everyone retired to a white open-air tent to dine on caviar, broiled swordfish, rack of lamb, lobster ravioli, and curried oysters—all downed with a Pinot Noir from northern California's Madonna vineyards. The all-white theme extended to the tablecloths, bunting, even the floral arrangements, and at the center of every table was a bejeweled gold Cinderella slipper—a copy of the bride's own handmade high heels. An entire room of the house was filled with wedding gifts, including an antique jukebox, tableware (Madonna had registered with Tiffany for dinnerware in the Carnival and Monet patterns), and a graffiti-covered silkscreen by Andy Warhol and Keith Haring showing a *New York Post* headline that read, "Madonna on Nude Pix: So What?!"

"It was the right mixture of everybodies and nobodies," recalled Warhol, who came as the "date" of Madonna's onetime roommate and friend Martin Burgoyne. "Really, it was the most exciting thing ever. . . .You could see everybody who was there, it was under a tent, and it wasn't too crowded. And those young actors seemed like they were in their fathers' suits, like Emilio Estevez and Tom Cruise." Indeed, the roster of "somebodies"—including Cher, Martin Sheen, Rob Lowe, Carrie Fisher, Christopher Walken, Rosanna Arquette (Madonna's costar in the film *Desperately Seeking Susan*), record mogul David Geffen, Timothy Hutton, David Letterman, and Diane Keaton—was impressive by design. Never one to leave anything to chance, Madonna had consulted a number of Hollywood insiders before deciding who was important enough to attend, then drew up the guest list herself—including the names of several stars she barely knew, and a few she had actually never met.

No matter. Cher, for one, was clearly thrilled to be asked to what some were already calling the Hollywood wedding of the decade. She was on the verge of yet another comeback, and her attentions to rock's hottest new star bordered on the sycophantic. "Oh, I can't *stand* Cher," Madonna had confided to friends. "I'm so sick of her. She just wants me to write songs for her. She's always calling me up and bothering me. But I guess I'd better invite her." At the wedding, about to cut the five-tiered hazelnut wedding cake, Madonna turned to Cher and blurted, "Hey, you've done this before. Do you cut just one piece or do you have to slice up the whole thing?"

When it came time for the bride and groom's wedding dance, the evening's deejay played Sarah Vaughan's soulful "I'm Crazy About the Boy." While the newlyweds spun around the dance floor that had been constructed over the tennis courts, Madonna flashed the wildly colored silk slip she wore beneath her dress. Then her husband entertained the crowd with what he called his "three-minute John Travolta impression."

Meanwhile, several of the guests, Madonna's closest cronies from her down-and-dirty early days in New York, gossiped about the marriage and what they all saw as its slim chance for success. "The other relationships weren't right because they weren't fifty-fifty," Martin Burgoyne speculated. "This one is. Neither one of them is in control; she can learn from him, and he can learn from her."

Burgoyne's optimism notwithstanding, Penn had never concealed his contempt for Madonna's crowd (particularly Burgoyne, whose presence in Madonna's life would later spark several marital spats). Penn routinely dismissed Burgoyne and company as "faggots, dykes, and freaks." And while theirs was one of the most publicized show business romances in history, it nonetheless came as a shock to even Madonna's closest friends when the couple issued a press release announcing their engagement. "She hadn't told any of us that she was seriously thinking of marrying this guy," a longtime friend said. "He was always so menacing, so violent—he could be such an insufferable asshole. Nobody from Madonna's world liked him, and I guess she knew it."

While the revelers danced below, in a powder room upstairs in the house, Madonna's longtime confidante and makeup person, Debi Mazar (known to everyone as Debi M.), was trying to wash Steve Rubell's vomit off her dress. Rubell, who had gained notoriety in the 1970s as the owner of New York's Studio 54 nightclub, had consumed too many Quääludes and thrown up on the limo ride from the Beverly Hills Hotel. Helping Debi M. was another close compatriot of Madonna's from New York, Erica Bell.

Enter Paula Ciccone. Gazing into the bathroom mirror as she

fixed her lipstick, Madonna's younger sister flew into a jealous rage. "I can't believe this is happening. This should be *my* wedding day, not *hers*," she seethed. "*I* should be the famous one. This should be *my* career. All this attention should have been *mine!*"

Madonna's girlfriends squirmed uncomfortably. "Honestly," Erica Bell said, "it was like a scene straight out of *Whatever Happened to Baby Jane?* It was totally crazy. We all just sort of looked at each other and said, 'Gee, she can't be serious.' Debi M. and I sort of backed out of the room. From then on, I always feared Paula might actually do something to Madonna—she was that insanely jealous of her sister's success."

At the vortex of this swirling chaos, like the quiet eye of a tropical hurricane, stood Madonna herself. Her skeptical New York cohorts notwithstanding, the bride managed, by sheer force of will, to persuade practically everyone present that somehow this bizarre union of two phenomenally temperamental stars could be made to work. Judge Merrick, for one, was convinced. "I felt they were as much in love as any couple I've married," he said, "and I've married hundreds of them."

Nevertheless, her undying devotion to Penn had not kept Madonna from instructing her lawyers to draw up an ironclad prenuptial agreement. "Of course I have much more money than he does," she told friends at the time, "and I'll have even more by the time this thing is over." Madonna, after all, had built her career on taking risks—so long as they were calculated ones.

The ensuing marriage would, of course, rank as one of the most turbulent and acrimonious even in a town fabled for its matrimonial catastrophes. Over the next four years the "Poison Penns," as they would come to be known, would veer from one headline-grabbing scandal to the next before finally falling victim to a lethal combination of alcohol, violence, and jealousy. Yet, on her wedding day, Madonna showed not a flicker of doubt. Why should she? She was already being compared to another legendary sex symbol, and to a large extent that comparison seemed valid. Madonna may well be a Marilyn Monroe for our times, but a Marilyn with a difference: Madonna, as Sean Penn and the rest of the planet would eventually learn, is nobody's victim.

2

"I have the same goal I've had since I
was a little girl: I want to rule
the world!"

"Are you ready?"
"*Si!*"
"Are you hot?"
"*SIIII!*"
"Good. Me, too. *Allora, andiamo!*"
With that, Madonna, clad in a black corset and stiletto heels,
twirled, strutted, and prowled before a screaming audience of
65,000 Italian fans jammed into a Turin soccer stadium on a hot
summer evening in September 1987. Two hours later, she got her
biggest ovation of the evening by telling her audience the one
thing they longed to hear: "*Io sono fiera di essere italiana!*" (I'm
proud to be an Italian.)
Signs of rampant hysteria were evident earlier in the day, when
police turned firehoses on thousands of fans who gathered outside
the stadium hoping for even a fleeting glimpse of Italy's favorite
daughter. "Animals," a weary officer muttered under his breath as
a dozen unconscious young "wannabe" Madonnas were passed
over the heads of the crowd to the relative safety of a hastily set up
Red Cross station.

While mayhem reigned outside the stadium, Madonna quietly met backstage with a couple of distant cousins and a solemn delegation of townspeople who presented her with a piece of parchment proclaiming her an honorary citizen of Pacentro, the tiny village her grandparents had emigrated from sixty-eight years before. One resident of Pacentro who had declined to make the pilgrimage to Turin was Madonna's eighty-two-year-old great-aunt, Bambina De Guilio. "Of course I'd like to see her and hug her—after all, it is an honor to have such a famous relation," she told a Rome newspaper, adding that she was just too weak to make the journey to Turin. When pressed, however, Bambina revealed her true opinion of Madonna: "What do you want from me? The girl is a singer, just a singer. In my times, we didn't behave like that!"

Three months after Madonna's departure from Italy, the people of Pacentro would still be squabbling over their most famous descendant. This time, however, the focus was not Madonna herself but a thirteen-foot-tall bronze statue proposed to honor the singer in the town square. At a Rome press conference, sculptor Walter Pugni unveiled his scale model for the planned statue, a scantily dressed Madonna singing into a microphone. At her feet: a battered suitcase held together with string—a symbol of the twenty thousand emigrants who had fled Pacentro for America, leaving the sun-washed medieval hamlet in Italy's impoverished Abruzzi region with a population of scarcely two thousand.

The bearded artist could barely contain his emotion as he described in detail his plans for the dedication ceremonies, complete with operatic accompaniment. One thing Pugni did not dwell on, however, was the cost—some $416,000, which, the statue's proponents insisted, could be raised from private contributors in Italy and the United States. Such a monument would also, Pugni argued, put sleepy Pacentro on the tourist map.

The local parish priest, Don Giuseppe Lepore, was the first to speak out against the proposed shrine to the not-so-virginal Madonna. Echoing the sentiments of the Vatican, which had already condemned the singer's flaunting of crucifixes and other religious symbols as sacrilegious, Don Giuseppe warned that any such figure would forever mark Pacentro as a modern-day Sodom.

For his part, Mayor Raffaele Santini opposed the statue on the grounds that it would bring "ridicule" on the community. Moreover, after he had gone to the trouble of personally bestowing honorary citizenship on Madonna, she had never even bothered to express her gratitude—either in person or in writing. "Madonna," Mayor Santini said bitterly, "has taken no interest in the problems of our town."

Gaetano and Michelina Ciccone could never have guessed when they left Pacentro for a new life in the New World that, sixty-eight years later, a controversy over their granddaughter would threaten to tear the town apart. Nor could they have imagined that their own flesh and blood would be simultaneously adored and reviled by millions, the object of endless scrutiny and speculation, a perpetual source of scandal and heated debate—in short, the most famous and talked-about woman of her generation.

Yet the roots of Madonna's magic ran deep in the soil of Pacentro, and in the strict Roman Catholic beliefs her paternal grandparents brought with them to America. Uneducated and unable to speak English, the Ciccones settled in the Pittsburgh suburb of Aliquippa, where Gaetano was able to find work in a steel mill. There, while they were living in one of the crowded, sooty tenements of Aliquippa's Italian neighborhood, Silvio was born on June 2, 1931—the youngest of the Ciccones' six sons, and the only one, it would turn out, to get a college education.

Since their parents never even attempted to learn the language of their adopted country, all the Ciccone offspring were proficient in Italian as well as English. Always more ambitious than his siblings—a trait he would eventually pass on to his eldest daughter—lanky, dark, aquiline-featured Silvio Ciccone appeared determined from an early age to shake whatever stigma remained from his immigrant-family upbringing. Working at a variety of jobs to pay his college tuition, Silvio was known to everyone outside the family by the less alien-sounding "Tony."

Like another Pennsylvania-born son of Italian immigrants named Lee Iacocca, hard-driving Tony Ciccone headed north to Detroit in search of a lucrative engineering job in the booming automobile industry. He found it as an optics and defense engineer with Chrysler, working on various weapons contracts with the government at the company's missile and tank plant in Warren, Michigan.

With memories of the Korean War still vivid and the draft remaining in effect, Tony Ciccone sought to fulfill his military obligation by joining the Air Force reserves. After duty in Alaska, he was briefly stationed in Texas. There, at the wedding of service buddy Dale Fortin, he was introduced to Fortin's little sister, and young Tony Ciccone was instantly smitten. She was a fragile beauty, with flowing dark hair, wide-set blue eyes, and a porcelain complexion. There was an ethereal quality about her, and that extended to her unforgettable name—Madonna Louise. She was not Italian. Her family, which lived in Bay City, Michigan, was French Canadian in origin.

Undaunted by the fact that she was already engaged to another man, Tony Ciccone began dating Madonna Fortin. Within a week of their first meeting, she broke off her engagement. Not long after, in 1955, Madonna Louise Fortin and Tony Ciccone were married at Bay City's Visitation Church. The couple moved into a cramped brick bungalow at 443 Thors Street in the suburb of Pontiac, some twenty-five miles northwest of Detroit. A year later, on May 3, 1956, their first child, Anthony, arrived, followed on August 9, 1957, by a second son, whom they named Martin.

In August 1958, Madonna Ciccone was again nine months pregnant. This time, she wanted the Fortin family physician, then sixty-two-year-old Dr. Abraham H. Jacoby, to deliver her baby. By prearrangement, the Ciccones journeyed to Bay City and awaited the baby's arrival at the home of Madonna's maternal grandmother, Elsie Fortin.

Unlike Pontiac, Bay City was a picturesque port community whose quiet, tree-lined streets were dotted with Georgian and Victorian mansions built by Midwest lumber barons during the turn of the century. But the town had not entirely escaped modern problems; Grandma Elsie (called Na-noo by all thirty-four of her grandchildren) lived downwind from the Dow petrochemical plant, and the memory of that aroma would stay with her for a lifetime. Still, the town was for the most part a decidedly suburban, all-American setting for the birth of Tony and Madonna Ciccone's first daughter at Bay City's Mercy Hospital on the morning of August 16, 1958. They named the little girl after her mother and called her Little Nonni to distinguish her from Madonna senior. Thus, contrary to popular belief, Madonna's name was not Italian but French Canadian in origin.

The year Little Nonni was born, Dwight David Eisenhower was halfway through his second term as president, Nikita Khrushchev came to power in the Soviet Union, "Gunsmoke" was the highest-rated series on television, and Elvis Presley was the nation's number one recording artist. It was also a time when the two-income family was a rarity. Yet Madonna Ciccone worked as an X-ray technician, pouring whatever energy she had left into cooking, cleaning, and raising her rapidly growing brood. Another daughter, Paula, was born barely a year after Little Nonni, followed by Christopher in 1960 and Melanie in 1962.

Madonna's earliest memories of life on Thors Street revolved around her mother. Madonna shared a room with her two sisters, and she would often awaken in the middle of the night, wander down the hall, and push her parents' bedroom door open. "They were both asleep in bed," she recalled, "and I think I must have done this a lot, gone in there, because they sort of sat up in bed and said, 'Oh, no, not again,' and I said, 'Can I get in bed between you?' I always went to sleep right away when I slept with them." What Madonna also remembered vividly was that, while her father opposed letting her into their bed, her mother welcomed her. "My mother had a really beautiful red nightgown, silky red. I remember getting into bed and rubbing against her nightgown and going to sleep—just like that. To me that was heaven, to sleep in between my parents."

Madonna was, by all accounts, equal parts nice and naughty as a child. Her first recorded act of hostility occurred when she was barely four. She was sitting in the driveway of the Ciccone house, fuming because her father had told her not to leave the front yard. When a two-year-old girl waddled up and presented her with a dandelion, Madonna shoved the toddler down. "I was so mad because I was being punished, and my first instinct was to lash out at someone who was more helpless than I. I saw in her innocent eyes the chance to get back at some authority." Besides, Madonna hated dandelions because, she said, "they're weeds that run rampant, and I like things that are cultivated."

Another clear recollection Madonna had was of her mother scrubbing the kitchen. "I remember her being a very forgiving, angelic person," she once recalled. "She did all the housecleaning, and she was always picking up after us. We were really messy, awful kids." It was from her mother that Madonna inherited her musical aptitude. "She loved to sing and knew all the words to all the songs," recalled Grandma Elsie Fortin. "That's what I missed most about her [Madonna's mother] when she left home."

Indeed, the Ciccone kids proved a handful—a fact that did not make them particularly popular with the neighbors. Big brothers Anthony (Little Tony) and Martin (Mard) would throw rocks through windows, start fires in the basement, and fight constantly. "I think my parents pissed a lot of people off," Madonna said later, "because they had so many kids and they never screamed at us. My brothers were very rambunctious, but my mother and father would never yell at them. They would just hug us and put their arms around us and talk to us quietly."

Despite their laissez-faire attitude toward their children's mischief, the Ciccones—Tony in particular—adhered to a strict moral code and expected their children to do the same. "My father was very strong," Madonna would remember. "He did have integrity, and if he told us not to do something, he didn't do it, either. A lot of parents . . . give you some idea of sexual modesty—but my father lived that way. He believed that making love to someone is a very sacred thing and it shouldn't happen until after you are married. He stuck by those beliefs, and that represented a very strong person to me. He was my role model."

Above all else, the Ciccones were devout Catholics. From infancy, Little Nonni's environment abounded with all the religious images that she would later employ to such effect in her career— rosary beads, pictures of saints, and most significantly, crucifixes. "Crucifixes are sexy because there's a naked man on them," she later observed. "When I was a little girl, we had crucifixes all over the house . . . Crucifixes are something left over from my child-hood, like a security blanket."

The family was so devout, in fact, that every morning the chil-dren were rousted out of bed around six A.M. so they could attend church for an hour before being bused miles away to parochial school. "It just seemed like such torture," Madonna said. "I mean, school was punishment enough." Grandma Ciccone taught Little Nonni another indelible lesson: "When I was tiny, my grand-mother used to beg me not to go with men, to love Jesus and be a good girl. I grew up with two images of a woman: the virgin and the whore. It was a little scary."

The world became a lot scarier for Little Nonni after her mother, pregnant with Madonna's sister Melanie, was diagnosed with breast cancer. She never complained and in her daughter's words, "never allowed herself to wallow in the tragedy of her situ-ation." After Melanie was born, Madonna Ciccone continued doing her household chores for a time, but as she grew more and more exhausted, she would stop abruptly in the middle of the day and "just sit on the couch," her daughter recalled.

As their mother's illness progressed, all the children grew in-creasingly impatient and confused. "We really tortured her when she was sick, because we wanted her to play with us," Madonna said. "I think little kids do that to people who are really good to them." One afternoon, as her mother sat on the couch, Little Nonni climbed on her back and demanded that they play together. Too tired to move, her mother began to sob. Little Nonni re-sponded by pounding on her mother's back and shouting, "Why are you doing this? Stop being this way, please, please stop, please stop. Be who you used to be. Play with me!"

It was then that Little Nonni realized her mother was crying and wrapped her arms around her. "I remember feeling stronger than she was," said Madonna. "I was so little, and yet I felt like she was the child. I stopped tormenting her after that. I think that made me grow up fast."

Madonna Ciccone spent the final year of her life in the hospital. Even under those emotionally trying circumstances, she was so upbeat—"always cracking up and making jokes"—that the Ciccone kids looked forward to their hospital visits. "She accepted things well," said Grandma Elsie, "because of her deep faith." During one trip to the hospital on December 1, 1963, five-and-a-half-year-old Madonna laughed when her mother, who had been unable to eat anything solid for weeks, jokingly demanded a hamburger. Then the little girl was escorted from the hospital room, and within an hour, her mother was dead. She was thirty. "My father told me she was dead," Madonna recalled, "but you keep waiting for her to come back, and we never all sat down and talked about it. . . . I saw my father cry just once." Madonna later speculated that her mother's on-the-job exposure to X rays may have contributed to her fatal cancer.

Elsie Fortin recalled that her daughter Madonna was "a beautiful girl. Everyone loved her. Her and Tony's marriage was a good one. I don't think they ever had a fight."

From her mother's death on, there was only one Madonna—and she was determined that no one would forget it, least of all her father. "Like all young girls I was in love with my father, and I didn't want to lose him. I lost my mother, but then I was the mother; my father was *mine*."

Madonna's dependence on her father bordered on the obsessive. Still demanding more attention than any of the other Ciccone children, she would crawl into her father's bed in the middle of the night, shivering with fear. It was only then that she could fall asleep, free of a recurring nightmare that someone was out to murder her. "I fell right to sleep," she later explained in her 1991 documentary film *Truth or Dare*, "after he fucked me. Just kidding."

Madonna had no intention of sharing her father's affections—not even with her siblings. "I kept saying, 'If you ever die, I'm going to get buried in the casket with you,' and my father would say, 'Don't talk like that. That's really disgusting.' "

Her father's admonitions were not enough to keep Madonna from dwelling on her own mortality. For the next two years, she became a hypochondriac. She convinced herself that, like her mother, she, too, had cancer. The house became her sanctuary. With the exception of time spent at church or in school, she became frantic and vomited if she left the house for any length of time. "It was," she later observed, "the sickest thing."

Her father continued to be the sole focus of her life. To hold on to Daddy's affections, Madonna learned to hone her feminine wiles. "I knew how to wrap him around my finger. I knew there was another way to go besides saying, 'No, I'm not going to do it,' and I employed those techniques." One of her techniques was to climb up on her father's lap and flirt outrageously. "I flirted with everyone—my uncles, my grandfather, my father, everybody. I was always aware of my female charm."

Another way she secured her place in her father's heart was to excel in school. Madonna's kindergarten teacher at St. Frederick's parochial school, Jo Ann Carpenter, had scribbled a note on her record for her first-grade teacher, Sister Norma: "12/1/63 Mother died. Needs a great deal of love and attention."

Judging by the little girl's academic performance, Sister Norma needn't have worried. Madonna's father rewarded his children with fifty cents for each A each little Ciccone received on his or her report card. Madonna always emerged the big winner. "There was a lot of competition in our family, and I was always vying for my father's attention, so I worked really hard in school. I was a straight-A student, and they all hated me for it . . . I just tried to be the apple of my father's eye. I think that everyone else in my family was very aware of it. And I kind of stood out from them."

That was largely by Madonna's own design. "She was really pretty," recalled Grandma Elsie Fortin, "and did she like attention! She liked attention from the family, and she usually got it. I used to feel sorry for Paula. They'd say, 'Isn't Madonna so pretty?' And there was Paula standing there."

Perhaps as a result of her desire to stand out, Madonna grew up "not feeling particularly close to anybody in my family—like an outsider in my own house." Athletic and aggressive, Paula emerged as the tomboy in the family, perhaps in response to her sister's success at charming their father. Paula then teamed up with her brothers to, in Madonna's words, "torture" her. One favorite trick was to get some clothespins and hang the diminutive Madonna from the backyard clothesline by her underpants. "Or they'd pin me down on the ground and spit in my mouth," she remembered.

Being incessantly picked on was not something Madonna took lightly. She became the family snitch, constantly tattling on her siblings. "I was the sissy," she claimed, "but I was the *loud* sissy. If I didn't like something, I let everybody know it, even then."

Madonna's closest playmate in Pontiac was Moira McPharlin, whose mother, Wanda, had been Madonna Ciccone's best friend. The McPharlins lived two doors away from the Ciccones. The two children put on shows in the backyard and charged tolerant neighbors ten cents admission. One of their favorite costumes was a wedding dress they had exhumed from Wanda's closet. "We fought over who was going to be the star of the show," McPharlin said.

The death of Madonna's mother changed her best friend profoundly, McPharlin recalled. "I remember feeling really bad when her mother died," she said later, "but it probably made her stronger because she hurt so bad. She probably wouldn't be where she is today if her mom hadn't died." Madonna agreed. "My mother's death left me with a certain kind of loneliness, an incredible longing for something. If I hadn't had that emptiness, I wouldn't have been so driven."

For the three years following his wife's death, Tony Ciccone went through a series of housekeepers. None could stomach the incorrigible Ciccone kids—until 1966, when Tony Ciccone hired blond, athletic Joan Gustafson to try her hand at managing his brood. Six months later, he married her.

Madonna, no longer Daddy's one and only, was devastated. She had clung to him for the three years since her mother's untimely death, and now she was replaced by this near-stranger. "My father made us all call her Mom," Madonna said. "I couldn't, I wouldn't say it." At the age of nine, she also suddenly found herself burdened with having to help raise her younger siblings. "I didn't resent having to raise my brothers and sisters as much as I resented the fact that I didn't have my mother. And that my ideal of my family was interrupted." Nor was Joan ready, in Madonna's words, "for a zillion kids who were extremely unwilling to accept her as an authority figure. So it was rough. We all resented it."

The differences between Madonna's mother and Joan were evident to all who knew them. Even while she was undergoing painful and exhausting chemotherapy, Madonna Ciccone "always had a smile on her face," Moira's father, Patrick McPharlin, said. "If you wanted to send a few more kids over to her house, that was always okay." He described Joan as "more of a disciplinarian—but she had to do a lot of work to take care of those kids. We always kidded Tony that he had two saints for wives."

Little Madonna was not so understanding. Feeling emotionally betrayed and abandoned by her father, she turned inward. "It was then that I said, okay, I don't need anybody," she would later reflect. "No one's going to break my heart again. I'm not going to need anybody. I can stand on my own and be my own person and not belong to anyone."

For the next twenty-five years, Madonna kept that promise to herself. If there were hearts to be broken, she would do the breaking. And she did.

3

"The angriest time in my life was my
teen years."

While Madonna struggled with the new family dynamics,
the upwardly mobile Ciccones moved to Rochester, Michigan—
an affluent community not far from the exclusive Detroit suburb
of Bloomfield Hills. By the 1990s, Rochester would be a booming
conglomeration of very upscale housing developments (mostly
newly built minimansions in various styles from Georgian brick to
pillared antebellum), gleaming office parks, shopping malls, and
golf courses—all surrounded by rolling hills and lush farmland.

When the Ciccones arrived in the mid-1960s, however, Rochester still clung to much of its small-town charm. All of the streets
in the housing tract they moved into—one of Rochester's earliest
—were named after states. The Ciccone house stood at the inter-
section of Oklahoma and Texas streets—a two-story brown
clapboard-and-brick colonial with green shutters, a blue front
door, lots of shrubbery, a split-rail fence, and a wagon wheel
embedded in the front lawn. These were hardly the mean streets
Madonna would later claim forged her indestructible persona.

Today the house at 2036 Oklahoma Street is much the same as

it was when Madonna grew up there, right down to children's construction-paper cutouts in the window and the swing set in the yard. Only in 1991, they decorate the day care center Madonna's stepmother Joan operates out of the Ciccone family home.

Back in the late 1960s and 1970s, the Ciccone kids maintained their familiar ritual: up at dawn to put on their uniforms, then straight to church for prayer. Only now, the commute from church to school was not taxing. St. Andrew's—a modernistic structure with a soaring, gull-wing copper roof—was situated directly across a parking lot from the church's bunkerlike, single-story brick schoolhouse.

"It was an ideal place to bring up a young family," a neighbor said. "There was no crime to speak of—people left their doors unlocked. It was the kind of place where the Cleavers would have felt right at home. Of course that was at the time of the race riots in Detroit, but that might as well have been happening on another planet. We felt that removed from the real world."

An idyllic setting for a carefree childhood? Like other kids her age, Madonna tore around the gravel roads of the subdivision on her Schwinn and spent hours playing no more serious games than Monopoly and Clue. But as she took on more and more responsibility for her younger brother and sisters, her anger and resentment grew. Her feelings of bitterness, of being the central victim in the Ciccone family melodrama, understandably became even more intense with the arrival of two stepsiblings—Jennifer and Mario.

Increasingly, as she was called upon to change diapers and baby-sit, Madonna came to see herself as a modern-day Cinderella, with Joan cast as the wicked stepmother. "I have to say I resented it, because when all my friends were out playing, I felt like I had all these adult responsibilities. I think that's when I really thought about how I wanted to do something else and get away from all that." In fact, she "couldn't wait to escape."

In all fairness, Madonna's workaholic father almost certainly had as much to do with her predicament. Tony Ciccone felt that idle time was wasted time, that virtually every waking moment should be filled with schoolwork, housework, or prayer. Television was forbidden. "It was a very regimented life until we got older," Madonna said. "My father didn't like us to have any idle time. If we didn't have schoolwork to do, he found work for us to do around the house. He thought we should always be productive and make good use of our time. He was very adamant about that." The notion of "always challenging your mind or body," said Madonna, "definitely shaped my adult life."

The Ciccones were not a particularly musical family, but Tony nevertheless insisted that all of his children pick a musical instrument and take lessons every day. Madonna took piano lessons, but "hated them." Eventually, she persuaded her father to enroll her at a local dance studio—"one of those places where you get ballet, jazz, tap, and baton twirling." Madonna flourished there.

Madonna was particularly resentful of her parents' insistence on conformity. When she wasn't wearing her drab school uniform, for example, she wore clothes identical to her sisters'—dresses her stepmother had made using fabric from K Mart. "The thing I hated about my sisters most was that my stepmother insisted on buying us the same dresses," she recalled. "I would do everything not to look like them." That meant tying bows in her dark, shoulder-length hair, wearing flashy socks and shocking pink sweaters —whatever she could think of to make herself stand out from the crowd.

One Easter, Madonna was sitting in the family station wagon on the way to church, complaining nonstop about the lime green outfits she and her sisters were forced to wear. "I mumbled something," Madonna recalled for *Rolling Stone*, ". . . and my stepmother just went *bam*," spattering the lime green dress with blood. "I always got nosebleeds when I was little. . . . Even though I was in agony I couldn't have been more thrilled. Not only did I not have to wear the dress, but I didn't have to go to church."

Madonna joined the Brownies ("I ate all the cookies") and then switched to the Camp Fire Girls because "they had the cooler uniforms." But she earned most of her merit badges as a playground tease. Beneath her parochial school uniform, she wore brightly colored panty bloomers—then spent most of recess hanging upside down on the monkey bars, surrounded by an ogling audience of nine-year-old boys. Eventually, she left the Camp Fire

Girls after she was caught trying to consort with a troop of Boy Scouts. "I'd camp out with the boys," she admitted, "and get into trouble." As a result, said Madonna, "my stepmother slapped me a lot."

Tony Ciccone managed to hold his anger over Madonna's irreverent behavior in check—until the day of the St. Andrew's talent show. Like the other proud parents, he sat, Polaroid in hand, waiting for his child to make her appearance. After the pint-size violinists, pianists, and tap dancers, Madonna twirled onstage—nude.

Actually, she wore a bikini and was covered from head to toe with fluorescent green paint that glowed beneath a black light. But the effect was the same. "I *was* practically naked," she remembered, "but the talent show was my one night a year to show them who I really was and what I could really be, and I just wanted to do totally outrageous stuff."

As Madonna wriggled her way through her tribute to Goldie Hawn's go-go dancer routine on television's "Laugh-In," Tony fumed. The audience of parents gave her the biggest ovation of the evening, but her father was mortified. "How could you do this to me?" he asked his daughter, and promptly grounded her for two weeks.

From the outset, Madonna did whatever was required to seize and hold the attention of those around her. Often that took the form of "mouthing off," as she put it, to friends, family, and teachers. "I always remember being told to shut up. Everywhere, at home, at school—I always got in trouble for talking out of turn in school." The toughest punishments were meted out at St. Andrew's, where nuns tried washing her mouth out with soap, and when that failed, taping it shut. She was also on the receiving end of some old-fashioned corporal punishment. "I got hit on the head with rulers by hostile nuns," Madonna recalled.

Curiously, that did not keep her from wanting to don a habit herself. If she had any idols as a young girl, Madonna said hers was Christ. "When I was growing up, I was religious, in a passionate, adolescent way. Christ was like a movie star, my favorite idol of all."

Next to Jesus, Madonna also idolized those very nuns who punished her. By her own admission, she was for a time—up until age twelve, in fact—"obsessed" with being a nun. "They seemed all-powerful and perfect. Above everything. Superior. And I also thought they were very beautiful. . . . They never wore any makeup and they just had these really serene faces. Nuns are very sexy."

Madonna continued to hold that view. In 1989, when she was asked to name her role models in life, she replied, "We didn't read magazines or watch much TV. The only person I could have based my look on was the Singing Nun."

Endlessly fascinated by the sisters who taught them, one day Madonna and her girlhood friend Carol Belanger climbed over a convent wall and peeked through the windows to catch a glimpse of the nuns without their habits. "We found out then," Carol said, "that they had hair."

For her confirmation name, Madonna chose Veronica—the woman in the New Testament who gave Jesus her handkerchief to wipe his brow as he carried the cross to Golgotha—because she thought the gesture was "really dramatic." Had she actually become a nun, Madonna would have faced the dilemma of changing her name, since nuns are not allowed to keep their real names after joining a religious order. "But how could I change my name?" she asked rhetorically. "I have the most holy name a woman can have."

At the age of ten, Madonna began to take serious notice of the opposite sex. "I remember liking my body and not being ashamed of it. I remember liking boys and not feeling inhibited. I never played little games. If I liked a boy, I'd confront him. I've always been that way. Maybe it comes from having older brothers and sharing the bathroom with them or whatever."

Not that she didn't play with Barbie dolls like other girls her age, only Madonna used them to act out her sexual fantasies. "They were having sex all the time," she said. "I rubbed Barbie and Ken together a lot." And Madonna's Barbie was "bitchy, man. Barbie was *mean*. Barbie would say to Ken, 'I'm not gonna stay home and do the dishes. *You* stay home! *I'm* going out tonight. . . . Barbie was going to be sexy, but she was going to be *tough*." Joan Ciccone was not exactly thrilled when she pulled back Madonna's bedcovers to discover that her stepdaughter had stripped Barbie and Ken and arranged them in a compromising position under the sheets.

Little Madonna's newfound interest in boys was the cause for some considerable concern among the nuns at St. Andrew's. At one point, she ripped off her blazer and blouse and began pursuing a boy named Tommy around the playground. After class, Tommy relented and planted Madonna with her first kiss—an experience she describes to this day as "incredible."

Madonna's appetite was merely whetted by her fourth-grade encounter with Tommy. "I wanted to chase after boys, and the nuns told me I couldn't, that good Catholic girls didn't chase boys," she later said. "I didn't understand what was so bad about it, so I would do it anyway. And I would get punished for it." As long as there was the promise of absolution, Madonna went right ahead and followed her instincts: "I did a lot of bad things because I knew I could go to confession at the end of the week and all would be forgiven."

Although much of her adulthood would be spent rebelling very publicly against the Church and its teachings, Madonna conceded that she was left with "a great sense of guilt from Catholicism that has definitely permeated my everyday life, whether I want it to or not. If I don't let someone know I've wronged, I'm always afraid I'm going to be punished. . . . The Catholic Church teaches you that you are a sinner—that *all* human beings are. You must constantly be asking God to cleanse your soul and begging Him for forgiveness."

Until Madonna was twelve, she would claim she was "very conscious of God watching everything I did. I believed the devil was in my basement and I would run up the stairway fast so he wouldn't grab my ankles. We had the kind of stairway where there were spaces between each step."

For Madonna, sex, family, religion, and guilt were all inexorably and hopelessly tangled. Often it was hard to tell if she was railing about the inequities of her faith or merely sulking over facts of biology. "You know how religion is," she once reflected. "Guys get to do everything. They get to be altar boys. They get to stay out late. Take their shirts off in the summer. They get to pee standing up. They get to fuck a lot of girls and not worry about getting pregnant. Although that doesn't have anything to do with being religious."

During this time, Madonna was so intent on trying to have that same kind of freedom that she experimented with ways to urinate without sitting down. She would lift up the seat and facing the toilet, straddle the bowl standing up. "Really weird," she later confessed.

At home, tensions mounted as Madonna grew increasingly assertive and independent. What was she like to grow up with? "She wasn't rich. She wasn't famous then," Martin Ciccone said of his sister. "But she was the same." Translation: "I was a bitch," Madonna conceded. "Well, I always thought I should be treated like a star when I was a kid. The biggest piece of the cake."

Tony and Joan Ciccone were not amused. Madonna remained an achiever at school and dutifully did more than her share of the household chores, but her increasingly rebellious attitude left them reeling. She was not, in the words of one sibling, "a whole lot of fun to be around."

As far as Madonna was concerned, the feeling was entirely mutual. "I certainly wanted really badly either to find out my parents weren't my real parents," she admitted, "so I could be an orphan and feel sorry for myself or wanted everyone to die in a car accident so I wouldn't have parents to tell me what to do. My dad used to send me to my room and I'd slam my door and say, 'I hate you' —not loud enough so he could hear it, but loud enough to hear I was saying something." In short, she shared the intermittent love-hate feelings harbored by most preadolescents—feelings that would grow much stronger in the coming years.

At age eleven, Madonna was already beginning to blossom. "At the same time as I began to rebel against the Church and my family," she said, "my breasts started to grow. I went through puberty before most of the girls in my class. . . . They hated me for it."

One day Joan Ciccone, who by now had formally adopted all of Tony's children, took it upon herself to give Madonna a birds-and-bees lecture over the kitchen sink as they washed dishes together. Madonna was stunned. Whenever her stepmother said the word *penis*, Madonna turned up the water to drown her out. "Absolutely horrifying" was what Madonna thought of this new information. To complicate matters, Joan informed her that using a tampon before she was married was "the same as having sex."

So Madonna turned to her friend Moira McPharlin for guidance. During one sleepover, the two girls slipped out of their nightclothes and explored each other's body. It was Moira, Madonna said, who taught her how to insert a tampon. ("I put it in sideways and was walking around paralyzed one day.") Madonna also said, using her own less-than-delicate terminology, that her friend "finger-fucked" her.

Years later, Madonna would confront her startled childhood friend with this story before millions of moviegoers in her hit film *Truth or Dare*. "All of my sexual experiences when I was young were with girls," she insisted. "I mean, we didn't have all those sleepover parties for nothing."

Another classmate, Colin McGregor, remembered that even in the sixth grade Madonna was quite well endowed physically—a fact that did not go unnoticed by the boys who attended St. Andrew's. "She kept wearing scanty panties and the shortest miniskirts in school to make the boys notice," said McGregor, who with several classmates tried to coax a few girls on the cheerleading squad to give them a private preview of their routine. All the girls refused—except Madonna. "She went through the whole cheerleader chorus and ended up doing cartwheels. Her skirt went up around her waist, and we all got a good look at her red panties."

The next day, Madonna sent McGregor a smoldering love note. After class, he asked if she wanted to take a walk through Samuel A. Howlett Municipal Park, a tiny wooded pond behind the school better known to locals as the Swamp. McGregor said he "had it all worked out. I'd physically stop her in her tracks, face her, and then plant a big kiss on her. I was nervous.

"When I finally did it, she didn't object, though. It was a really long kiss. My knees were trembling, I was feeling dizzy, and I expect she was, too. I realized I'd actually kissed a girl, though in my case it happened to be Madonna. After that we used to dash to the Swamp every lunchtime for necking sessions."

Eventually, McGregor worked up enough courage to ask Madonna out on a date—by all accounts, it was her first. They went to see a horror movie, *The House of Dark Shadows*. Once again, McGregor had a plan: "The minute a vampire came out, I had my arm around her, and then I let my fingers creep down her shoulder to see how she would react. She did nothing, so I started undoing her shirt buttons and slipped my hand into her bra." McGregor expected Madonna's bra to be stuffed with Kleenex, but it wasn't. "She was a very well-developed girl for her age. And her breasts were her best assets."

When she entered seventh grade in 1970, Madonna was enrolled at West Junior High School, a single-story, white brick structure on Rochester's Old Perch Road. West Junior High gave Madonna her first taste of life at a public school, and she savored the comparative freedom. Her best friend at the time, Lori Sargent (now Lori Jahns), recalled sleepovers and slumber parties spent drawing up lists of the boys they most wanted to kiss. Madonna's was a long one, including the names of no fewer than a dozen neighborhood boys. Although she continued to make excellent grades, Madonna (who now called herself "Mudd") was already beginning to cultivate a "reputation" at school. She was a frequent participant at the "make-out" parties that included both boys and girls, but guarded her virginity by sometimes wearing a purple turtleneck leotard.

Just how notorious Madonna had become was evident when a pretty blond classmate name Katrina, generally regarded as the most popular girl at school, walked up to her one afternoon after school. "Her boyfriend started flirting with me, and I think I may have kissed him once," said Madonna, "but that's all, and I remember she *slapped* me on the street, right in front of everybody. I was devastated."

Madonna's unsavory reputation concerned the parents of her friends. "Madonna would come to my house and we'd go into my room and talk about boys and stuff," Lori Sargent recalled, "but my mother didn't want me around Madonna. The way she dressed, and the way she acted, just turned my mother off."

Most of the time, the girls just listened to music—Motown, Aretha Franklin, Joni Mitchell ("Her *Court and Spark* album was my bible for a whole year," Madonna said.) Madonna's first music idol was Nancy Sinatra: "Go-go boots, miniskirt, blond hair, fake eyelashes—she was cool." What most appealed to Madonna was the explicit message of Nancy Sinatra's first No. 1 hit "These Boots Are Made for Walkin'." "That made one hell of an impression on me," she later told *Time*. "And when she said, 'Are you ready, boots, start walkin',' it was like, yeah, give me some of those go-go boots. I want to walk on a few people."

Ironically, Lori Sargent thought nothing of Madonna's voice at the time. "It was nothing special. She really showed no interest in becoming a singer back then. None at all."

After graduating from the eighth grade, Sargent and Madonna spent the summer of 1972 visiting Madonna's maternal grandmother in Bay City. Grandma Fortin was much less strict than her father. ("I loved going there; we could have twelve desserts at Grandma's and stay out past ten and go out with boys and drink beer.") Madonna's uncles had their own rock band, and she hung out with them. For the first time in her life, she wore tight jeans, smoked cigarettes, plucked her eyebrows, and started feeling "like, yeah, this is it. I'm *cool*."

When she returned home to Rochester, Madonna was promptly branded a "floozy" by her stepmother. From then on, Madonna and her friend Lori jokingly tried to live up to the title. "We got bras and stuffed them so our breasts were overlarge and wore really tight sweaters. We wore tons of lipstick and really badly applied makeup and huge beauty marks [in addition to Madonna's natural beauty mark] and did our hair up like Tammy Wynette." Then they struck poses on Madonna's bed and took photographs of each other. "These were our ten-cent floozy pictures. We were going to look back at them and laugh, because we knew how ridiculous it was."

It was about this time that Madonna chose to make her movie debut, in a Super 8-mm short directed by another of her West Junior High schoolmates. In it, an egg was "fried" on Madonna's stomach—the first on-camera exposure of what would become one of the most celebrated navels in history.

Beneath the bravura, however, was a soul in turmoil. Madonna's fear of cancer had returned, and she became convinced that any new mole or freckle was a sign of melanoma. She was also suffering from a recurrent dream—a nightmare in which she was being brutally murdered by a faceless, nameless man. This disturbingly graphic image would haunt her for years.

4

"I saw losing my virginity as a
career move."

In 1972, Madonna graduated to Rochester Adams High School.
Situated at the corner of Tienken and Adams roads not far from
the Meadowbrook Village mall, Rochester Adams, like so many
high schools in America's more affluent communities, looked
more like a country club than a public facility. The sprawling
brick, cement, and stucco main structure sat on a broad plain,
surrounded by willows, pines, and tennis courts. A mural depict-
ing Olympic figures adorned the athletic building. Most of the
sports cars in the parking lot were of recent vintage, and many
belonged to students. Madonna would later talk of growing up as
one of the few whites in a predominantly black neighborhood, and
of her years attending a racially mixed high school. Yet Rochester
Adams was (and remains) overwhelmingly white.

During her four years there, Madonna would, on the surface at
least, lead a completely normal, middle-American existence. She
shopped for clothes with her stepmother at the Mitzelfield's Department Store, and bought candy at the D&C Dimestore on
Main and Fourth. Like the other teens, she spent hours at the one

movie theater in town, then headed for Knapp's Dairy Bar or the Dairy Queen for a hamburger and a shake. On crisp autumn afternoons, there were hayrides to Yates Cider Mill for hot apple cider. Later, when she became a high school varsity cheerleader, Madonna would help transform a hay wagon into a homecoming float.

On paper, Madonna was still a model student. In intelligence tests, she rated in the top 2 percent with an IQ of over 140. She lived up to it, garnering straight A's in courses that ranged from adolescent psychology, poetry, black history, and French to anatomy, drama, music theory, and modern Russian history. She even got an A in a course titled "Marriage and Family."

Madonna's extracurricular life was equally impressive. She was a member of the volunteer Help a Kid program and spent summers as a life guard and swimming instructor at the tony Avon Hills Swim Club. During her freshman and sophomore years, she was a cheerleader for the Rochester Adams Highlanders (the school newspaper, curiously enough, was called *Under the Kilt*), joined the French Club, and sang in the school choir. All of her brothers played musical instruments, and some performed in school plays. Madonna founded the school drama club, the Thespians, and starred in every student production from *Cinderella* and *The Wizard of Oz* to *Godspell* and *My Fair Lady*. "The ingenue role was always mine," she said. "But when there was a role for, like a forward, bad girl, everybody sort of unanimously looked over at me when they were casting it."

There was a reason for this. Madonna's reputation had preceded her. "When you're that aggressive in junior high," she later said, "the boys . . . mistake your forwardness for sexual promiscuity. Then when they don't get what they think they're going to get, they turn on you."

Madonna did not try to dispel any of these notions. Karen Craven, who was on the cheerleading squad with her, remembered the day they made a human pyramid and Madonna "vaulted up, then flipped to the top." The crowd gasped when her skirt flew up to reveal that she was not wearing underwear. Or at least that's the way it appeared; she was actually wearing flesh-colored tights. "She was always out to shock," Craven said. "But that's Madonna for you." Added another friend, Mary Conley Belote: "She'd come right out and say what she thought, no holds barred. She never censored or edited herself the way the rest of us do. Absolutely fearless."

Not everyone appreciated Madonna's candor. Her friend Carol Belanger recalled the day she and Madonna were spending the afternoon at a local lake. Several bikers began tossing lit firecrackers at them. "Madonna yelled up and told them to knock it off," Belanger said. Suddenly one of the bikers' girlfriends ran up and began punching Madonna in the face, giving her a black eye. From that point on, Belanger would "literally put my hand over her mouth to shut her up."

Madonna could not be controlled so easily. Together with a close-knit group of fellow outcasts, she would go on shoplifting sprees at Mitzelfield's and the D&C Dimestore, always emerging with more pilfered merchandise than anyone else. Although her father gave Madonna a red Mustang once she got her driver's license, she repaid him by skipping Mass and driving her friends to Dunkin' Donuts for coffee. On the way back, they would pick up the church program to prove to her father that she had been there.

More and more, Madonna got into arguments with her father about religion, questioning the basic tenets of Catholicism. She began asking him why she had to go to church to pray, and why she had to go to a priest for confession, rather than to God directly. "These things didn't make any sense to me," she said. "My father would always have this stock response, 'Because I said so.' And that wasn't good enough. I started to think it was all stupid, and hypocritical . . . These were all silly rules somebody made up, not God."

On those increasingly rare occasions when she did actually attend church, Madonna would sometimes go with her friend Carol, the two girls wearing nothing under their overcoats. They would spend the entire service trading knowing glances, barely able to contain their laughter. All of which was beginning to add up to a persona with which her name would ultimately become synonymous. "I went through this whole period of time when the girls thought I was really loose and the guys called me nympho," Madonna recalled. "I was necking with boys like everybody else. . . . So I didn't understand where it all came from. I would hear words like *slut* that I hear now. It's sort of repeating itself. I was called those names when I was still a virgin. I didn't fit in and that's when I got into dancing. I shut off from all of that and I escaped."

Christopher Flynn was forty-two and Madonna barely fourteen when she enrolled as a student at his Rochester School of Ballet. The school occupied the second floor of 404 Main Street, a stone building at the corner of Main and East Fourth streets that had been constructed in 1899 to serve as the town's Masonic temple. Situated six doors down from the movie theater and just opposite Mitzelfield's Department Store, it was in the very heart of Rochester—and at the same time, at least as far as Flynn and Madonna were concerned, a million miles away.

The day she arrived at the school, Madonna's self-esteem was at an all-time low. Yet Flynn, a frustrated former ballet dancer, was intrigued by this child-woman. "She was very young, still an adolescent," he remembered, "playing the little child—dark hair, nothing special." Curiously, Flynn recalled that she often brought with her to class "a little girl doll, about two feet high, with a little dress. Madonna looked like the most innocent child in the world."

Whether she was imitating Carroll Baker's child-woman in the sensational movie *Baby Doll* or borrowing a page from Vladimir Nabokov's *Lolita*, the sight of Madonna carting a thigh-high dress-up doll to ballet class was nothing if not attention-grabbing. If seduction was her motive, then she was wasting her time. Christopher Flynn was devoutly homosexual.

Madonna's primary motivation for such behavior was simple fear. She had studied only jazz up until this point, and suddenly she found herself in the company of young women who had devoted their lives to classical dance. Hurling herself into Flynn's demanding regimen ("I had to work twice as hard as everybody else"), Madonna quickly impressed her teacher with her fierce determination. The strenuous routines were also sculpting her voluptuous form into a more ascetic-looking dancer's body.

After one particularly grueling session, Madonna wrapped a towel around her head turban-style and gazed out the window as she tried to catch her breath.

"God," said Flynn, startling her, "you're really beautiful."

"What?"

"You have an ancient-looking face," he went on. "A face like an ancient Roman statue." Then he walked away.

"I was fourteen and feeling horribly unattractive and unpopular and uninteresting and unfabulous," Madonna later said of that moment. "And Christopher said, 'God, you're beautiful.' No one had ever said that to me before. He told me I was special, and he taught me to appreciate beauty—not beauty in the conventional sense, but really about beauty of the spirit." From that point on, Madonna said, "my whole life changed. Not just because studying dance with Christopher was so really important, but because he gave me a focus and took me out of what I considered my humdrum existence."

Madonna played a willing Galatea to Flynn's Pygmalion. To explain what he meant by likening her to a Roman statue, he took her to museums and art galleries. "She was a blank page, believe me," he recalled, "and she wanted desperately to be filled in. Madonna knew nothing at all about art, classical music, sculpture, fashion, civilization—nothing about life, really. I mean, she was just a child. But she had this burning desire to learn, that girl. She had a thirst for learning that was insatiable. It was something that would not be denied."

Madonna herself was characteristically blunt about her relationship with Flynn: "I latched on to him like a leech and took everything I could from him."

Flynn found Madonna's candor—and her offbeat, guileless brand of humor—refreshing. Once, while driving through the Michigan countryside, she told knock-knock jokes nonstop for over an hour. "Normally, that kind of thing turns me off—I never know when to laugh," said Flynn. "But she loves knock-knock jokes, and the way she did it, just rapid-fire like some kind of machine rattling off these cornball puns with such enthusiasm, you *had* to laugh."

Yet there were times when Madonna's mood turned somber, and she confided in Flynn that her mother's death had so devastated her emotionally that she still suffered nightmares about it. She left no doubt that she still harbored great resentment toward her father, and toward the stepmother, who, in her view, usurped her role as the woman of the house.

"Madonna hated her stepmother, and she was very bitter toward her father for betraying her by remarrying. Or at least that's how she saw it," said Flynn. "Madonna felt her entire family hated her, and she even dreamt about killing them all. If anything drove her at that point, I think it was a desire to show her family that they'd all be sorry for not paying attention to her, for not loving her. I guess I was the first person who ever told her she was a star—or at least that she had the potential to be one."

Toward that end, Flynn's tutelage extended well beyond museums, concerts, and art galleries. When she was just fifteen, he began taking Madonna to gay discos in downtown Detroit. "It was like nothing," Madonna recalled, "I'd ever seen before." Indeed, she felt strangely at home as the only female among hundreds of writhing men. And while she would have a lifelong aversion to drugs, she was not put off by the huge quantities of cocaine and amyl nitrate snorted at these establishments. "Men were doing poppers and going crazy," she remembered. "They were all dressed really well and were more free about themselves than all the blockhead football players I met in high school."

Away from the watchful eye of her strict Catholic family and the snickering of scornful classmates who viewed her as the girl with the "bad reputation," Madonna could set her spirit free on the dance floor. "She loved to dance, period," said Flynn. "She loved it. And God, was she hot. She just cleared the floor and we just cut loose and everybody loved her. It's not that she was showing off. She just thoroughly enjoyed dancing and it just sprang out of her."

At the gay dance clubs, Madonna often played the tease just as she always had in school—only now to hilarious effect. She would go out on the floor alone and end up dancing suggestively with two or more gay men at a time. "Everybody thought it was hysterical," Flynn remembered. "She was total fun in that outrageous way. Boys practically knocked each other over to dance with her." On occasion, fights would erupt between lovers over the attention being paid to Madonna. "Gays really love me, don't they?" she asked rhetorically. It was then, Flynn later theorized, that it first dawned on Madonna that, at least as a dancer, she appealed strongly to the gay audience. "She was wild," he said, "and her wildness excited them."

As for the sexual practices at the establishments they frequented, Madonna was unabashed in her curiosity. "There would be boys off in the corner doing, well, *everything*," said Flynn, "and she would just walk right up and stare."

However worldly she was about the sexual practices of gays, Madonna herself was still a virgin. But once she had made up her mind to lose her virginity, she acted on that decision with characteristic efficiency. She was fifteen and a standout member of the cheerleading squad when she met seventeen-year-old junior Russell Long in the fall of 1973. Long thought she was sixteen, and admitted that, "if my parents had known she was only fifteen, they would have hit the roof."

Madonna selected Long to be her first lover because "he had the guts. I danced very wildly and other boys were frightened of me. Russell won my heart because he had the courage, really." On weekends, the couple tooled around Rochester in his 1966 light blue Cadillac ("Boy, did she love that car," said Long), but she resisted his attempts to lure her into the backseat.

When Long's parents went away for the weekend, Madonna invited him out for a movie followed by a hamburger and a Coke at Knapp's Dairy Bar. They sat staring at each other until she finally suggested they go back to his place. "I was surprised at the forwardness," he later said, "but it gave me a kind of charge, too."

It was not Long's first sexual experience, but he conceded that he "wasn't the local stud, either. I was so nervous I couldn't get her bra strap undone." In fact, they lay atop his bed fully clothed for a half hour, trying to overcome their embarrassment and work up the nerve to do something. Finally, Madonna turned to him and blurted, "Do you want to do it or not?" They shed their clothes awkwardly. "There was a lot of fumbling going on. I had this great urge to start laughing, but Madonna was pretty methodical about it. It was like she'd made up her mind she was going to lose her virginity, no matter what."

Madonna was a tender if inexperienced partner. "She called me 'baby' a couple of times while we were huffing and puffing," Long later remembered. And as they climaxed, she yelled " 'Oh, Baby,' or something like that." Long was surprised that she didn't "cry out or burst into tears like you'd expect. It was like she felt she'd achieved something."

In truth, Long now says he "wouldn't call it making love." That was not what he told Madonna at the time, however. She pleaded to know if her performance was satisfactory, and Long recalled that Madonna was "tickled pink when I said it was great. Actually, neither of us had that great a time that night, but there you go." Madonna later confessed that she still felt she was a virgin after this first bona fide sexual experience. "I didn't really lose my virginity," she said, "until I knew what I was doing."

From then on, Russell Long's Cadillac was their usual trysting place. The normal routine began with parking on a deserted country road, then climbing into the backseat. He would light up a joint (after experimenting a few times, Madonna abstained), then they talked while kissing and fondling one another.

Madonna proved to be faster at stripping off her clothes. "She'd curl up on the seat telling me to hurry up and make her warm," Long said, "while I fiddled with my shoes and my zipper." After sex, Madonna often spoke of her mother's early death and the resentment she felt from all her siblings. "She was always saying how she was going to show them. She was going to show everyone."

Determined not to disappoint her public even then, Madonna continued her performance as the class tease. She necked with boys in the hallways—eyes always open—and even let a few, in the adolescent vernacular, "feel her up." But for the remainder of high school at least, Russell Long would be her only lover.

It was a fact she freely shared with the rest of the student body. "Madonna left us in no doubt," Madonna's school chum Mary

Beth Glaser, recalled, "that she and Russell were sleeping together." Former class president Bart Bedard concurred: "It was common knowledge that Russell and Madonna were making love regularly in the back of his Cadillac. We called it his passion wagon."

It was less well-known around school that, according to Madonna, she was also experimenting with homosexuality. She would later claim that at fifteen she had had her first real experience with a woman—a childhood friend.

Long may have been her first and only male lover in high school, but Flynn continued to be the most important man in Madonna's teenage life. Even as she and Long fogged up the windows of his Cadillac, Madonna's attachment to the gay dance teacher twenty-eight years her senior grew stronger. At sixteen, she seduced him, but their sexual relationship was short-lived; Flynn's brief dalliance with bisexuality was strictly "experimental. I loved her, of course. She was my little Madonna," he mused years later. "We were soul mates. Much more important than anything physical."

Increasingly, Madonna felt less the high school girl and more the liberated, avant-garde artiste who belonged in Flynn's world of classical dance and gay discos. Determined to cast herself in the role of school oddball, she dropped out of the cheerleading squad in her junior year. She gave up Dairy Queen hamburgers and became a vegetarian. She wore pants with gaping holes held together with giant safety pins. She also stopped shaving her legs and under her arms—all part of a rather obvious attempt to shock her fellow students and the faculty.

"It was gross," recalled a fellow student. "Here Madonna had been this straight-A student and all of a sudden she's a brooding, European-intellectual bohemian type. It got to the point where she could practically braid the hair on her legs." Her guidance counselor, Nancy Ryan Mitchell, said, "Her new look shocked me, all right, but I pretended not to notice."

At about this same time, Madonna faced other pressures that sorely tested her family loyalty. Her brother Marti's problems with drugs were, according to one classmate, "a source of constant embarrassment to her. He was a freak and she hated it. She was never into drugs, but if someone went for Marti, she and her sister Paula would leap to his defense."

If Madonna abstained from drugs, alcohol was another matter —or so it seemed. "Madonna's big kick in high school was drinking," former boyfriend Colin McGregor said. "At all the parties she was always the one who fell off the chair 'drunk.' But the thing was, she wasn't drunk at all." Appearing to be under the influence gave her the excuse she needed for some of her more outlandish actions. "She drove guys up the wall," a former friend claimed, "do everything but go to bed with them, and the next day act as if nothing happened—like she didn't remember a thing." "You see," McGregor concluded, "for Madonna life has always been one big, long act."

5

"I'm a sponge. I soaked up everything
in my life and this is how it
manifested itself."

"Lf you've ever seen Madonna," Nancy Ryan Mitchell said, "the
one thing you will never forget is her eyes—those incredibly beautiful, haunting blue eyes." Behind those eyes, according to Mitchell, was a keen intelligence and a steely determination to succeed.
Mitchell knew what she was talking about. In addition to being
Madonna's guidance counselor throughout high school (and for
that matter, the guidance counselor for all the Ciccone children
over the years), she became a valued friend of the family.

Despite her outstanding academic record (not a single B her last
two years in high school), Madonna was not, insisted Mitchell,
"your standard college prep student. Even then, those of us on the
faculty were sort of in awe of her. On an instinctual, gut level, she
just seemed more streetwise than the other suburban kids at the
school. It's strange, because obviously she grew up in the same
upper-middle-class area that everybody else did. Madonna had all
the advantages. But she was resourceful—she made it clear to
everybody that she knew how to take care of herself."

Where other students sought advice on what classes to take and which colleges to aim for, Madonna "never asked our opinion about anything," Mitchell said. "Madonna always knew exactly what she wanted, and how to get it. Usually, she'd come to me to sign authorization slips. I can still see her come breezing into my office, chewing gum frantically. She'd slap a form on my desk—completely filled out—and say, 'Hey, I need you to sign this application for me.' Not rude—she'd always thank me—but very direct."

Mitchell and other faculty members were not unaware of her wild reputation ("Madonna really cut loose at student dances—always more sexually suggestive than anyone else would dare," Mitchell recalled), but her classroom behavior remained exemplary. "Madonna came into my class as a junior," said Marilyn Fallows, who taught a course in Russian history. "She sat right in front of me. I focused on her. She engaged me. There was such a quality of charisma about her."

Madonna graduated from Rochester Adams a semester early and at Christopher Flynn's urging, applied for a dance scholarship at the University of Michigan's School of Music. Flynn had already accepted a teaching position in the dance department there and helped pave the way. For their part, Nancy Ryan Mitchell and Marilyn Fallows wrote glowing recommendations.

Asked by the university to list Madonna's strengths, Mitchell wrote that she was "extremely talented, dedicated, motivated, experienced, open to improvement," and possessed a "sparkling personality." Asked how best to describe her character, Mitchell said Madonna was "dynamic, vivacious, truly alive."

On April 2, 1976, Marilyn Fallows wrote to the University of Michigan that she found Madonna to be "an intelligent, sensitive, and creative young woman. She has an inquiring mind that probes the causes of events rather than the mere acceptance of facts. She has a delightful sense of humor, but never at the expense of anyone. She is sensitive and kind to her fellow students."

Upon graduation, Madonna gave her favorite teacher an autographed class photo of herself. On the back, she scrawled, "Mrs. Fallows, I can't begin to tell you how I feel about you, and how I will always treasure your words of encouragement. Sometimes

I think you might explode with so much energy inside of you. I think you are crazy, and I am really in love with your craziness, and of course, you."

Madonna was accepted by the University of Michigan's School of Music and arrived in Ann Arbor in the fall of 1976, once again determined to stand out in the crowd of swan-necked, would-be ballerinas. In this artificially rarefied atmosphere where the Audrey Hepburn gamine look was de rigueur, Madonna wore a short, spiky, black punk hairdo and shredded leotards barely held together by safety pins. Although they were initially impressed by her full scholarship, Madonna did not win any popularity contests among her fellow students. "She tried so hard to be 'different,'" said one, "that it came off as an obvious grab at attention. She wasn't outstanding as a classical dancer by any means, but she made up for her lack of technical expertise with sheer guts. She liked to stir things up, to give the impression of being a real troublemaker. Nobody thought it was all that funny, though."

As for her relationships outside the classroom, the people Madonna called friend were few and far between. "I don't know if she had any friends at all," one classmate recalled. "If she did, they weren't fellow dance students. None of us socialized with her, to my knowledge."

Keeping to herself, Madonna devoured the dark poetry of Sylvia Plath and Anne Sexton. Off campus she made the rounds of the clubs, often alone. The clientele at the Blue Frogge was overbearingly preppy, but it was at this popular student watering hole that a black waiter named Steve Bray caught her eye. Tall, lean, and quietly self-assured, Bray was also the drummer of an R&B group that played some of the local clubs, but all Madonna knew when she first spotted him was that he seemed "real cute. Someone all soulful and funky-looking you couldn't help but notice. First time in my life I asked a guy to buy me a drink."

Bray would turn out to be, for want of a better term, Madonna's first important pickup. She then began tagging along on all his club dates, usually to local Holiday Inns and Howard Johnsons—

any motel with a lounge and a need for some sort of live entertainment. Frequently, Madonna and a girlfriend would be the only ones dancing. It was, albeit small-time, her first exposure to the music business.

"She wasn't really a musician back then; she was just dancing," said Bray. But there was no doubt in his mind that she had something "truly unique. She stood out. Her energy was really apparent. What direction she should put that energy in hadn't been settled, but it was definitely there."

Almost as soon as Madonna arrived at the university, it became clear to Christopher Flynn that his protégé would find what she was looking for only in New York. "I told her to get off her ass and go there," he said. "There can be something thrilling about academic dance, but it has its limits. Madonna was just so much bigger than that—I could see it, even if she couldn't. There were just so many more things for her to explore, and they were all in New York. Stop wasting your time in the sticks. Take your little behind to New York. Go! Finally, she did."

"He was constantly putting all that stuff about New York in my ear," Madonna remembered. "I was hesitant, and my father and everyone were against it, but he really said, 'Go for it.' " Madonna had no choice but to listen to the man who had become the greatest single influence in her life. "He was my mentor, my father, my imaginative lover, my brother, everything" she said, "because he understood me."

Madonna saved up enough money for a one-way ticket to New York and informed Flynn of her decision to drop out of school and make the journey. Her mentor breathed a sigh of relief. "I lit a fire under Madonna, sure. I've lit fires under lots of people, only their kindling was wet. Madonna was the only one to burst into flame."

Had he known he was playing with fire, Steve Bray might not have been burned so badly when Madonna left town without saying good-bye. "Looking back," she told *Rolling Stone*, "I think that I probably did make him feel kind of bad, but I was really insensitive in those days. I was totally self-absorbed." It was a trait, her critics would later charge, that came to characterize her entire career.

6

"I'm tough, ambitious, and I know
exactly what I want. If that makes me
a bitch, okay."

On a warm July morning in 1978, nineteen-year-old Madonna
Louise Veronica Ciccone ignored her father's protests and
boarded a flight for New York. It was her first plane trip and by
any measure, her most important. Debarking at La Guardia with
nothing but a suitcase and the clothes on her back, her dance
slippers and $37 in cash crumpled in her purse, Madonna hailed a
cab. Totally unfamiliar with Manhattan, she simply instructed the
taxi driver to take her "to the center of everything." The cabbie
thought for a minute, then drove her straight to gaudy, seedy,
crime-ridden Times Square. "He must have had quite a sense of
humor," Madonna's brother Christopher Ciccone later quipped.
The cab fare: $15—not quite half of Madonna's entire stake.

Wearing a heavy winter coat in the middle of a typical New York summer heat wave, Madonna lugged her suitcase east, past the porno houses that lined Forty-second Street, then took a right on Lexington Avenue. A few blocks farther downtown, she came upon a street fair. Making her way through the crowd, she realized that she was being followed. Rather than trying to escape the man following her, she spun around and said hello.

"Why are you walking around with a winter coat and a suitcase?" he asked.

"I just got off the plane," she replied.

"Why don't you go home and get rid of it?"

"I don't live anywhere," Madonna told the stranger.

With that, he invited her to stay at his apartment, and she accepted. "I pretty much had to charm people into giving me things," she later said. For the next two weeks, the stranger (whose name she could no longer recall) made her breakfast while she looked for a place of her own and a job to pay for it. All she could afford was a roach-infested, fourth-floor walk-up at graffiti-covered 232 East Fourth Street between avenues A and B. "I really wouldn't go visit her there," Steve Bray later confessed. "I thought I was going to be killed by junkies."

To pay the rent and finance her dreams of dance stardom, Madonna landed a job behind the counter at a Dunkin' Donuts across the street from Bloomingdale's. But no sooner was she settled in New York than she received a call from Christopher Flynn, who informed her of the annual American Dance Festival, a six-week workshop being held that year at Duke University in Durham, North Carolina. The course in advanced technique was being taught by choreographer Pearl Lang, cofounder with Alvin Ailey of the American Dance Center in New York. Several months earlier, when Lang was teaching as an artist-in-residence at the University of Michigan, Madonna had attended a performance of her work on campus and was mesmerized.

Madonna scrounged up bus fare for the trip to Durham and was among the three hundred aspiring dancers competing for one of a half dozen scholarships to the six-week program. She was one of the winners. "When we announced her name," Lang later remembered, "Madonna walked right up to the table and looked straight at me and declared, 'I'm auditioning for this scholarship so I can work with Pearl Lang. I've seen one of her performances and she's the only one I want to work with.' Of course," said Lang, who had been lead soloist for Martha Graham before starting her own company, "Madonna's eyes popped out of her head when I told her I *was* Pearl Lang."

All of which came as a surprise to one classmate. "Pearl Lang was pointed out to her before the audition," she said. "Madonna knew *exactly* who she was talking to. Corny, but it worked."

At the end of the first week of classes, Madonna brazenly asked Lang if there was an opening for her in Lang's New York company. "I was kind of taken aback," Lang said. "I told her I had to see, but that we could probably make room. I asked her how she was going to get back to New York. She said, 'Don't worry—I'll manage.' "

Contrary to the claims in her later press releases that she "performed with the Alvin Ailey dance troupe," Madonna in fact began by taking classes with the American Dance Center's third-string troupe. Yet the experience was exhilarating and challenging, for it marked her first exposure to young performers who were as consumed with ambition as she was. "I thought I was in a production of *Fame*," she told *Rolling Stone*. "Everybody was Hispanic or black, and everyone wanted to be a star." Feeling very much alone in New York Madonna often went to Lincoln Center, sat by the fountain, and cried. "I'd write in my journal," she said, and "pray to have even one friend. . . . But never once did it occur to me to go back home. Never."

Faced with such stiff competition, Madonna switched from Ailey's classes to Pearl Lang's Dance Company in late November of 1978. Lang's style was very disciplined and demanding. Her approach to modern dance was, like Martha Graham's, Spartan, dramatic, angular. Madonna chose to describe Lang's choreography as "painful, dark, and guilt ridden. Very Catholic."

Unlike the other dancers, who came to class in leotards, Madonna wore a baggy sweatshirt ripped up the back and held together with a gigantic safety pin. But her unorthodox getup did not detract from her talent as an interpretive dancer. Lang recalled that Madonna was "exceptional. She was very talented—very fragile, but fierce. Many people can do the acrobatics required, but she had a poetic quality about her."

Because Madonna was so skinny, her first appearance in a Lang production was in the role of a starving ghetto child in the Holocaust drama *I Never Saw Another Butterfly*. "She was emaciated enough to pass for a Jewish child in the ghetto," Lang remembered. "And she danced marvelously." But her most persistent memory of Madonna the dancer was a single pose she struck in another modern piece, *La Rosa en Flores*. "It involves a very dramatic, high arch in the back. Madonna did it so beautifully, I can still see her dancing that role and doing that movement in my mind's eye."

Lang recognized that Madonna had "the power, the intensity, to go beyond mere physical performance into something more exciting. That intensity is the first thing I look for in a dancer, and Madonna had it."

Madonna also had an impetuous streak that appealed to Lang— for a time. It was not long before she was dating some of the wilder male dancers in the company, and arriving at the studio late for rehearsals. Lang did not take this blatant challenge to her authority lightly, and before long they were squaring off before the whole company.

"It was like watching two tigresses prowling around, sizing each other up," a former Pearl Lang dancer remembered. "Pearl was very demanding of all her students, but Madonna was not one who took commands easily, particularly when she felt she was right." The two argued bitterly, and on several occasions Madonna stormed out of the studio in a rage. "Eventually," the dancer said, "she always came back and did it Pearl's way. Madonna wanted to get ahead as a dancer, and she wasn't stupid."

Madonna had other equally pressing concerns. Still living on East Fourth Street, she was scarcely able to eke out a living and was having to rely more and more on friends for meals and handouts. She had even taken to rummaging through garbage cans in search of food. If she spotted a paper bag bearing the Burger King or McDonald's logo, she would, being a vegetarian, throw out the meat but eat the bun and the french fries that came with it. It was now not unusual for her to go a day or more without eating at all, although her fellow dancers said it never showed in her performances.

To earn a few extra dollars, Madonna began moonlighting as a nude model—a trade she had first plied as an undergraduate back at the University of Michigan. "I was in really good shape," she later recalled, "and I was slightly underweight so you could see my muscle definition and my skeleton. I was one of their favorite models because I was so easy to draw. So I sort of made the rounds." She discovered she could earn up to $100 for a day's work —compared to $50 for eight grueling hours waitressing. Soon, she was modeling nude for private groups of three or four. "So I got to know these people in a friendly kind of way."

Madonna had already modeled for several art classes in Manhattan by the time she strolled into the West Twenty-seventh Street studio of veteran photographer Bill Stone shortly before Christmas of 1978. He was impressed with her dancer's grace, she with his experiences photographing the original Ballet Russe de Monte Carlo in the late 1930s.

A former staff photographer for *Life* and *Esquire* magazines, Stone was perhaps best known for his highly romantic, sepia-toned portraits of nude women posed in the style of Titian, Botticelli, Modigliani, and other artists. He was planning to make Madonna look like something out of Matisse, but she posed herself—much to the delight of Stone, who felt she "knew exactly what she was doing. She was an accomplished dancer and was very helpful in improvising poses."

They chatted about the dance world during the photo session, and Stone's mysterious new model vamped outrageously, playing with her nipples as she luxuriated atop a Victorian settee, then leapt up and struck several of the "painful, guilt-ridden" modern-dance poses she had perfected under the watchful eye of Pearl Lang. The results of the session were striking; with her dark hair, huge eyes, and a lean-to-the-bone figure that bordered on the androgynous, Madonna on film was every inch the timeless, ethereal beauty.

After two exhilarating hours, Madonna announced she had to

be going. And when she signed the model's release form simply "Madonna," Stone asked her for her last name.

"I'm just Madonna," she answered.

"Darling," said Stone, "everyone has a last name."

"Would Madonna Madonna suit you better?" she said with a smile.

"No, no," he said, laughing. "Madonna will do just fine."

Before leaving, she spun around and asked Stone what he thought of her. "You've photographed a lot of women who've gone on to make it big. Do you think I'll make it big someday?"

"Darling," replied Stone, "you have the looks and the talent, and with the right promotion and backing, you just might."

Stone paid her $25—nearly twice her usual $7-an-hour modeling fee—and asked where she lived so he could get in touch with her for future work. Her cryptic answer: "Here and there."

Martin Schreiber's encounter with Madonna was equally memorable. Schreiber was in the middle of teaching a ten-week photography course at the New School in Greenwich Village when Madonna showed up on February 12, 1979, to model for his students. "Sometimes models would come in and be flamboyant and gregarious and talk with everyone," Schreiber said. "Madonna came in very quiet." Although he had no role in selecting her—the school hired all the models—Schreiber remembered that she was not only "a welcome relief from the average, lumpy but sweet art-class model, but she was also one of the loveliest models I ever photographed. She came in wearing pajama bottoms, like a little girl. When she took off her clothes, she had a terrific body. It was beautifully proportioned, muscular, strong. She had lovely skin. She was an ideal."

Her long dark hair tumbling over her shoulders, Madonna seemed oblivious to the dozen or so amateur and professional photographers—all male—who crowded around her. "I don't think she was all that comfortable," Schreiber suggested. "She was taciturn. Her face didn't reveal much. Her strength revealed itself in her silence, what she *didn't* say."

Unlike the pictures taken by Stone, Schreiber's had a more stark, urban quality about them. In some frames, Madonna is kneeling down on her hands and knees, staring straight into the camera. In others, she is caressing a cat, or reclining before the metal grill of an electric space heater. Throughout the ninety-minute session, for which Schreiber paid her $30, she remained totally at ease, the cool professional.

After the class, Madonna gave Schreiber her phone number and they began dating. Madonna accepted Schreiber's invitations to come to his loft, and in return for her companionship he bought Madonna expensive dinners and hired her for his private advanced photography class. At times, he found her bohemian personality off-putting. "Once we went to a party in a loft on the Lower East Side, and she wore those same pajama bottoms! There were people of all ages there, and a couple of little kids. She preferred to sit on the wooden floor and play with them. I wanted her to be interested in me, but she wasn't."

Schreiber later felt that his fleeting relationship with Madonna had less to do with his charm than his ability to advance her modeling career: "She may have seen an opportunity." Whatever her motive, it was clear to Schreiber even from this brief exposure that Madonna "was strong emotionally and she had ambition. I felt that nothing nor anyone was going to stand in her way."

With the possible exception of Pearl Lang. During the early months of 1979, tensions between the two strong-willed women continued to mount. "She would not come in once a week, or twice a week," Lang said, "and I became concerned about her lack of discipline. If I asked her to do a movement over, she'd say, 'I didn't know it was going to be so *haard*.'"

Every day Lang ordered her rebellious pupil to repeat routine after routine until, on several different occasions, a "humiliated" Madonna collapsed in tears before the entire troupe. At one point, Lang pressed her to do a single difficult step over and over again. Unable to perform it to Lang's satisfaction after seven attempts, Madonna slammed her head against the wall before the stunned company. "Is that what you want?" she screamed. "Is that better?"

For her part, Lang took Madonna's attitude in stride. "I liked her. She would talk back, but not to the point where I couldn't handle it," she said. "That's just part of being an artist. Madonna can be belligerent, but I think that comes from growing up with so many brothers and sisters and having to stake your claim."

It was about this time, in the spring of 1979, that Tony Ciccone, concerned about his daughter's welfare, showed up unexpectedly on Madonna's doorstep. "When my father came to visit," she once recalled, "he was mortified. The place was crawling with cock-roaches. There were winos in the hallways, and the entire place smelled like stale beer." Predictably, Tony pleaded with her to abandon her "foolish" dream of becoming a dancer and return with him to Michigan to finish college. Just as predictably, she refused.

She was, in fact, mulling a career switch—partly because of her tempestuous relationship with Pearl Lang, but mostly due to the simple fact that the competition was too stiff. The field was so crowded that it would take at least three, perhaps five, years for Madonna to earn a spot with a major touring dance company.

Although she had never expressed an interest in a music career before, Madonna began auditioning for singing and dancing parts in musicals and later videos, as well as for acting roles in films. Among the many roles she would be turned down for in the com-ing months were the lead in the hit film *Footloose*, and a part in the television series "Fame." Undaunted, Madonna scanned the trades for work daily; where there was an open "cattle call," she could be counted on to line up with the other gum-chewing hope-fuls.

Between auditions and dance classes, Madonna took up with a series of graffiti artists. Several of these aspiring Picassos, such as Futura 2000, Keith Haring, and Jean-Michel Basquiat, would soon become high-paid darlings of the New York art world. Then, how-ever, they were street-savvy paupers, and Madonna felt comfort-able in their company. Not one to be outdone, she carried a Magic Marker in her pocket at all times, defacing the sides of buildings, buses, and subway cars with her sprawling signature.

One entrepreneur who managed to turn a tidy profit by putting his graffiti art on T-shirts was Norris Burroughs. Within weeks of their first meeting, Madonna moved in with him. After three months, their relationship fell victim to the irrefutable fact that both possessed a wandering eye. Having found a new love for himself, Burroughs played matchmaker for Madonna. He threw a party and invited Madonna and Dan Gilroy, a pleasantly goofy-looking musician/songwriter/comedian whose wardrobe of porkpie hats and slouchy coats mirrored Madonna's own offbeat look. Sparks did not exactly fly when they first met. She found him brusque, and he found her "depressing." But they warmed to each other in the course of the evening, and by night's end Madonna turned to Gilroy and asked point-blank, "Aren't you going to kiss me?"

He did, and not long after they were making love in the converted Corona, Queens, synagogue Gilroy shared with his brother Ed. The synagogue, still resplendent with carved stone Stars of David and other Judaic symbols, also served as a studio for the brothers, who at various times worked as musicians or comics under the name Bil and Gil.

It was sometime during that first night at the synagogue when Gilroy strapped a guitar on Madonna and taught her her first chord. That moment, she recalled, "really clicked something off in my brain." That "something" was the realization that music—not dance—might be her ticket to stardom.

Madonna's relationship with Dan Gilroy was barely two weeks old when Jean Van Lieu and Jean Claude Pellerin, the two French music producers behind the success of European disco star Patrick Hernandez, held open auditions in New York for fresh young faces to back Hernandez. Virtually unknown in the United States, Hernandez's single "Born to Be Alive" was nevertheless an international hit, grossing more than $25 million.

Madonna went to the audition, and after watching her dance and belt out a generic disco tune, Van Lieu and Pellerin were so impressed with her passionate delivery that they offered to bring her to Paris and mold her into a star. "We saw right away that she had more punch than the others," Hernandez said. "Instead of selecting her to dance like an idiot behind me, we separated her from the other performers. We wanted to bring her to France so she could record." Tired of sifting through garbage cans for her next meal, she accepted.

The news that Madonna would be leaving for France in a few weeks came as something of a relief to the commitment-shy Gilroy. Now that the end of their time together was clearly delineated, he could relax into the romance. "It was like a roller coaster," Gilroy said of their relationship. "You go on for a few thrills, then it's over."

Madonna arrived in Paris in May of 1979 and was whisked from Charles de Gaulle Airport by limousine to the elegant Right Bank apartment of Jean Claude Pellerin. In addition to her lavish accommodations and round-the-clock access to her own chauffeured limousine, her new employers supplied their find with her own maid, secretary, vocal coach—and an unlimited wardrobe budget.

Evenings were spent ricocheting from one chic party to another, dining at Maxim's and Tour d'Argent, tearing up the dance floor at Regine's. Wherever they went, Madonna was proclaimed by her patrons to be "the next Edith Piaf." Van Lieu and Pellerin also took great pains to introduce her to the jet-set scions of some of France's oldest families. She was not amused. "They made me meet all these awful French boys," she remembered, "and I would throw tantrums. They would just laugh and give me money to make me happy."

"She was very beautiful and dated a lot of French boys," Pellerin's wife recalled. "But she thought they were very old-fashioned, and she was very free. Very free. Very liberal. She wanted a lot of boys."

"Madonna went out every night in Paris," Hernandez said. "Concerning male friends at the time, let's just say she had a healthy appetite."

The attention paid by these fawning playboys, all sporting Italian suits and Riviera tans, only fueled Madonna's suspicion that she had been brought to Paris as a trophy, not an aspiring star. Her Parisian benefactors had delivered on all their promises, and spectacularly. For the first time in her life, Madonna was savoring a taste of la dolce vita. Yet the career guidance that had been promised her had not materialized. Furthermore, no one was permitted to speak to Madonna in English—presumably part of their master plan to transform her into the new Piaf. Their perception of her became all too clear when, at one of the many social events to which she was carted, Madonna was introduced to the Eurotrash crowd. "Look what we found," Van Lieu said, patting her on the head, "in the gutters of New York."

Accordingly, Madonna made no secret of her contempt for the French. "Madonna had no interest in European culture," Hernandez recalled. "She never even tried speaking French; she only spoke English. She was not interested in trying French gourmet dishes. It all appeared to be a waste of time to her."

Once again casting herself as the enfant terrible, Madonna rebelled the best way she knew how. She demanded even more money, and when her French sponsors gave it to her without hesitation, she spent her francs on men, and not the aristocratic European variety. "I hung with Algerian and Vietnamese lowlifes who didn't have jobs but just drove around on motorcycles and terrorized people," she remembered. "I've always been attracted to people like that because they're rebels and they're irresponsible and challenge the norm. I'm attracted to bums!"

Zigzagging through the narrow side streets of the Left Bank and Les Halles on the back of someone's Harley-Davidson, the leather-jacketed, smart-mouthed Madonna was understandably much in demand among Parisian postpunkers. They worshiped everything American, particularly if it smacked of James Dean. A favorite pastime of Madonna and her biker friends: swerving close to hapless American tourists, then yelling epithets at them in French.

Madonna bulldozed through a dozen or more lovers during her brief European sojourn, although for a time she clung to one in particular, whom she later described as a Vietnamese street tough. In truth, her "rebel" lover was the pampered son of a wealthy South Vietnamese businessman. "Oh, he was very handsome and he did own a motorcycle," said a friend, "but he also had a trust fund."

Hernandez believed that Madonna's career as a French disco star was doomed from the start. "The minute she set foot in France," he said, things didn't go well between Madonna and her producers. "She didn't want to do what we had in mind for her. She did not want to sing; she had to do it. She just wanted to dance. It came as a big surprise for her that we wanted to turn her into a singer." Even when it came to dancing, Madonna and her French sponsors could not agree on what direction to take. "She was interested in the avant-garde and the times demanded disco," Hernandez recalled. "We wanted her to dance like Donna Summers and Madonna wanted to move otherwise." Stymied by this insurmountable impasse, she grew more and more dissatisfied.

Throughout her French interlude, Madonna took some solace in the letters she received from Dan Gilroy, her old flame from Corona, Queens, who wrote her impassioned pleas to "return to America. We miss you." Meanwhile, her tantrums escalated in both frequency and intensity. But to her chagrin, they only served to convince Hernandez, Pellerin, and Van Lieu that their discovery from the "the gutters of New York" had the fiery temperament of a true star.

Madonna was torn. These were the first people in the industry who had recognized her promise as a performer, and who backed up their faith in her with cold cash. Yet they had done nothing to further her career since she'd arrived in Paris. She had yet to write a single song or deliver a single performance. When Pellerin and Van Lieu commissioned a song for her entitled "She's a Real Disco Queen," Madonna refused to sing it. "At the time, she was interested in punk and New Wave," Hernandez said. "Funny, when she became a success years later, it was by singing the kinds of pop dance tunes we were trying to get her to record in the first place. In the end, her music was not at all avant-garde."

After three months in France, Madonna was feeling manipulated and worse, neglected. She wanted out of the arrangement. The letters from Dan Gilroy, each more insistent than the last, buoyed her spirits, but also reminded her that her luxurious life in Paris might be costing her the chance to achieve the stardom she coveted back in the United States. She grew increasingly homesick, and the psychic strain took its toll on her health. In the summer of 1979, she fell ill with a bad cold, and within a week, she was battling pneumonia.

Recuperating in bed, Madonna took stock of her situation. As soon as she was well, she told her bosses that she wanted to pay a brief visit to her family in America. To prove that she intended to return to Paris, she asked for a round-trip ticket and left all of her expensive new clothes behind with the Pellerins. Yet Madame Pellerin was never fooled. "Madonna wanted only one thing," she said, "to be a star. And when she left Paris, she promised that she would come back a star."

Patrick Hernandez credited Madonna's Parisian sojourn with "putting the bug in her ear that she could sing. Maybe if she had never come to Paris, Madonna would have continued taking dance lessons, going to auditions—and never even tried to make it as a singer!"

Madonna did not return to Paris, and while her French producers bitterly resented her blatant ingratitude, Hernandez was impressed by her "courage and single-mindedness. She once told me, 'Success is yours today but it will be mine tomorrow.' I was surprised at the time. I mean, was she bluffing, or did she really believe what she was saying? Back then in Paris, Madonna was pretty insignificant, but she was resolute. Success was a certainty in her mind. She knew she would be a star."

True to her word, Madonna would not return to Europe until she had achieved stardom the hard way—by earning it in America. "You have to work for something and you can't have anything handed to you," she said. "If it's handed to you, it's not gonna last."

7

"All those men I stepped all over to get
to the top—every one of them would
take me back because they still love
me and I still love them."

Her bittersweet Parisian escapade behind her, Madonna returned to New York in August of 1979. On the surface at least—
homeless, penniless, with no visible career prospects—she appeared no better off than when she left. Yet she did manage to
salvage from her junket to France one precious possession—a con-
viction that she could make it as a rock performer. But that would
mean placing her dance career on the back burner and concen-
trating on music.

Dan Gilroy was not entirely surprised when Madonna, her
brown hair shorn gamine length à la Leslie Caron, arrived back on
his doorstep in Queens. He knew she had been frustrated and
lonely in Paris, and that she would not long be placated by the
empty promises of her French sponsors. When she asked him to
help her get started by teaching her an instrument, Gilroy didn't
take long to decide which instrument she would be temperamentally best suited to: the drums.

While Dan Gilroy and his brother Ed were out busing tables
during the day and performing their comedy gigs around town at

night, Madonna made use of their converted-synagogue studio, practicing the drums six hours or more a day. She had also begun writing songs, strumming tunes on Ed Gilroy's battered guitar. Dan Gilroy was an enthusiastic audience of one. "It was one of the happiest times of my life," Madonna later said of that period. "I really felt loved. Sometimes I'd write sad songs and he'd sit there and cry. Very sweet."

Although Dan Gilroy's largesse made it possible for her to concentrate on her musical self-education without the distraction of full-time employment, Madonna took the occasional job to help out. She worked as a coat-check girl in several nightclubs and restaurants, the most notable of which was the venerable Russian Tea Room on West Fifty-seventh Street near Carnegie Hall. Boasting a festive green and red decor, gleaming samovars, and paintings of the Ballet Russe, the Russian Tea Room was a celebrity-watcher's paradise—one of the few places where movie stars, rock stars, and politicians mingled freely with best-selling authors, television news anchors, socialites, fashion designers, and classical artists.

The restaurant's manager, Gregory Camillucci, recalled the day he hired Madonna for the $4.50-an-hour job in 1979. "I remember our first meeting vividly," he said, "because she was very striking in a kind of jungle way. Not that she was raw. She was a sweet thing, but rather like a sculpture that isn't quite finished yet." He was also impressed by her name: "Even then it was just Madonna —such a striking, eye-opening, and ear-awakening name." Physically, Camillucci remembered that she was "gaunt. She definitely had a dancer's body, and I got the impression that the one meal we fed her was the only food she was getting. She had very dark hair, she was very Italian looking, very beautiful."

Sequestered in the tiny cloakroom to the immediate left of the restaurant's entrance, Madonna made no friends. "She was very quiet, never buddy-buddy with any of the other employees—a loner," Camillucci said. She was a "hard worker, conscientious," but that did not make up for her wardrobe. Dressed in wild animal prints, ankle socks, and high heels, Madonna did not exactly fit the Russian Tea Room's uptown image.

After two months, Camillucci fired her. "She took it well," he said. "I didn't come right out and say she was terribly dressed or anything of that sort. I felt sorry for her. I felt badly because you could feel that she was alone. The others who work here—you know if they don't make it as actresses or singers, they will survive nicely. They have that sense of security, of having a family to fall back on. Madonna never gave that impression. She was obviously driven."

More than a decade later, Camillucci was still haunted by Madonna's "intense eyes. When you would look at her, in returning that look there was an almost mystical stare. You never forget it."

Madonna's work life during this period did on at least one rare occasion include a foray into acting.

When she picked up the August 1979 issue of *Back Stage*, one particular ad caught Madonna's eye. In it, an avant-garde film-maker said he was seeking a very specific type of actress to star in his next movie: "a dark, fiery young woman, dominant, with lots of energy, who can dance and is willing to work for no pay." Madonna was not exactly thrilled with the notion of working gratis, but she knew that what she needed now was experience, and exposure.

For three days straight, Stephen Lewicki had been holed up in his un-air-conditioned West Side studio, poring over hundreds of ré-sumés and accompanying eight-by-ten glossies and agonizing over who should be picked for a part in his film. Despondent, he began tossing out résumé after résumé. When one of the envelopes fell out of the wastebasket, he bent over to pick it up, and a three-page handwritten letter fell out. He had somehow managed to overlook this one application, so he sat down to read it.

"Dear Stephen," it began, "I was born and raised in Detroit, where I began my career in petulance and precociousness. By the time I was in the fifth grade, I knew I either wanted to be a nun or a movie star. Nine months in a convent cured me of the first disease. During high school I became slightly schizophrenic as I couldn't choose between class virgin or the other kind. Both of them had their values as far as I could see.

"When I was fifteen, I began taking ballet class regularly, listening to Baroque music, and slowly but surely developed a dislike of my classmates, teachers, and high school in general.

"There was one exception, and that was my drama class. For one hour every day, all the megalomaniacs and egomaniacs would meet to compete for roles and argue about interpretation. I adored it when all eyes were upon me and I could practice being charming or sophisticated, so I would be prepared for the outside world.

"My infinite impatience graduated me from high school one year early, and I entered fine arts school at the University of Michigan, studying music, art, dance, and participating regularly in most theatrical productions. After two years of isolated utopic living I was dying for a challenge, so I moved to New York City and became a college dropout."

As he finished her letter, the photograph that Madonna had enclosed with the wry résumé of her life slipped out of the envelope. Lewicki was immediately struck by her looks. He was also struck by similarities in their backgrounds. They shared the same birthday: August 16. Both were middle-class misfits who landed in New York on their own, with plenty of creative energy but lacking in direction. And both were determined to make it, against all odds. Madonna got the part and since he had to scrounge up financing as he went along, it took Lewicki two years and an almost unbelievably paltry $20,000 to make the erotic thriller *A Certain Sacrifice*, the story of Bruna (played by Madonna), a Lower East Side denizen with her own family of three "sex slaves." No sooner does Bruna find true love than she is brutally raped in a coffee shop rest room. To avenge the crime, Bruna enlists the aid of her slaves, who hunt down, abduct, and execute the rapist, then drink his blood in a bizarre sacrificial ritual.

From the beginning, Madonna proved a thorough and willing professional—particularly when it came to her nude scenes. At one point, Lewicki took the actor portraying the rapist aside and told him to rip her blouse off—an action not described in the script. Madonna's shocked reaction on camera lent an undeniable authenticity to the scene.

Yet she could not be described as the ideal ensemble player.

According to Lewicki, she became visibly restless and distracted when the camera wasn't on her. That didn't stop Lewicki from being smitten by his egregiously self-centered star. They were never lovers, although Madonna could hardly be faulted for trying. One afternoon while they sat on a bench in New York's Battery Park, she invited her director to lick blueberry yogurt out of her ear. He did. "That woman has more sensuality in her ear," he remembered, "than most women have anywhere on their bodies."

When Lewicki contacted her months later to do some reshoots, Madonna was willing—for a price. She needed money to pay her rent, so Lewicki agreed to write out a check for $100. This was not only the total amount he paid Madonna for working on the picture, it was Lewicki's total outlay for actors' salaries.

Madonna got her first exposure in a music video in 1980, when Ed Steinberg, a pioneer producer in the field, put out a call for extras to appear in a video starring an up-and-coming group called Konk. The entire video was shot on location at a downtown Manhattan spot called David's Loft. "While we were shooting," Steinberg said, "this one extra kept jumping out in front of the crowd, dancing really wildly, hogging the camera. She was one of the most energetic people I'd ever seen, but I had to ask her to cool it down a bit." The scene-stealing extra was Madonna.

Madonna was not living at the Gilroys'—despite the fact that she spent all day every day there practicing drums and writing songs. She was bouncing from one apartment to another, pushing the collective tolerance and generosity of all her friends to the limit. Finally, since it had become clear that Dan Gilroy was not about to invite her to stay, she invited herself. He grudgingly agreed, on the condition that they first ask his brother Ed for permission. "Ed?" Madonna replied, dumbstruck. "You have to ask *Ed?*"

Once she moved in, Madonna launched her campaign to be included in the new band the Gilroy brothers were putting together. There was hesitation. Despite his respect for her songwriting talent, Dan was not convinced that Madonna was enough of a musician to pull it off in front of a paying audience. He soon relented, however, and Madonna recruited another disaffected dancer friend, Angie Smit, to join their new group.

At Madonna's insistence, the band rehearsed relentlessly at the Gilroys' synagogue-studio. The all-night sessions spilled over into morning, when the exhausted musicians would stumble over to a local coffee shop for breakfast. After several weeks of this, the choice of a name seemed obvious. From now on, they would be known as The Breakfast Club.

The Breakfast Club began doing gigs at all "the Lower East Side hell holes"—clubs with names such as UK, My Father's Place, and Botany Talk House. Even with Madonna flailing away earnestly behind a drum set, it soon became apparent that the star attraction was Angie Smit. Wearing little more than lingerie, the lithe dancer-turned-guitarist barely sang an audible note. But she did sway seductively throughout most of the act, leaving Madonna and the Gilroys completely upstaged. At Madonna's insistence, Smit was politely but firmly asked to leave the band.

The departure of their only girl singer offered Madonna a unique opportunity, and she seized it. She pleaded with Gilroy to let her come out from behind her drum set and sing a couple of the songs she had written. Reluctantly, he agreed. Her greatest asset to the group, however, was as a hustler. She spent all day every day on the telephone, chatting up record producers, club owners, agents, and managers—anyone who could conceivably advance the band's fortunes with a record deal or club date. "I think I was just naturally more charming to these horny old businessmen," she said, "than Dan and Ed Gilroy."

Madonna's partners were pleased that their girl percussionist was so adroit at drumming up business, but they were also taken aback by her unabashed ambition. Like so many denizens of the downtown New York scene, they were too immersed in their music to figure all the angles. "They weren't as interested in the commercial end as I was," Madonna said. "It never occurred to me to get into this business and *not* be a huge success. It doesn't help to be the best singer in the world or have the most talented band if only a few people know it. I wanted the world to notice me, always have."

Audiences did indeed begin to notice Madonna. It was hard not to when she jumped out from behind her drum set, grabbed a microphone, and belted out her songs, gyrating wildly about the stage. Trouble was, the rest of the band at times looked more like backup for a solo act. Ed Gilroy in particular resented Madonna's constant maneuvering to be the main singer. There were doubts on the part of both Gilroys that she was a singer at all. Even Madonna would acknowledge that Dan had "created a monster" by nurturing her musical aspirations. Yet she needed to be center stage, and if the Gilroy brothers were not ready to move aside, she would have to start a band of her own.

For over eight months, Dan Gilroy had not only provided Madonna with a basic musical education, but worked nine-to-five so that she could stay home and concentrate on honing her talents. Now that she had, in her own words, "sucked what I needed" from them, she announced to Dan that the affair was over, and that she was moving from Queens back into Manhattan to start her own band.

Gilroy was not surprised. At the time her talents may have seemed meager to him, but not her chutzpah. He was shaken, and perhaps even a bit bitter when she packed up to leave—but also, he confessed, a little relieved. Madonna's demands had strained the relationship between the Gilroy brothers to the breaking point. At least now they would be free to proceed at their own laid-back pace.

Back on the Lower East Side, Madonna wasted no time setting out to recruit members for her new group, even though she was afraid she lacked the credentials to discriminate between a solid musician and one who was merely run-of-the mill. And once she had settled on drummer Mike Monahan and bass guitarist Gary Burke, she was again forced to play the name game. Calling themselves The Millionaires, then Modern Dance, they performed for several weeks as Emanon ("no name" backwards) before finally landing on Emmy—another of Madonna's many nicknames.

For most of the spring of 1980. Emmy played at whatever "hellhole" would have them for the going price of $25 per night. Since that amount was split three ways, Burke and Monahan were not about to give up their day jobs. Their leader persevered, however, but just as Madonna sensed the band was on the verge of a breakthrough, Monahan announced he was getting married and leaving the group.

"The Chinese symbol for crisis is also the symbol for risk," mused Madonna's old friend Christopher Flynn. "She had a knack for turning a crisis around, for capitalizing on it. All it took was luck, which she has always seemed to attract like a lightning rod."

Providence did indeed intervene within days of Monahan's decision to leave. Unexpectedly, Steve Bray, Madonna's ex-lover from Ann Arbor and her first pop music mentor, called to say that he was fed up with life in the Midwest and ready to attack New York. "Oddly enough," recalled Bray, "she needed a drummer. So I said, 'I'll be there next week.'"

Up until Bray's arrival, Madonna had been illegally squatting in a loft. There she slept on a scrap of carpet and kept warm with three electric space heaters placed strategically around the room. One night she woke up to find that one of the heaters had set her little piece of carpet ablaze, and that she was surrounded by a "ring of fire." She doused the flames with water, but to no avail. As she spun around to get more water, her nightgown caught fire. Madonna stripped it off, gathered what little she had together, and fled before the entire loft was gutted by fire.

It was then that self-described "soul mates" Madonna and Bray rekindled their romance. "He was a lifesaver," she said. "I wasn't a good enough musician to be screaming at anybody about how loudly they were playing." Together they moved into the Music Building, on Eighth Avenue in mid-Manhattan a charmless, Depression-era edifice that now housed dozens of recording and rehearsal studios.

"It was supposed to be like the Brill Building," said another musician who rented space there in the early 1980s. The Brill Building was the legendary midtown art-deco structure that housed several music publishers and spawned such songwriting legends as Carole King and Gerry Goffen. "The only trouble was, the Music Building was filthy *and* dangerous—the neighborhood was crawling with cockroaches and addicts. The hallways smelled of urine, there was graffiti everywhere; the place was truly disgusting."

To this inhospitable locale gravitated the down-and-dirty bands that sought to fill the void left by the departure of New Wave. An as-yet-undiscovered Billy Idol was among them. Most of the rockers, however, did not live on the premises. Yet Madonna and Bray actually squatted there off and on for nearly a year, working between gigs on their own material and subsisting on tuna fish and popcorn. ("I still love popcorn," Madonna said later. "It fills you up and it's cheap.")

Plopped down in the middle of a community of musicians, she was quick to make enemies. "There was a lot of resentment of someone who's obviously got that special something," said Bray. "There are so many musicians out there, but only a few who really have that charisma. The community out there kind of frowned on her about that. She had trouble making friends." Another Music Building alumnus was less charitable: "Confidence is fine, but she was unbelievably pushy. No class. No consideration for others. She was this kind of Sammy Glick character—naked ambition, but not the talent to back it up. *That's* why nobody liked her."

Bray took Madonna's lack of finesse in stride. Remembering the co-ed in Michigan who tagged along with his band when they performed at the local Howard Johnsons, he was now inspired by Madonna's gutsy determination to make it in the music field. "She'd written fourteen songs by then," he said, "which was really impressive to me because I'd had a lot of training but I still hadn't written one song. So if that person came out of dance school and by sheer volition became a songwriter, I figured I could do that, too."

Bray was impressed, but not so impressed that he could go along with Madonna's repeated demands to change the band's name again. This time, she wanted to drop Emmy in favor of the simple and compelling Madonna. As the months passed, Bray also began to harbor reservations about the direction Madonna was taking musically. She was an outspoken fan of Chrissie Hynde and the Pretenders, as well as Pat Benatar, the Police, and several other leather-jacketed, hard-rock groups that aspired to be their generation's answer to the Rolling Stones.

As convincing as Madonna could be as the street-smart, hollow-eyed diva, her accompaniment, in the words of one club owner, "stank. She sounded terrific. She knocked herself out onstage. But the guys with her screwed things up. Madonna was every bit as good as Chrissie Hynde, in my opinion, but the band was so awful that it really distracted from her." Bray concurred: "If we found that right guitar player, I think that's when things would have taken off . . . but there are so many horrible guitar players in New York, and we seemed to get them all."

By early 1981, Emmy had unraveled. Left to her own devices, Madonna now concentrated on promoting the one product in which she had absolute confidence: herself.

8

"I am ambitious, but if I weren't as
talented as I am ambitious, I would be
a gross monstrosity."

One morning Adam Alter of Gotham Productions was walking briskly through the Music Building's shabby lobby when a gum-snapping girl in torn jeans stopped him. "Hey," she said before walking on, "you look just like John Lennon."

At the same time, unbeknownst to Alter, his business partner Camille Barbone had encountered an offbeat young girl on the elevator. "We had the whole second floor to ourselves," said Barbone, an attractive, no-nonsense New Yorker who had worked over the years with such stars as Melba Moore and David Johansen and for such companies as Columbia, Polygram, Buddha Records, and Arista. "When I got on the elevator one morning, I noticed this striking young lady. She had red hair, chopped off in a Prince Valiant style."

The next day, the young girl in the Prince Valiant bangs showed up again. "Did you do it yet?" she asked.

"Excuse me?" Barbone replied.

"Did you *do* it yet?"

"No."

"Okay."

This bizarre exchange on the elevator was repeated for several days. "She was teasing me, and I was intrigued," Barbone admitted.

A few days later, Barbone was searching for the keys to her office corridor when the same sassy young woman in dark glasses opened the door for her. "Don't worry," the mysterious girl said matter-of-factly. "You'll be opening doors for me someday."

Meanwhile, Alter had persuaded Barbone to listen to a demo tape recorded by this spectacular new talent he had discovered. Her name, he told his partner, was Madonna. Barbone thought most of the tape forgettable, except for one cut—an early rendition of "Burning Up." Alter then dragged Barbone to watch this Madonna woman rehearse. It was only then that she realized the Madonna on the tape and the mysterious woman she had been repeatedly bumping into were one and the same. "I was shocked," she recalled. "Madonna had obviously planned this all along, and I never realized it."

Rather than feeling manipulated, however, Barbone was struck by Madonna's "waifish charm. She had evolved as a personality even then." Barbone agreed to catch Madonna's act upstairs at Kansas City, a seedy downtown establishment, but didn't go because of a debilitating migraine. The headache pain she experienced that night was nothing compared to what was in store for her the following morning when Madonna paid her a visit.

"She came flying into my office," Barbone recalled. " 'You're just like everyone else,' she screamed. 'How *could* you not show up? This is my *life*.' "

Barbone sat speechless on her side of the desk. "I was impressed," she conceded. "Here she was *screaming* in my face, but I admired her. No one had ever been so ballsy before."

Barbone apologized, agreed to catch the show the following Saturday, and reached across her desk for her datebook to make a note of the place and time. Madonna grabbed the book and shoved it into Barbone's chest. "No," she said, "you just *remember*." Then she left.

At Kansas City, Barbone remembered sitting in the audience

when Madonna "poked her head out from behind the curtain looking for me. When she saw I was there, the show began. She wore men's gray pajamas with red stripes and the fly sewn up. She had dyed her hair from red to dark brown. The minute I saw her, I knew she was a megastar. Wow, I thought, what I could do with that face."

Barbone was so excited, in fact, that after the first number she walked downstairs to the bar to cool off. "She had been on stage for one and a half minutes with a lousy band, but there was something about her that was sensational. I was so worked up I couldn't stand still. Afterwards, she came up to me and said she had a sore throat. So I got her some tea with honey it. Then I said, 'How would you like a manager?' She screamed, 'Yeah!' and threw her arms around me."

Not long after, on St. Patrick's Day 1981, Madonna sat on the floor of Barbone's office drinking green beer as her new manager explained each clause of her contract with Gotham Productions. Barbone then recommended a lawyer to approve the contract for Madonna. "I knew she would be big," she said "so I did my best to forestall any trouble down the road. I didn't want there to be any misunderstanding when it came to our legal arrangement." The initial contract called for Barbone to act as Madonna's sole manager for six months, then wound up being extended for three years.

The first order of business was to find Madonna a decent place to live. She went out and found a place for $65 a week—one room on Thirtieth Street just across from Madison Square Garden. Barbone wrote her a check for the apartment, gathered all Madonna's worldly possessions—a guitar with a broken neck, some soiled and frayed secondhand clothes—and piled into a cab for the ride to Thirtieth Street. "When we got there, I was appalled at the squalid conditions," Barbone said. "This was not decent, this was not safe. But she was a free spirit, and she didn't seem to care at all."

Neither did she complain about being hungry, although it soon became apparent to Barbone that Madonna often went hungry. "Every morning I'd come to the Music Building and she'd be sitting outside the office. It would always be 'Bring me an apple' or

'Bring me a yogurt' or 'Bring me a cheese popcorn,' and pretty soon I realized that this was probably the only meal she could count on."

On signing the contract, Barbone had given Madonna enough cash to tide her over for a week. Part of the money was used to repair Madonna's bicycle—her only means of transportation. "She wasn't shy about asking for more money after that," recalled Barbone, whose interest in Madonna was more than professional.

Although at age twenty-nine she was only seven years Madonna's senior, Barbone's initial feelings for the struggling singer were maternal in nature. Following a break-in at Madonna's Thirtieth Street apartment, Barbone and Alter agreed to set their new protégée up in a comfortable apartment on Riverside Drive and Ninety-fifth Street (her roommates were a handsome middle-aged man and his grown-up twin sons), pay her a weekly salary of $100, and allow her free run of their recording studio. In return, she agreed to allow Gotham Productions to mold her act, select her musicians, and guide her career—and collect 15 percent of the gross.

Realistically, Barbone and Alter could not expect to see any real income from Madonna for months, possibly years. To help make ends meet, Barbone found a housekeeping job for Madonna. Just a few days after she was hired, Madonna phoned in a panic. She had cut her finger on a broken glass while washing dishes, and she wanted Barbone to drive her to the hospital. "There was a lot of blood," Barbone admitted, "but after all it was just a cut finger. Madonna wanted to be babied, specifically by me."

Barbone would later describe Madonna as "almost innocent back then, in a lovably obnoxious sort of way. And she was always asking people to teach her things." Once she admired the way one of Barbone's more sophisticated friends held a cigarette. "She walked up to my friend and said, 'Teach me to smoke.' My friend was startled, but she stood there showing Madonna how to light a cigarette and hold it, how to take a drag. She walked away knowing the proper way to smoke a cigarette for effect. It was classic Madonna."

While Madonna vacuumed during the days and wrote songs at

night, Barbone fired her ragtag group of backup musicians and put together a new band. It would take months ("I can still hear Madonna whining, 'I *want* my *band*. I want it *now*,' " Barbone recalled.), but the results were impressive. In the end, she had signed up such respected sessions players as John Kaye (formerly David Bowie's bass guitarist), guitarist John Gordon, keyboardist Dave Frank, and drummer Bob Riley.

Madonna's only caveat: that Steve Bray be hired as her drummer. Barbone refused. Madonna already had a drummer, Bob Riley. Besides, Barbone knew that Bray and Madonna had been lovers. As a manager, Barbone strongly disapproved of love affairs among band members because of the friction that usually results.

"I laid down the rules to Madonna," she said. "No romantic involvement with the band. There were so many heartbroken men running around I didn't want to add to the list. She said, 'Don't worry about it,' and then proceeded to go to bed with Riley." Confronted by Barbone, Madonna denied the affair at first, then demanded that Riley be fired and replaced with Bray. "I had to fire Bob," Barbone remembered "and he was heartbroken." She then called the band members together. While Madonna sat there chewing gum, dangling her legs and blowing huge bubbles, Barbone told the other band members in no uncertain terms to "stay away from Madonna."

Barbone's motherly concern also involved keeping a watchful eye on Madonna's health. When she had four impacted wisdom teeth removed, it was Barbone who paid the dentist bills and put Madonna up at her home in Bayside, Queens. "She wanted to get it over with so she had all four removed at once," Barbone recalled. "That night, Madonna was swollen, she bled all night, and she cried all night. She woke me up, and I held her and took care of her."

Barbone's involvement extended far beyond dental care. She even took Madonna to Planned Parenthood and arranged for birth control pills. "The last thing I wanted," she said, "was a pregnant Madonna."

As long as Barbone showed concern, Madonna was not averse to being mothered. For twenty months, Barbone would be the single most important person in her life, nurturing her talent, orchestrating her career, and massaging her ego. "Madonna would actually sit on my lap," Barbone said. "She needs to feel physically close to other women—she needs that nurturing. Her mother's death is still doing a number on her. She's still searching for mommy."

From the beginning, Barbone recognized Madonna's potential and, more than anyone else, convinced her that she was star material. She was destined for greatness, Barbone and partner Adam Alter told her, if she changed her sound from hard rock to lighter, more commercial fare. Madonna's tastes were undergoing a dramatic metamorphosis, but in the opposite direction—toward beat-heavy urban funk. To please her patrons, she played the more mainstream music they wanted her to play, then stayed up until dawn with Bray writing and recording the sort of gritty tunes they were hearing on the street.

Throughout the remainder of 1981, Barbone and Madonna forged an intense personal relationship. The two women shared the same birthday, August 16, so when Madonna turned twenty-three and Barbone thirty, they celebrated together. "Being raised in Detroit, she had never been to the ocean," Barbone recalled. She drove Madonna to the beach at Far Rockaway, Long Island, in her father's white 1975 Chevrolet Impala. Once there, they walked on the beach, and Madonna "rolled around in a rock pool for about two hours." They capped the day with a lobster dinner —Madonna's first. "She said to me later," Barbone remembered wistfully, " 'That was the greatest day of my life.' "

Curiously, Madonna had a difficult time comprehending the notion of impending stardom. "We walked along the beach, and she was completely mesmerized by what I had to tell her," Barbone remembered. "I told her what it would be like to ride around in limos, to have total artistic freedom, what it would be like to be unable to walk down the street without being mobbed. I told her I wanted her to be prepared for the loss of privacy and the pressures that would come with being a star. She seemed sort of embarrassed at first; she really didn't believe it would happen."

Madonna often seemed to take nothing seriously, and her playful streak could get out of hand. Once, Barbone asked Madonna to take care of her two poodles, Norman and Mona, while she was out of town for a few days. When Barbone returned, she found that Madonna had spray-painted Norman orange and Mona pink. She had also painted a word on each of the pets: SEX and FUCK. "I was bored," she told Barbone. "I had to do *something*."

For a time, Barbone kept Madonna happy "with the little things." The two were insatiable moviegoers—"Madonna especially. She went nearly every day." Another favorite pastime was prowling through the racks of secondhand stores in search of off-beat items for Madonna's already distinctive wardrobe. "She could put on horrible clothes and pull it off," Barbone said. "She'd buy a shirt for fifty cents and cut it up. She usually wore oversized clothes, men's paint-stained pants, high-heeled shoes, a rag in her ratted hair." Madonna's favorite article of jewelry: a turquoise rosary that had belonged to her grandmother.

They also spent weekends together perusing art galleries, strolling through Central Park, or going to the movies. As long as she did not have to pick up the check, Madonna seemed content to take whatever Barbone offered. With one major exception. Looking beyond Madonna's musical career, Camille Barbone envisioned a time when her young client might make the switch to becoming an actress. Toward that end, Barbone enrolled her in classes with the renowned acting teacher Mira Rostova.

Madonna quit after one day because she found the experience "too hard" and the teacher "mean." According to Barbone, Rostova was happy to see her go. "This girl will never be an actress," Rostova told Barbone. "She is too vulgar, and she thinks she knows it all. Besides, I do not like her."

"The acting thing was a big bone of contention between Madonna and me," Barbone said. "I wanted her to evolve. She wasn't interested in the hard work it would take to become a real actress." Madonna seemed more content lolling around on the floor of her living room taking Polaroids of herself. "The character she would later play in *Desperately Seeking Susan* was Madonna," Barbone said. "I saw her do the things she does in that picture a thousand times."

By mid-1981, it was time for Madonna to break in her new act. Her first gig would be at a biker club on Long Island called U.S. Blues. A few days before the club date, Barbone was walking through Times Square when she noticed a crowd gathering around three young breakdancers. She put a $20 bill in their cigar box, along with her business card.

The night Madonna made her first appearance under Barbone's auspices, she walked onstage wearing a man's tuxedo shirt and a gold beaded sweater with a huge red M printed across the chest "like a cheerleader's outfit." Backed by her top-caliber band and the three breakdancers, she twirled, strutted, and bounced to her own "Sidewalk Talk" (the tune would later appear on future boy-friend Jellybean Benitez's debut album).

"She sweated so much that people in the front row got wet," said Barbone of that memorable first gig. At one point, Madonna walked up to the edge of the stage and picked out a little boy to sing to. "Afterwards, I told her to touch the boy while she sang to him," recalled Barbone. From that point on, it would be part of Madonna's modus operandi to have a very young boy—seldom older than thirteen or fourteen—in the front row so she could stroke him affectionately while she sang. "She really liked to per-form with a kid," Barbone said, "but away from the spotlight she didn't like kids at all. Her interests were more of the adult variety."

Those interests did not include drugs. While nearly everyone around her was sucked into an addiction of one sort or another, Madonna remained essentially abstinent. According to Barbone and others, she did occasionally take a hit of marijuana. "One time she snorted some coke and then screwed up her face and said, 'Get this awful shit away from me!' "

Madonna's personal "just say no" approach to drugs stemmed less from health or legal concerns than from her desire to remain in control of her faculties at all times. "She could look out over this sea of people," said an acquaintance from those days, "and know she was practically the only one there who wasn't completely out of it. I'm sure she felt like God."

A decade in the music business had prepared Barbone for just about any form of aberrant behavior, or so she thought. But she claimed to have been dumbfounded by the sexual games Madonna would play. Whenever Madonna's close friend from the University of Michigan came to visit, Barbone felt at times as if she were the mother of two giggling teenagers. "They were like two little girls," she recalled. "They would switch clothes and play together. The two used to sit in the back of my car and just kiss."

Whenever they were interested in a man, Madonna and her girlfriend put him through a special test. The two women would kiss each other passionately in front of him, then wait for his reaction. "If he didn't get flustered," Barbone said, "they decided he was okay. Then whoever wanted him would have him."

Was she bisexual? "Madonna loves beautiful women," Barbone claimed, "and she is into anyone sexually, male or female, who is beautiful." Madonna made no attempt to conceal her sexual ambidexterity. Barbone remembered that Madonna, who "sweats profusely on stage," would end each show by running to her dressing room, tearing off her soaking clothes, and instructing Barbone to "towel me off. She was teasing me, of course."

Madonna did even less to conceal her particular brand of eclectic sexuality when she attended a series of concerts in New York given by one of her idols, Tina Turner. Madonna insisted on standing near the stage, Barbone claimed, "so she could look up Tina's legs."

When it came to the opposite sex, Madonna was employing essentially the same disarmingly direct approach she had used on the boys back at St. Andrew's to such great effect. "She loves sex," observed Barbone, "and would go after any man she wanted. There's a stong maleness in Madonna. She seduces men the way men seduce women." According to Barbone, even in the days she was struggling for recognition while performing in some of lower Manhattan's sleaziest clubs, "men were always overwhelmed by Madonna. She's seductive and alluring. She touches men's shoulders, necks, and faces a lot if she likes them." As a result, Barbone concluded, "she has an amazing ability to manipulate men, based on her sensuality and the possibility of sexual favors. The entourage of young men she had hanging around was just waiting to get into bed with her. But she was a great tease. She kept them at a distance, but always interested and intrigued. She never *had* to go to bed with anyone."

Madonna's strategy was always to keep men off balance. "She knew how to intimidate men by standing close to them," said Barbone. "She singles someone out and says something like, 'Do you want to stay after rehearsal and play a little music?' So they play music, then she says, 'Why don't you take me for a drink?' Then she looks the guy straight into the eyes and says, 'You have great lips, why don't you kiss me?'"

When Barbone brought her darkly handsome sixteen-year-old cousin to catch Madonna's show, she spent the evening seducing him. "Stand in front so I can see you," she told him. Then, during the performance, she grabbed him by the collar and sang directly to him. Later, Barbone discovered the two necking in Madonna's dressing room and pulled them apart. "He's awfully young, isn't he?" Barbone said. "Yes," said Madonna, shrugging, "but he's awfully cute." Barbone was convinced they would have wound up in bed together that night if she hadn't taken him home to his family. Even then, Barbone insisted, "A man couldn't be around her without falling in love."

No one was more aware of Madonna's prowess than Madonna herself. During a photo shoot, her favorite turquoise crucifix slipped off her neck and fell into her jeans while she was zipping up. "You see," she yelled gleefully, "even God wants to get into my pants!"

"She's a sexual human being," sighed Barbone. "She can only communicate in that way. It's all she knows. It's got her everything. At the same time, sex means nothing to Madonna. It's a means to an end. She thinks of sex in the same way as some men —very promiscuous men."

One man who succeeded in turning the tables on Madonna was artist-musician Ken Compton. Blond, blue-eyed, and angular, Compton did not appear to be Madonna's type physically. "Madonna usually goes for Latin or light-skinned black men," Barbone said. "Kenny was very Aryan-looking, and very much in control of his feelings. He did the kind of number on Madonna that she did on everybody else—not returning phone calls, being late, cheating with other girls. She'd be on the phone to him screaming, crying. Ken drove her *crazy*."

Ken Compton aside, Madonna's pride in her power over men sometimes led to friction with Barbone. One night Madonna, her girlfriend from Michigan, and Barbone were stopped at the door of the Underground and denied entrance into the trendy New York club. Barbone protested that they were on the list to get in, but the man at the door refused to budge. Then Madonna yelled at the top of her lungs: "Hey, don't you remember me? We made out the other night." The trio was immediately ushered in.

Barbone found Madonna's lack of propriety disconcerting, to say the least. That night, she drove home with Madonna and her girlfriend necking in the backseat. "The entire ride, I kept calling her 'slut.' Madonna was very proud of her sexual escapades. She wanted everyone to know about them. I, on the other hand, wanted her to present herself to the public as a nice person. Pure folly on my part."

Their battles over this and other aspects of Madonna's life and career intensified. "We yelled and screamed at each other constantly," Barbone said. "We fought so ferociously that the band members would get up and leave. She was a bitch, but I could be an even bigger bitch. I was the only one she couldn't bully."

Despite their differences, Barbone saw to it that Madonna was always pumped full of self-esteem. Even at seedy, sawdust-on-the-floor joints where she was performing for $100 a night, Madonna behaved as if she were about to play before a standing-room-only crowd at Madison Square Garden.

"She acted every bit the star even then—even though she was nothing," recalled *Village Voice* writer Michael Musto, who was part of another downtown group at the time. "She tested her microphone from every angle. She wouldn't let us have a mike check at all. And after we did our opening act, she wouldn't let us share the dressing room with her. Her manager would say, 'You have to leave. Madonna's getting dressed.' Even though that was the only dressing room for all of us. We insisted on staying anyway. I thought, 'This girl is not going anywhere. She's a major bitch. She's going to offend so many people and she's going nowhere fast.' "

On the contrary. It was precisely by offending people—millions of them—that Madonna would eventually become the most famous woman in the world. But first she had to land a major record deal. At Gotham Studios, Madonna teamed with Bray and two other musicians to record a demo tape that included four singles: "Get Up," "Society's Boy," "Love on the Run," and a ballad Madonna wrote for Barbone, "I Want You."

Barbone circulated the tape, and by the autumn of 1981 agents, producers, booking agents, and packagers of every stripe were vying for a piece of Madonna. No fewer than nine record companies called Gotham to say that, on the basis of the demo tape, they were on the verge of signing up the hot singer with the provocative name. Barbone and her partner, Adam Alter, were eager to sign a deal and replenish the company coffers that had been drained to support their up-and-coming star. "There were days," Alter said, "when I would go to the bank and there was nothing there. *Nothing*. It had all been spent promoting Madonna." Added Barbone: "We had kept the Madonna Telethon going as long as we could. Now we needed an infusion of capital."

But while those about Madonna scrambled for power, Barbone noticed that the object of everyone's affections was beginning to behave strangely. She spoke in hushed tones about the impact her mother's tragic death had had on her, and the fierce competition within her family. One evening, she told Barbone she was convinced that Elvis Presley died on her birthday "for a reason. His soul has gone into me," Madonna said, "and has given me the power to perform." Reincarnation aside (Madonna turned nineteen when Presley died on August 16, 1977), Barbone was quite convinced at the time that she was serious.

She was. Over the years, Madonna had also come to believe that she possessed certain precognitive powers. "Madonna was very sensitive, very attuned spiritually," said Christopher Flynn. "There were things that other people might chalk up to coincidence, but we knew better."

Madonna was haunted by the recurring premonition that she would be assassinated on stage, like the country-western star who is gunned down before an audience in the hit movie *Nashville*. For Madonna, that scene took on a fresh and frightening reality.

"She always felt that there was somebody out there in the audience who was going to jump onstage and shoot her," Barbone claimed. As a result, Barbone hired Roman "Fundy" Fundador to be Madonna's bodyguard long before she had achieved star status. "She was already whipping audiences into a frenzy," Barbone said. "So when she was finished, Fundy would literally scoop her up and carry her above the heads of the crowd to safety. She was *terrified*." Even after each performance, Madonna was "afraid of being alone," Barbone said. "So I would drive her around for hours until she felt safe again. She hated being alone."

Madonna seldom was alone, dancing wildly with a whole new cast of friends and admirers at such yuppie discos as the Roxy, the Paradise Garage, the Continental, the Pyramid Club, and Danceteria—not the hard rock clubs handpicked for her by Barbone. Madonna, who still had no qualms about asking for handouts from near-strangers, did not resist the blandishments of industry producers and executives who wanted to do an end run around Gotham.

"I was her mommy for over two years, and she was just grateful for the simple things I could do for her," Barbone recalled. "Then Madonna realized she could have anything she wanted. I watched her change from a really sweet girl into someone who really believed her own publicity. My efforts at building her confidence had backfired. I knew I was losing her. All the people I had introduced her to were now slipping her tickets to concerts behind my back and taking her out to dinner."

Tensions escalated as Barbone sought to protect her sizable investment in Madonna. During one of their bitter arguments, Barbone flew into a rage. "I screamed at her and told her she was manipulative, an egomaniac who didn't give a damn about anyone." Madonna cried, but her tears were unconvincing. "At that moment, I realized I had no control over her. I knew I had created a monster who would turn on me." Enraged by what she viewed as Madonna's betrayal, Barbone smashed her fist through a door, fracturing her wrist. Madonna did nothing to help. "She wouldn't hold the door open for me, or anything," Barbone recalled. "I was in tremendous pain, but she had no sympathy at all. Madonna has no compassion. To her, that would be a sign of weakness."

In a moment of desperation, an emotionally spent Barbone confessed to Madonna that she could no longer meet the singer's needs. "I can't ever do what you want," she said. "I can't please you."

Madonna agreed, "I'm a bitch." She shrugged. "I always want more."

"Madonna is a sponge all right," observed Barbone. "She soaks up everything she can from you, then when you're totally drained, she goes on to the next victim."

By the middle of 1982, with Gotham's cash reserves depleted and no firm record deal, Madonna's band members left for paying jobs. It seemed an opportune time for Madonna to reevaluate her situation. Both she and Bray were forced to admit to themselves that they were not merely dissatisfied with the pop rock songs they had been ordered to write by Barbone, but that they hated them. In an emotional confrontation, Madonna blurted out to Barbone, "I can't do this anymore. I'm going to have to start over."

The blow proved devastating to Barbone. "I risked my entire career on Madonna," she said, "and she nearly destroyed me. But," she added years later, "I don't hate her. I miss her."

On reflection, Barbone believed that Madonna viewed herself "as part of the immaculate conception. The rules that apply to the rest of us didn't apply to her. She wasn't intentionally malicious, but she was incapable of seeing life from anyone else's point of view. She wanted what she wanted, and if you didn't give it to her, she turned her back on you."

Gotham was not about to take Madonna's decision to depart lying down. Barbone and Alter announced their intention to sue Madonna on the grounds that their contract had never been legally dissolved. As for the "Gotham Tape," as the four-tune demo would become known in music circles, Barbone and Alter would be enmeshed for years in a legal battle for control of the potentially valuable recording—a battle that remained unresolved into the 1990s. Jointly owned by Gotham, Madonna, and the studio where it was recorded, Media Sound, the demo tape can only be released with the consent of all three parties. "There is no way Madonna would allow me to make millions off that tape," Barbone said. "I'm still being punished."

One who refused to become bogged down in this legal quagmire was Madonna. She moved back into the Music Building with Steve Bray, where their only furniture was some battered egg crates retrieved from a Dumpster. Once again left to their own devices, Madonna and Bray went back on their forced diet of cheese popcorn and the occasional can of tuna fish.

After Pearl Lang, Patrick Hernandez, Dan Gilroy, and now Gotham's Camille Barbone, Madonna was finding it easier to jettison friends and lovers when they no longer served her purposes. Bray remained, but having already been unceremoniously deserted when Madonna fled Michigan for New York, he harbored no illusions about the future of their relationship. With the faithful Bray in tow, Madonna dove headlong into New York's smoky, swirling nightlife in search of the sound that would rocket her to stardom—and of the man with enough influence and power in the music industry to light the fuse.

9

"Sometimes I feel guilty because I feel
like I travel through people. That's true
of a lot of ambitious people. You take
what you can and then move on."

Lt was Erica Bell's first visit to the Continental Club, and everything she had heard about the place was true. "People said that
the minute you walked in the door, somebody would thrust cocaine in your hand," said Bell, a graduate student in sociology at
New York University who had just opened her own downtown
nightclub on Ninth Street off Third Avenue, Lucky Strike. "It was
worse than that. Outside the door, somebody offered me coke,
which I didn't do."

Everything about that night in 1982 would remain clear in Erica
Bell's mind. Once the striking black dancer/model/sociology stu-
dent/nightclub owner passed through a billowing curtain into the
main room, she was instantly struck by the blue-and-white high-
tech decor. "It was straight out of the Jetsons," Bell said. "There
was a huge fish tank, a bar that went on forever, and these white,
four-foot-high Corinthian columns for dramatic effect. It seemed
like everything was covered in glitter. Very Hollywood."

At the opposite end of the long bar, sitting cross-legged atop one
of these columns, was "this woman, dressed all in white—wear-

ing a white tuxedo suit with a very wrinkled white shirt. She had this dark hair sticking up all over the place, and of course, she was surrounded by men."

It was Madonna. "My eyes went right to her," Bell recalled. "I just could not take my eyes off her. And she had such beautiful eyes. Incredibly gorgeous. She was staring at me and I was staring at her. To me it seemed like an eternity. It's one of those strange things that happen in your life. When you meet someone you fall in love with. It sounds so corny or trite, but it's like the movies when time stops. We've talked about it many times since."

The men talking to Madonna melted away, several with her phone number in hand, until the only one left was Bell's own roommate, Peter Schultz. Bell strode up to them and told him to go away. " 'Come on,' I said, 'she's not going out with *you*. I want to talk with her.' " Then, turning to the beautiful girl in white, Bell explained, "I live with him." Schultz quickly added that he and Bell were just roommates and not involved romantically. "Peter was worried that Madonna would think we were lovers— not that she would care. If she wanted to go out with him, she would have gone out with him." (Schultz, too, left with Madonna's phone number and dated her twice).

Erica Bell and Madonna had much in common. Bell, quickly nicknamed Rica by her new friend, had also been brought up in an affluent suburb—in her case, Great Neck, Long Island. Like Tony Ciccone, Bell's father was highly educated—a scientist who worked for years with the Nuclear Regulatory Commission. Much was demanded of Bell, and like Madonna, she had excelled in school. She, too, had gravitated to dance and now found herself trying to carve out a niche for herself in Manhattan's sense-blurring, neon-lit nightlife. Both young women were articulate, attractive, and confident—although one considerably more so than the other.

The one thing they did not share at this juncture in their lives was hunger. Bell was impressed with Madonna's resourcefulness when it came to scrounging up a meal. "Even later, when she started to make it and we were driving around town in limousines," Bell claimed, "she'd point to an alley and say, 'I used to dig through the garbage cans in there looking for food. It's amazing how much perfectly good stuff people throw away.' Delicatessen and restaurant owners would come up to Madonna, and she'd recognize them right away. 'Rica, I love this guy. He used to feed me, save food for me out back.' These were very lean times. I mean, there were times when she'd have to decide whether she was going to eat an apple or take the subway. Hearing these stories made me want to cry."

But not Madonna. "She isn't the emotional type," said Bell, who soon became Madonna's closest female confidant. "Madonna has this force. She has the most phenomenal will of anyone I've ever met. How close were we? Well, we slept in the same bed," said Bell, who would recall Madonna's curious six A.M. ritual of gargling with salt water—"for her voice, I think."

Sympathetic to her new friend's plight, Bell hired Madonna to tend bar at her club, Lucky Strike. That lasted for only two nights —"She wanted to focus all her energy on her career, which she talked about incessantly"—but that brief stint marked another milestone in Madonna's life. A tall, blond Floridian with a cherubic face and a disarming smile was the bartender at Lucky Strike, and Bell introduced Madonna to him. Like her first mentor, Christopher Flynn, Martin Burgoyne was gay. He also clicked with Madonna and would soon wear the mantle as her closest friend— male or female. "Everybody loved Martin," Bell recalled. "He was sweet and funny and handsome and wonderful. But he and Madonna had this very special way of communicating. If he had been heterosexual, of course they never could have been so close."

Most nights, according to Bell, she and Madonna went out— often to the trendiest of the downtown clubs, Danceteria. "We would go there on a date," Bell remembered. "We went terrorizing —that's what we called it because that's what we did—terrorize people. She would say, 'Rica, I am the best-looking white girl here, and you are the best-looking black girl here, so let's do it.' Then we'd push people off the dance floor and take over.

"We'd pick out the cute boys," Bell continued, "go right up and without saying a word kiss them on the mouth. Then we'd take their phone numbers, walk away, and while the guy was still watching, crumple up the number and throw it away."

A favorite gambit involved waiting to get on an elevator with a man, then ambushing him inside. "I remember this one up-and-down session Madonna had with this guy," Bell said. "They just rode up and down the elevator, and when he got off, he was cross-eyed. He talked about it for months."

Madonna was nothing if not an Olympic-caliber kisser. "She must be great in bed because she is so uninhibited and athletic," Camille Barbone observed, "but it's kissing that turns her on." Citing Madonna's open bisexual overtures, Erica Bell stressed, "I was intrigued with Madonna before she kissed me. But I can tell you one thing: once Madonna kisses you, you stay kissed."

When they weren't prowling the clubs, Madonna and Bell revealed to one another their hopes and fears. While she may have appeared dauntless, Madonna did have a tangible dread of death, or more precisely, oblivion. "She used to tell me that she wanted to be famous," Bell said, "that she *had* to be famous. Madonna would say, 'I don't just need attention. I need *all* the attention. I want everyone in the world to know who I am, and to *love* me.' That was two years before she had a hit record. I think the strongest fear she had then was that she might die and be forgotten."

One evening, as the two sat on the floor of Madonna's room ("We had to—there were no chairs," said Bell), Madonna surprised Bell by pulling out of an envelope the nude photographs that had been taken of her during her hand-to-mouth modeling days. "Rica, you won't believe this," she said to her gaunt friend, pointing to the photos, "but back then I was just as flat-chested as you!"

"We were rolling around laughing, these nude pictures seemed so hysterically funny to us," Bell recalled. "Oh, I just can't wait until I'm famous and these get out," Madonna said. "Someone's going to want to sell these to *Playboy*." Then she paused, screwing up her face. "But they won't want these. Look how flat-chested I am." (Years later, when both *Playboy* and *Penthouse* published the photos, causing a national furor, Madonna would telephone Bell. "Rica, I can't believe this," Madonna said, shrieking with laughter. "But I'm so *flat-chested*.")

Another evening, Madonna, intent on pursuing her tough-girl persona, decided there was one street art at which she would have to become proficient. "She asked me," said Bell, "to teach her how to spit. So we stood on the curb and spit and spit and spit—until she felt satisfied that she could spit like a tough New Yorker. People on the street were horrified, but we thought it was hysterical."

Less amusing to Madonna was the progress of her musical career. Since she had no independent claim on the four-song Gotham Tape, Madonna and Bray recorded another demo, this time containing four of their own streetwise dance tunes: "Everybody," "Ain't No Big Deal," "Stay," and "Burning Up."

Madonna waged a one-woman campaign to get the demo heard by the right people. Her chosen arena was midtown Manhattan's Danceteria. Carrying on in the media-pandering tradition of Studio 54, the Mudd Club, and Xenon, Danceteria was opened by nightlife impresario Rudolf in 1981 and overnight became one of the city's most talked-about and written-about avant-garde hangouts. While it catered to the requisite contingent of Eurotrash, overpaid Wall Street tyros looking for unsavory ways to spend their cash, and the sort of bicoastal personalities who routinely wind up in the "Star Tracks" department of *People* magazine, much of Danceteria's clientele was genuinely on the cutting edge of fashion, art, and music. Artists Andy Warhol, Keith Haring, and Jean-Michel Basquiat, designers Willie Smith and Betsey Johnson, groups such as Blondie, Kid Creole and the Coconuts, Tuxedomoon—even the bizarre pioneers of a new music form known as rap (including the Beastie Boys and Run-D.M.C.)—were among the Danceteria regulars.

Even in this Day-Glo crowd, Madonna was a standout as she tore up the dance floor every Saturday night with her best pals Martin Burgoyne (who also worked as a bartender at the club) and Erica Bell and Bell's friend Bagen ("Bags") Riles. "It was very sudden," Bell recalled. "Everybody asked us, 'Who is this girl?' Madonna *made* herself known."

Indeed she did, with the help of a well-connected expatriate Frenchwoman named Maripol. At least a decade older than Madonna, Maripol, like Camille Barbone before her, became the aspiring star's mother-figure-of-the-moment. While working part-time at the disco as a hatcheck girl, Madonna indulged in an affair with British-born busboy Joe Jones. "One night Joe Jones and Madonna decided to dye their hair the same color," Bell recalled. "The next day they both showed up at work as platinum blonds.

He looked awful, but she looked great. It was the first time any of us had ever seen Madonna as a blond."

Madonna remained her own best public relations woman. And unquestionably the single most important person she made herself known to at Danceteria was Mark Kamins. The Manhattan-born son of jazz aficionados, Kamins grew up listening to the music of John Coltrane and Miles Davis. After he graduated from Ithaca College with a degree in film, he went on to postgraduate studies in Paris and Athens. Returning to New York in 1978, he capitalized on his lifelong love of music by doing a stint as a disc jockey at a trendy club called Tracks. When Rudolf opened Danceteria, Kamins signed on as the club's sole deejay, and his flamboyant style quickly earned him the reputation as king of the New Wave deejays.

What Kamins really wanted to do was produce records. "I was always the guy at the parties who played the records," he said. "But once I actually got inside a studio, I made the decision to become a producer." After writing a song called "Snapshot," he had landed a deal to produce an album for Capitol Records vocalist Delores Hall. He followed that up by working on a record with David Byrne of the group Talking Heads.

It was at this critical juncture that Madonna sidled up to Kamins at Danceteria's deejay booth. She left no doubt as to her intentions. "I'd been watching her dance," Kamins said, "and she was spectacular—but always from a distance. When she came up and introduced herself, I was struck by her innate sexuality. She is beautiful, but it is her sense of style, of individuality. She has this aura about her."

Bell watched in amazement as her friend implemented her plan to conquer Kamins. Her technique was always the same. "She seduces people," Bell said. "She tells them they are wonderful, flatters them, flirts with them, then sucks whatever it is she wants out of them."

Before long, Kamins and Madonna became lovers, and one of the night's most visible couples. "She always was sexually aggressive, and it wasn't just her image," Kamins said. "She used her sexuality as a performer, but it's also how she got over offstage."

Not that she left any doubts as to her intentions. "She was always straightforward. She always made it clear that she wanted to be a star. But there was also an innocence about her. An innocence," he added wistfully, "that soon vanished."

After a few days together, Madonna felt comfortable enough to spring her demo tape on Kamins. He did more than just listen to the demo; he played it at the Danceteria. The crowd went wild for the homemade tape—and Kamins was convinced that in Madonna he might have the makings of a star.

Kamins had done some free-lance scouting for the Artist and Repertoire department of Island Records and had recently signed a British group called U2 that would by the mid-1980s become one of that label's biggest-grossing rock bands. He took Madonna's demo to Island executive Chris Blackwell, who promptly turned it down. It was not the first time Blackwell had passed on an act brought to him by Kamins. Two years earlier, he also turned down a chance to sign an offbeat group called Culture Club, apparently not sufficiently impressed by the talents of its lead singer, Boy George.

Kamins's next step was to take Madonna's demo to Warner Brothers, where he had just completed work on the new David Byrne album. He had become friendly with an up-and-coming artist and repertoire man at Warner's Sire label named Michael Rosenblatt. At a time when most record executives were stumbling over one another to sign up the next snarling, leather-encased punk rocker, Rosenblatt had championed upbeat dance-club acts such as the B-52's and the English duo Wham. Kamins called up Rosenblatt and invited him to drop by Danceteria to meet a young singer who would, Kamins promised him, "knock you out."

Several days later, Rosenblatt was playing host to visiting Wham at Danceteria when the group's lead vocalist, George Michael, spotted an attractive young woman (whose blond hair was growing back dark) in a jaunty cap and garish, mismatched stockings prancing up to the deejay booth. She was chewing gum frantically; a crucifix dangled from her left ear. Without having to be introduced to her by Kamins, Rosenblatt knew instantly that this "incredibly wild-looking" woman was Madonna. He introduced himself—as well as the gawking George Michael—then invited her to drop by his office with her demo tape.

Kamins brought Madonna to Rosenblatt's office at Warner headquarters in Rockefeller Center several days later. He placed a Sony tape recorder on the desk and switched it on. The first song was "Everybody." As they sat there, waiting for his verdict, Rosenblatt listened to the four songs on the demo, then rewound it and listened again. "The tape was good," he recalled, "but not outstanding. But here was this girl sitting in my office, radiating that certain something. Whatever it is, she had more of it than I'd ever seen. I *knew* that there was this star sitting there."

Rosenblatt paused for a minute after listening to the demo, then turned to Madonna. "So, what do you want to do?" he asked her.

"I want to make records," she answered.

"Okay," Rosenblatt replied, extending his hand. "Let's go!"

Rosenblatt, Kamins, and Madonna sketched out the terms of a contract on a yellow legal pad. Madonna would be paid an initial advance of $5,000, plus royalties and publishing fees of $1,000 for each song she wrote.

Now all that remained between Madonna and a bona fide recording career was Sire president Seymour Stein, whose final stamp of approval was needed on all Sire contracts. Less than an hour after Madonna and Kamins departed, Rosenblatt took the tape to the mercurial Stein, who was in Lenox Hill Hospital recuperating from heart surgery. Stein was so excited by the demo tape that he ordered Rosenblatt to bring Madonna straight to him. The next afternoon, Madonna, Kamins, and Rosenblatt walked into Stein's hospital room to meet the powerful president of Sire Records, who greeted them, Madonna recalled, "in his Jockey shorts, with a drip-feed in his arm!"

For the first time since her stint with Patrick Hernandez in Paris, Madonna could stop rummaging through garbage cans in search of her next meal. She went right out and spent half of her $5,000 advance on a Roland synthesizer.

Stein and Rosenblatt may have been confident of their new discovery's potential, but not so confident that they were willing to gamble everything on the release of an album. Rosenblatt devised a strategy for promoting Madonna built on the release of a series of dance-oriented singles. The first single would be Stein's favorite song on the demo tape, "Ain't No Big Deal." On the B side of the record, intended initially as a throwaway, was to be "Everybody."

Who would be given the opportunity to produce Madonna's first record? Madonna felt it was time to reward the loyal Steve Bray. "She told me," Kamins recalled, "that she wanted Bray to do it. I told her, 'Hell, no. This is my opportunity as well as one for you.'" By way of compromise, Kamins and Madonna offered Bray the chance to arrange the single. Bray replied with a bluntly worded ultimatum: "Fuck you," he told Madonna. "Either I produce or nothing." Left with no choice, Madonna bowed to Kamins's wishes. Bray, understandably bitter over what he believed to be another betrayal by Madonna, would not speak to her for nearly two years.

After two weeks in the studio, Kamins and Madonna emerged with the single they were convinced would catapult her into the Top 40. Yet when Rosenblatt heard what was thought to be the surefire hit, he was crestfallen. "Ain't No Big Deal" turned out to be just that. There was no time to record a new tune. Instead, they would put the rollicking "Everybody" on *both* sides of the record. Rosenblatt's unorthodox solution paid off spectacularly. Within weeks, "Everybody" surged to the top of the dance charts.

If they were not ready to spring for an album, Rosenblatt and Stein did gear up Warner's publicity department to give Madonna the kind of send-off seldom accorded a first-time artist. "We were surprised at first," a former Warner publicist recalled. "The amount of money being spent on Madonna's publicity was more than we were spending on some of our established stars—and she was only releasing a single, not even an album. But then we got a look at Madonna, and we were no longer surprised. The powers-that-be clearly had a thing for her, and they were determined that we make her happy."

Although Rosenblatt was never romantically involved with Madonna, those close to them at the time said he was smitten. So much so that when Rosenblatt married Madonna's roommate, Janice Galloway, some wags speculated that he was virtually wedding Madonna by proxy. "It was as close to marrying Madonna," said a mutual acquaintance, "as Michael could get." Galloway and Rosenblatt later divorced.

The next phase of Rosenblatt's concentrated Madonna campaign was to concoct a sizzling stage act that would highlight her new single and at the same time prepare for the inevitable tour. Howie Montaug, who had managed Erica Bell's Lucky Strike and now ran his own No Entiendes ("You Don't Understand") cabaret, was tapped to produce a live show for Madonna. Clad in top hat and tails, the flashy impresario introduced Madonna and her dancers—Martin Burgoyne, Bell, and Bags—to a standing-room-only crowd at Danceteria. While the top brass of Sire Records looked on, Madonna whipped the sweating crowd of nearly four hundred into a frenzy. Rosenblatt turned to Stein and straining to be heard above the crowd, yelled a single word: "Video!"

It was early 1983, and in the three short years of its existence, MTV had given a thrilling new spin to the world of pop music—and stood to pocket hundreds of millions of dollars in the process. Yet the music video was still dominated by a handful of men—most notably Michael Jackson, whose "Billie Jean," "Thriller," and "Beat It" videos had established him as the master of the medium.

Before she could attempt to challenge the master at his own game, Madonna took her small troupe (including Erica Bell and Martin Burgoyne) on the road to polish their act. It was while rehearsing for an engagement in Florida that they decided to settle one nagging but important question once and for all. "We called it the Week of the Seven Hair Colors," Bell recalled. "Martin, Madonna, and I changed our hair color every single day. We had red, brown, black, blond, orange, even white." Madonna settled on a "reddish brown" and anxiously awaited her record company's approval. "Oh, I hope Michael [Rosenblatt] likes my hair when he sees it," she told Bell.

He didn't. "When he saw her, his jaw dropped," Bell recalled. "He said, 'We've spent so much money on your publicity, there is no way I'm going to let you look like this. *No way!*' " Rosenblatt ordered Madonna to dye her hair back to blond—and keep it that way.

10

"Wouldn't you rather read an article
about a slut than a plain-Jane
wallflower? I know I would."

Warner executive Michael Rosenblatt realized that much of Madonna's appeal was visual—she was nothing if not intriguing—but he fretted that her dance-oriented music would not be considered mainstream enough for MTV. Still, Sire was sufficiently buoyed by the steady movement of "Everybody" up the dance charts, and Madonna's galvanic presence onstage at Danceteria, to commit to a video—more or less. Rosenblatt and Sire chief Seymour Stein agreed that this video should be aimed not at a mass audience, but squarely at dance clubs around the country. As for the budget, out of the millions at Warner's disposal, they allotted an infinitesimal $1,500 for Madonna's first video—less than 1 percent of what was routinely budgeted for videos by the likes of Michael Jackson, Prince, Duran Duran, Lionel Ritchie, the Police, or any of the other big acts of the time.

The producer they chose to bring in Madonna's debut video on schedule and under budget was Ed Steinberg, the soft-spoken president of Rock America and supplier of videos to hundreds of clubs across the nation. Steinberg was not altogether unfamiliar with Madonna. This was the same producer who, only the year before, had hired Madonna as an extra in his video for the group Konk, then watched in amazement as she vamped outrageously before the camera.

From the outset, Madonna impressed Steinberg with her cool professionalism. When one of her three dancers failed to show up the morning of the shoot, Madonna devised a solution on the spot. "Anybody else might have been thrown," Steinberg said, "but she just said, 'Okay, so I've got two dancers instead of three. It's no big deal.' Then she redid the choreography right on the spot." He was also impressed with her apparent lack of temperament during the filming of the "Everybody" video. "She was great, a real trouper," he remembered. "Sometimes you'll tell an artist you've got to do another take, and they'll walk off the set. But Madonna did twenty takes without complaint. She wanted to get as close to perfection on tape as humanly possible, and she was willing to sweat if that's what it took."

Her work paid off. Boosted by the video, "Everybody" raced up to No. 3 on the dance charts, then crossed over to *Billboard*'s pop Hot 100. This achievement—it is rare that a single makes it onto the charts without the backing of an album—did not go unnoticed at Warner's head office. Rosenblatt, Michael Alago, and the other Young Turks who made up Warner's "kiddie corps" were now convinced it was time to take the next giant step and produce an album.

Thus far, however, Warner had managed to reap handsome profits on a tiny investment. To justify the substantial cost of producing and distributing an album, Seymour Stein wanted to make sure that "Everybody" was not just a fluke—that Madonna's appeal was broader than just the club scene. Toward that end, Stein authorized a twelve-inch "mini-LP" to test the waters. If it showed remotely as much movement as "Everybody," the green light would be given for Madonna's debut album.

Knowing all that was riding on this effort, Madonna met with Warner executives and insisted on hiring a more experienced producer than Kamins. Kamins's strength was handling musicians, she told them, not vocalists. In much the same way that George Cukor was a "woman's director," there were several record producers known for bringing out the best in female singers. Reggie Lucas, who had just produced a hit album for Stephanie Mills, was one of them. Madonna wanted him.

"Yes, I was hurt, and very pissed off!" said Kamins, who now lined up behind Gilroy, Bray, Barbone, and the growing number of people who had helped Madonna only to be cast aside. "She wanted someone who was better on vocals, and she was right," Kamins said. "That's not my forte. But it was the way it was handled. Madonna never told me to my face that I was replaced by Reggie Lucas. I had to find out from the guys at Warner." There remained one saving grace: Madonna had signed a document giving Kamins a percentage of all her royalties. And like Camille Barbone, Kamins would later become embroiled in a bitter and protracted legal battle with Madonna to enforce that agreement.

Madonna's new producer wasted no time writing a hit for her. Reggie Lucas had seen her act at Danceteria, and her sweaty persona inspired him on the spot to write "Physical Attraction." Seymour Stein and his colleagues at Sire would not be disappointed. "Physical Attraction" reached the top of the dance charts, and Rosenblatt was given the green light to proceed with an album.

Again, Kamins and Bray both demanded the assignment. "It was really awful," said Madonna, "but I just didn't trust Steve enough." As for Kamins: "I didn't think that Mark was ready to do a whole album."

While preparations were under way to record the album, Madonna was cutting a wide sexual swath through Manhattan. Her tempestuous affair with Kenny Compton continued, as did her relationship with Kamins—despite her decision to bypass him in favor of Reggie Lucas.

As focused as Madonna was on her music, the surreal world of SoHo's graffiti artists still held a special fascination for her. Only a few years earlier, Madonna's friend Keith Haring had been caught scrawling his bizarre chalk figures on subway walls and thrown in jail for defacing public property. Now those same otherworldly chalk figures—barking dogs with alligator jaws, crawling babies emitting a radiant glow, faceless humans beneath hovering

UFOs—were selling for as much as $350,000, making Haring the darling of the downtown art world.

Haring was homosexual and in less than two years would be diagnosed with AIDS (the disease would kill him in 1990, at the age of thirty-one). Yet several of the young graffitists Madonna was introduced to by Haring were heterosexual, and by 1983 she numbered several of the nation's most promising modern artists among her lovers.

Like Haring, Lenny McGurr was still in his teens when he ventured into subways to spray-paint the tiled walls and train cars with his iridescent abstract designs signed, enigmatically, "Futura 2000." By 1983, the slender black artist was being celebrated around the world, his paintings fetching $10,000 apiece and more.

"Madonna zeroed in on Futura 2000 like a missile," Erica Bell said. "Futura did not stand a chance. He was exactly her type—a light-skinned black, creative, rebellious but not threatening. They had a really hot thing going for a while, and for a while he was devoted to her."

At one point Madonna, who by now had moved into a modest East Village flat, invited Futura 2000 to cover the walls with his famous signature. "You have to put your name everywhere," she declared. The landlord viewed the matter somewhat differently and evicted her.

No matter. With the money from Warner, she could now afford a loft in SoHo. As for Futura 2000, her passion for him abated when she became infatuated with another black graffiti artist named Michael Stewart. Not yet out of his teens, Stewart appeared to be on the threshold of a brilliant career. Now finding herself attracted to younger and younger men, Madonna did not try to hide her affection for Stewart.

Although he appeared briefly in Madonna's debut video "Everybody," Stewart would not be allowed even the brief glimpse of fame and fortune afforded the doomed Keith Haring. In 1987, Michael Stewart was allegedly beaten by New York transit police as they arrested him for vandalism in the subways. He died as a result of those injuries, igniting a storm of protest that ultimately led to an investigation.

Tragedy, in fact, would befall many if not most of Madonna's closest friends. Jean-Michel Basquiat was not yet twenty-three and with the help of his friend and mentor Andy Warhol was already an established painter when he caught Madonna's eye at a party in 1983. The Brooklyn-bred son of a Haitian accountant and his Puerto Rican wife, Basquiat ran away from home when he was fifteen. His father, with whom he had an intense love-hate relationship similar to that between Madonna and her father, found Jean-Michel four days later sitting on a bench in New York's Washington Square Park. Jean-Michel's head was completely shaved. "Papa," he said, "I will be very, very famous one day."

The similarities between Basquiat and Madonna did not stop there. Leaving home for good at seventeen, he lived on handouts and slept on the floors of friends' apartments as he tried to gain a foothold in the art world. To survive during this period, he worked the streets as a male prostitute. And just as Madonna had forged vital contacts at downtown dance clubs, Basquiat hung out at Club 57, the Mudd Club, Hurrah's, M.K., Danceteria, CBGB, and other night spots that, in the words of one social commentator, "spawned the stars and sycophants of the eighties." By establishing the same sort of surrogate-parent relationship with art dealers that Madonna had established with Christopher Flynn, Pearl Lang, Camille Barbone, Maripol, and others, Basquiat gained visibility. And by early 1983, he was selling his paintings for upwards of $10,000 to the likes of Richard Gere and Paul Simon.

Basquiat also reveled in his growing reputation as the downtown art world's enfant terrible. He was thrown out of the Whitney Museum for scribbling on the walls. While dining at the exclusive restaurant Mr. Chow, he threw food at a woman at a nearby table. When Club 57 nearly burned down, the place was evacuated—with the exception of Basquiat, who stood in a corner smoking pot, laughing hysterically.

Indeed, drugs had already caused Basquiat's life to unravel by the time he and Madonna met. He had graduated from pot to LSD, then cocaine and finally heroin. He began freebasing. Despite the huge prices his canvases were commanding, Basquiat's costly habit ($2,000 a week on coke alone) and spendthrift ways—

he could easily spend $10,000 on designer suits in a single day—created financial pressures that occasionally forced him to return to hustling.

None of this mattered to Madonna. "She came up to me at a party and asked me to introduce her to 'that beautiful black boy in the corner,'" recalled Ed Steinberg. At the time Basquiat, who would later become known for his wild dreadlocks, was sporting a dyed-blond punk hairdo. Their affair would be intense and brief, ending in part over his drug addiction. "Being seduced and abandoned by Madonna," said a friend, "is something I don't think Jean-Michel ever got over." Five years later, Basquiat would be found on the floor of his bedroom, dead from a heroin overdose.

Another of Madonna's graffiti-artist lovers was sixteen-year-old Bobby Martinez. If Madonna was drawn to Michael Stewart and Jean-Michel Basquiat because of their touching vulnerability, it was the wildness in Martinez that she found appealing. Streetwise and later to serve time in jail for petty crimes, Martinez first heard of Madonna from his friend Keith Haring. "I was at Keith's," he recalled, "and he said, 'Do you want to go over to Madonna's apartment?' I said. 'Who is that?'"

Madonna and Martinez hit it off, dancing late into the night, and the next day he brought her one of his paintings as a gift. Two weeks later, she called him over for a private party, and he stayed the night.

For the next four years, Bobby Martinez would weave in and out of Madonna's life. "Madonna's not afraid of anything," Erica Bell said. "But Bobby was one of the boys who made her feel like she was living on the edge. He had this aura of danger about him, like so many men in her life. It makes her feel alive."

In the early spring of 1983, Madonna added to her list of conquests John "Jellybean" Benitez, an ambitious young musician from New York's barrio who had already built a reputation as mix master extraordinaire at Danceteria's rival disco, the Fun House. Benitez and Madonna, although from very different backgrounds, shared a burning ambition and a penchant for brazen self-promotion. With his first paycheck as a deejay at the Fun House, Benitez hired a personal publicist. "Jellybean is the type of person," observed Johnny Dynell, a singer and friend of Madonna's during this period, "who walks in, says hi, then scans the room to see if there is anyone more important he should be talking to."

Benitez, like Kamins, wielded enough influence on the club scene to make him a worthwhile person for Madonna to know. "Madonna sought Jellybean out," Johnny Dynell recalled. "She had heard about him, she knew he could help her. So one night she walked right up to the deejay booth, grabbed him, and kissed him. They are so much alike, it was inevitable."

Madonna's aversion to monogamy did not go unnoticed. "Madonna always had at least three guys going at a time," Mark Kamins said. "Each one of us was there to fulfill a separate need in her life. For a while it was me, Jellybean, and Ken Compton. The cast of characters changed practically every week. There was jealousy, sure. We didn't like it, but we knew what she was doing."

No more qualified an authority than Steve Bray, who would later be rewarded in very tangible ways for remaining loyal to Madonna, publicly forgave her for dumping him as a lover. "It seems like you're leaving people behind or you're stepping on them," he told a reporter, "and the fact is that you're moving and they're not."

To Madonna, men were incidental at best. And now that she had two hits under her belt, she was not about to lose momentum. She stepped up her networking efforts. The well-connected French socialite Maripol now seemed to be a constant presence in her life, hovering at her elbow, introducing the new star to all the "right" people, and tending Madonna's ego in much the same way Camille Barbone had done two years before.

"I can still hear Maripol with that ridiculous accent," Erica Bell said. " 'Oh, *Madonna*. If you are to be zee beeg superstar, you must meet zees people.' She practically pushed Madonna onto Mick Jagger. Not that she needed that much pushing, mind you." By the same token, Maripol could be quite blunt about whom Madonna should not bother with. "Maripol would tell Madonna not to waste her time with people who were no longer on top," Bell said. "Power and influence were the name of the game. If a person couldn't do Madonna's career any good, she ignored them. Madonna could be very brutal that way."

"Oh, yes," Maripol agreed. "I knew Madonna is zee superstar

before anyone else—even before Madonna knew it. Zat is why she loves me, and I love her."

On an almost nightly basis, Maripol escorted her celebrity friends, such as Jagger, Andy Warhol, and Blondie's Debbie Harry, over to meet Madonna. "Which is terribly ironic," Johnny Dynell recalled, "because Madonna stole so much of Debbie Harry's look and sound. Madonna worshiped Debbie Harry back then, but she felt even more strongly about Jessica Lange. She always used to say that who she really wanted to be was Jessica Lange—not the classy actress Lange became, but the flashy bimbo in *King Kong*."

Debbie Harry and Jessica Lange were not the only women from whom Madonna borrowed heavily. "Madonna always talked about being a comedienne," Dynell said. "That is what she wanted to be—a comedienne in the movies like Carole Lombard or Judy Holliday or Marilyn Monroe. That came later. I always got the feeling that she viewed the whole music thing as just a stepping-stone to movie stardom."

At the same time "Everybody" was climbing the dance charts, Dynell had his own hit called "Jam Hot." But neither could match the celebrity candlepower of Boy George, who caused a major stir the night he popped in unannounced with his transvestite boyfriend Marilyn. "Madonna was dying to meet him," Dynell recalled, "but when she walked up and stuck out her hand, he snubbed her completely. That really set her off. Madonna turned to me, fuming, and said, 'That little fuck! I'll be bigger than him, and when he wants to meet me, *I'll* do the snubbing.'"

Two years later, Dynell was on hand to witness Madonna's revenge. "By then, she was the biggest thing in music and his career had taken a nosedive. Boy George was so excited when he saw her, like some star-struck fan. But when he approached her, she literally spun around and started talking to somebody else. A lot of people were there, and it was pretty humiliating for Boy. Madonna couldn't have been more pleased with herself." Dynell claimed the incident taught him a valuable lesson about Madonna. "She forgets *nothing*," he sighed, "and she is perfectly capable of holding a grudge forever."

11

"The very best thing about being
single is that there's always someone
else. Besides, I wouldn't wish being
Mr. Madonna on anybody."

That spring of 1983, Madonna juggled at least a half dozen lovers while managing to record a debut album that Warner executives felt could sell at most 250,000 copies. Reggie Lucas, all agreed, had done a phenomenal producing job—with one notable exception. "Ain't No Big Deal," which now was intended to be the lead song on the album, *still* did not work. It would have to be replaced. But would Warner dip into its pockets to fund yet another song? Rosenblatt put his newest star on a plane for Los Angeles and dispatched her with orders to win over Warner's moneymen.

When Madonna walked into the Los Angeles offices of her record label, jaws dropped. "She sounded black," said a former Warner executive who had not seen her early videos, "and in pops this blonde. Everybody was stunned. She charmed the pants off everyone there."

The ploy worked and Madonna returned to New York with the go-ahead for a new song. But where would they find a replacement for "Ain't No Big Deal"? "Seymour Stein called in a panic," Kamins recalled, "and said, 'We need another song!' " So Madonna went to Jellybean Benitez, who just happened to have a tune handy. It was called "Holiday."

Within days, "Holiday" was recorded and added to the LP, but there remained the problem of what to call the album. As a bittersweet acknowledgment of the contribution he had made to her career, Madonna had written a tune called "Lucky Star" for Mark Kamins. She recorded it for the LP and that, Stein decided, would be the title of the entire album.

With the jacket design came another dilemma. If they were to call the album "Lucky Star" rather than use her name on the cover, then Madonna would at least have to be depicted in some way on the album. This they were not eager to do. If the record executives had assumed from listening to her sing that Madonna was black, then the public would make that assumption as well. In addition, her early records had received their best exposure on black radio stations. Would black radio stations continue to play her records and young black audiences buy them if they were confronted with the fact that Madonna was not one of them? Finally, the decision was made to call the album *Madonna*, but to leave her face off the jacket. "They didn't put her face on the album," Kamins said, "because they didn't want people to know she was white." At least not until she had that all-important hit album under her belt.

Released in July of 1983, the album, dismissed by most critics as little more than a bland collection of disco tunes, did not score an instant hit. Unfazed, Madonna launched a one-woman campaign to get the album national exposure. Performing her sexually charged dance routines at New York's top discos, she managed to keep the opinion-shapers in the music business focused on the album. Through club exposure and radio airplay, the lead single from the album, "Holiday," crawled up the charts over the next eight months. By early 1984, two more cuts from the album—"Lucky Star" and Reggie Lucas's "Borderline"—had made it into the Top Ten.

Equally important was Madonna's breakthrough into MTV. The videos for "Everybody" and "Holiday" were, as the executives at Warner had expected, successful in clubs but too dance-oriented for a television audience accustomed to ZZ Top's leggy blondes and Van Halen's daredevil acrobatics. As proof of his company's commitment to its new star, Stein approved the filming of a state-of-the-art video for "Burning Up." A laser-filled confection of special effects, the result was both surreal and mildly sado-masochistic. Throughout much of the video, Madonna, a heavy chain tightening around her white neck, slithers sexily in the middle of a highway while a determined-looking blond man in a blue convertible bears down on her. "Unlike the others, I'll do anything," go the overtly submissive lyrics. "I'm not the same, I have no shame." In the final scene, however, the man in the convertible has vanished and it is Madonna who sits triumphantly in the driver's seat.

By way of working out a private conflict in a very public way—a hallmark of her approach to her art—Madonna cast her on-again, off-again lover Kenny Compton as the man behind the wheel. In life as well as her videos, she clearly intended to wind up behind the wheel in their stormy relationship.

The groundwork having been laid, Warner now invested a major amount in the video for "Borderline." In this, the first Madonna video to be given sustained play on all-important MTV, she is torn between a possessive young Latino and a middle-aged fashion photographer who recruits her off the street to model for him. Ingeniously shot in black and white and color (the scenes involving the high-living photographer are in black and white, the street scenes with the young Latino in color), the story bounces along to its inevitable conclusion. After defacing the photographer's studio and his expensive sports car with spray paint, Madonna returns to the arms of her T-shirt-clad Latino boyfriend.

"Lucky Star," her next video, gave MTV audiences their first long look at Madonna the stage performer. Her exposed midriff, thrift-store wardrobe, and sexy strut contrasted sharply with the sleek, high-tech style of other videos. "The look she has in the video is mine," said Erica Bell, who performed as one of the two backup dancers in the video. "I made every stitch of clothing in 'Lucky Star,' from the knot in her hair to her socks and shoes, her black top—everything you see is mine. I even ripped the T-shirt in just the right spot to show off her belly button."

The Madonna Look that would soon sweep across America was taking shape. The fingerless lace gloves and ripped clothes were augmented by rubber bracelets, dangling cross earrings, and huge crucifixes now designed by Madonna's confidante/surrogate mother Maripol. Splashed across one of her jackets was a design by graffiti artist Kano and the words WEBO GALS. "Webo," Madonna took discernible pride in explaining, "means 'ball-shaker' in Spanish." (Madonna would later call her music publishing company Webo Girl Inc.)

She had already taken to wearing a belt emblazoned with her soon-to-be-famous "Boy Toy" logo—a leftover from her days hanging out with her breakdancer and graffiti artist friends at the Roxy. "Everybody had a tag name," she later explained. "One day I just thought of Boy Toy, and when I threw it up on a wall, everybody said they thought it was funny, too. It's a tongue-in-cheek statement, the opposite of what it says."

During the shooting of the "Lucky Star" video, Erica Bell served another function as well. "For her close-ups, Madonna told me to stand where she could see me," she recalled. "She said the video would be that much better if she could sing the song to someone she loved."

For reasons that would only become apparent much later, "Lucky Star" turned out to be a milestone for Madonna. The single was the first of fifteen consecutive Top Five hits—a feat that surpassed even the Beatles' record.

Across the Atlantic, meanwhile, "Holiday" was tearing up the European charts. It was the height of Fashion Week in Paris, and designer Elio Fiorucci flew Madonna and her small entourage to France to entertain at a party attended by such fashion luminaries as Yves Saint Laurent, Givenchy, Issey Miyake, and Karl Lagerfeld. Warner Records sent a Mercedes limousine to pick her up at the airport, and Madonna wasted no time scrawling BOY TOY in indelible marker across the upholstery. "The driver's name was Guy," recalled Erica Bell, who was along for the ride, "and he, needless to say, was *furious*. It got awfully sticky, but that was us in those days."

Madonna, Bell, and Martin Burgoyne were then ferried to Place Vendôme, where they checked into the swank Hôtel Meurice. "At first it seemed great," Bell said. "I mean, there we were in our rags. But then Madonna began having these horrible nightmares." According to Bell, Madonna dreamed that she was a nun being hunted down by Nazis. "She got so upset over this that she couldn't eat. It was only later that we realized that the Meurice had been German headquarters during World War Two."

"She hated her hotel," said a Warner employee in Paris at the time, "and she didn't like the chauffeur-driven car we provided her with. She didn't like the French press, so she refused to give interviews. In short, she was on a huge star trip way before she was a huge star and alienated everybody she came in contact with."

Philippe Manoeuvre, producer and host of a popular French television show called "Sex Machine" was no exception. "I thought 'Holiday' was superb," Manoeuvre said, "so as producer, I wanted her to appear on my show. It was like 'Saturday Night Live,' and I knew she'd be right for it." Madonna made enemies from the moment she arrived. Her segment was to be shot on the beach, but when star and crew arrived on location, she was not pleased.

"I don't want to dance in the mud," she complained to Manoeuvre.

"But it's not mud," he replied. "It's wet sand."

"I say it's mud!" she shot back. Then one of the letters of her Boy Toy belt fell into the sand. "She exploded," recalled Manoeuvre. "She made the Warner public relations woman, the driver, and two dancers look for the missing letter."

"Find the letter," Madonna screamed, "or I am not doing this fucking thing!"

"She had people on their knees," Manoeuvre said. "We were scrambling in the sand looking for the missing letter for half an hour." His assessment of her behavior: "Madonna was vile! She behaved very badly. I suppose if she did that kind of thing now, people would find her brilliant. At the time, everybody said, 'Why are we putting up with this?' She was nobody then."

From Paris, Madonna, Bell, and Burgoyne made their way to Germany, where again Madonna claimed to be weighted down by a "terrible feeling of dread." As their train pulled into Munich, Bell recalled, "we had this awful feeling. It turned out that this station was where Jews were jammed into cattle cars headed for concentration camps. Madonna is very psychic," Bell added. "She's always had this hypersensitivity, but she doesn't let people see it." In another one of her recurrent dreams at this time, Madonna, Bell said, saw herself as someone who was "so pure that she didn't defecate, or when she did, it was white."

The last leg of their journey was to Morocco, where they boarded a small, rickety bus to take them over the foothills of the Atlas Mountains. Halfway to Marrakech, the bus broke down. "The engine fell out *on the road*," recalled Bell. "There we were stranded in the middle of nowhere. We waited for hours before someone came to our rescue."

Tensions were already running high because of the fact that Madonna had chosen to bring a stranger into their midst. She had hired a female trainer to accompany her on this brief promotional tour, and it soon became evident to everyone that the trainer was quite taken with the boss.

While the two women carried on their training sessions behind closed doors, Erica Bell and Martin Burgoyne were left to brood. "Madonna likes to shake things up," Bell contended. "She's only happy if there's trouble brewing. Otherwise, she gets bored."

Back in the States, as her first records and accompanying videos did a slow burn up the charts, Madonna used the time to map out her next career moves. She intended to be the biggest pop star in the world, so now she wanted Michael Jackson's manager, Freddy DeMann, to handle her affairs. Madonna asked Seymour Stein to arrange a meeting with the superagent, unaware that Jackson was no longer his client.

"Freddy really got lucky with Madonna," said Melinda Cooper, DeMann's assistant at the time. "Seymour Stein gave Freddy Madonna as a gift. Freddy did not have a clue. He had never heard of Madonna before she was handed to him on a silver platter."

When Madonna walked into his Beverly Hills office in July of 1983, DeMann was not entirely won over. Although he would later tell reporters that "she has that special magic that very few stars have," he did not sound quite so favorably impressed after their first meeting. "Who *is* this girl?" he asked his assistants, shaking his head. "Who in the hell does she think she is?"

DeMann's skepticism evaporated when Madonna's debut album went on to sell 9 million copies and spawn six hit singles. And a decade later, he would still be Madonna's manager—although she never made it easy for him. "Madonna taunts Freddy mercilessly," Cooper said. "She calls him any hour of the day or night, gets him out of the bathroom, really treats him like a lackey."

A handsomely paid lackey, to be sure. As Madonna's manager, DeMann collected 15 percent of her gross earnings. Despite this, it was generally agreed that it was Madonna who managed her own career—right down to the smallest detail. "Madonna created Madonna," Cooper said. "She arrived ready-made on Freddy's doorstep."

DeMann quickly learned to defer to his headstrong client in all business matters, and she expected the same arrangement to prevail in her personal life. Jellybean Benitez was not so easily cowed. Ken Compton's infidelities had driven her to slam down the receiver occasionally, but Madonna's affair with Benitez was punctuated with knock-down, drag-out, plate-smashing rows. "Jellybean was the only one who could drive Madonna crazy," Erica Bell contended. "The only time I ever saw her cry hysterically over a guy was after they had a fight and Jellybean had stormed out. She was devastated, really pathetic, on the floor on her hands and knees sobbing. It was totally unlike Madonna, of course, but he could really get to her."

What their friends were witnessing was the collision of two titanic egos. Even Benitez admitted to journalist Christopher Connelly that they were held together by one thing: ambition. "We both started to move," he said, "at the same pace. My career has exploded in the industry, and hers has exploded on a consumer basis. We're both very career oriented, very goal oriented."

Benitez would be widely credited in later years for helping mold Madonna's musical *ouvre*, but those closest to them believed the opposite to be true. "Jellybean was no rocket scientist," Bell said. "We had to tell him that osso buco wasn't a Japanese dish. Musically, Madonna knew way more than he did. He owes his career to her."

Johnny Dynell was among the close friends from those early days who felt that Madonna and Jellybean Benitez were "meant to be together. They are true soul mates." Unfortunately their tempestuous on-again, off-again relationship, which lasted two years and nearly led to marriage, was undermined by one of the very traits they shared: an undeniable aversion to fidelity. Slightly built, standing barely five feet six inches tall, and wearing his dark hair shoulder length, Benitez fancied himself a lady-killer. He was also a classically hot-tempered male who frequently flew into fits of jealous rage.

Where Madonna was concerned, he had cause. In mid-1983, she was lip-synching onstage at a hip-hop club on New York's Union Square called Fresh 14 when she caught the eye of a young journalist named Steve Newman. The editor of a struggling underground monthly called *Island Magazine*, Newman was won over immediately. "I thought, 'Wow, she is great!' My staff wasn't that impressed with her, but I wanted to put Madonna on the cover right away. For some reason I knew this girl was going far."

Newman watched from the wings as Madonna had her picture taken for the cover. "At the photo shoot," he said, "I got really turned on." Several nights later, at another one of artist Keith Haring's parties, Madonna and Newman met again. "We danced, and she flirted outrageously," Newman remembered. "Afterwards, I sat on one arm of this big chair, and she sat on the other. Then she crooked her finger at me, leaned over, and gave me this deep, deep kiss. Right then I fell head over heels."

Newman was already aware of Madonna's reputation as a heartbreaker and was reluctant to embark on a romance that would leave him "wounded. So I took Madonna out for a drink and told her that I wasn't interested unless she wanted something full-tilt, all or nothing—because I felt so strongly about her I knew that's the only way it could be." When Madonna proclaimed that she was just as committed to a "full-tilt" relationship as he was, they began what Newman described as "the hottest thing you can imagine. She is unbelievably passionate, totally uninhibited. Madonna was wild. She liked to make love with the windows and shades open. I think even then she needed an audience."

Their idyll was rudely interrupted one morning when Jellybean Benitez, to whom Madonna was by now officially engaged, arrived unannounced on Newman's doorstep. "I was sitting in the window with just my jeans on smoking a cigarette, because Madonna didn't smoke," Newman recalled. "Suddenly Jellybean came bursting in, grabbed Madonna, and dragged her in the back room. I was in a daze; I just went in the kitchen and made toast. There was a lot of screaming. She and Jellybean were still engaged, and she was trying to get out of it. But he wouldn't let her."

Newman and Madonna continued to see each other, but the incident reminded him that he was far from the only man in her life. At one point, Newman told her point-blank: "I know your game, bitch. I know what you're doing. You're going to torture me."

"Oh, no," Madonna replied. "I love you, Steve. I'd never do that."

"She did, of course," sighed Newman, "but much later. Even after we stopped seeing each other frequently, she'd call me in the middle of the night to talk. She kept me hanging on for a very long time." Their breakup was not over other men per se, but over her success—or more to the point, Newman's comparative lack of it. "We sat down at a bar, and she said, 'Here you are, just this chump publishing a little magazine on the Lower East Side that's never going anywhere. I'm making two hundred thousand dollars this year, and I'll make ten times as much next year. It's just never going to work.' Madonna was very sentimental about it, though. Before she walked away, she gave me this nice bracelet. . . . I can't really be bitter toward her. Everything she said was true."

Newman took solace from the fact that he was far from alone. "Steve Bray told me that Madonna taught him never to trust a woman. Madonna indulges in everybody's fantasies—but only for a short while, until she becomes bored. Then she moves on to the next man, or woman—the next fantasy. She plays everybody every which way."

After their romance had cooled, Newman discovered that it still had its residual effects. Even though he brought two dates to a Halloween party at Madonna's apartment, an angry Jellybean threatened him. "He walked up to me and said, 'I'm going to have you killed.' That was all. He knew some pretty scary people, and I had no doubts that he meant it. I was really scared."

Fortunately for Newman, their mutual friend Erica Bell intervened to assure Jellybean that Madonna and Newman were no longer an item. "Erica saved my life," he said. "No doubt about it."

Had he known about Bobby Martinez, Benitez might not have been quite so understanding. Not yet out of his teens, Martinez still drifted in and out of trouble—and in and out of Madonna's bed. "We would get together at clubs, or we'd go to hotels," Martinez recalled. "If she wanted to have sex, she'd say, 'Let's go fuck,' and we did."

None of these torrid antics distracted Madonna from the task at hand: her career. She was already contemplating the inevitable stab at acting and had met with producer Jon Peters to discuss a possible role for her in his upcoming movie *Ruthless People*. Peters wound up hiring Bette Midler instead. But that September of 1983 he needed someone to perform a small role as a club singer in *Vision Quest*, a romantic comedy about a teenage wrestler's affair with an older woman. "They didn't want to get someone they had to direct," Madonna said. "They didn't want to get an actress to pretend she's a singer. They wanted someone with a lot of style already."

Even Peters's former girlfriend Barbra Streisand was impressed by this newcomer. Madonna arrived at Streisand's house wearing a rag in her hair, a midriff-baring blouse, and her grandmother's lucky turquoise crucifix. Over dinner at a Chinese restaurant, Streisand pumped her for over two hours: "She wanted to know everything about the way I dressed, the jewelry I wore, the way I sang, and how I grew up in Detroit."

Madonna walked away feeling she had had a genuine exchange —"as one singer to another." Streisand, however, was less than charitable in her assessment of her dinner guest. According to a friend who spoke with her shortly after the dinner date, "Barbra looked at Madonna as a curiosity. She admired the girl's chutzpah, but I got the impression she thought Madonna's singing was a joke."

That November, Madonna went on location to Spokane, Washington, with the cast and crew of *Vision Quest*. Bored, cold, and lonely, she called her agent Freddy DeMann's office and begged to have Benitez flown out first class to join her. When shooting was completed, she phoned her father and announced that she would be paying the Ciccone clan a surprise visit. "Jellybean's with me, and we're coming to Detroit," she told him, "so be ready!"

Since it was an occasion, Madonna decided to dress appropriately—or at least not in a manner that would send her aging grandmother into cardiac arrest. "I wore black pants, a black T-shirt, no jewelry at all, and my hair just sort of not combed—that's pretty conservative," she remembered. "No boots or spikes or anything, and my father spent most of the time looking at me going, 'You always dress like that? Is that a costume?' "

As last-minute as it may have seemed, Madonna's decision to bring Benitez home to meet her family was no chance occurrence. Rather than being put off by his pyrotechnic flashes of jealousy, Madonna found his passionate rages exciting. She was, by all accounts, in love with Benitez. More than once, according to Erica Bell, she declared her feelings for Benitez in no uncertain terms. "I'm going to marry Jellybean," she told Bell, "and I'm going to have his baby."

She would ultimately choose neither—although more than once she had the opportunity to have Benitez's child. "Madonna had several abortions when she was with Jellybean—at least three that I know of," Erica Bell said. "She didn't make any secret about it. It wasn't something she tried to hide. She told all her friends."

When Madonna returned to New York in December of 1983, the first item on her agenda was a session with the celebrated portrait-photographer Francesco Scavullo. During the shoot, Madonna rolled around seductively on the floor. Scavullo, dissatisfied, ordered her to lower her eyelids. When she did, he dropped the camera. "Oh, my God," he gushed, "it's Baby Dietrich!" The comment sent the nickname-loving Madonna into convulsive laughter, and for a time she insisted on having her friends call her Baby Dietrich.

As far as her developing image was concerned, Madonna was already proving herself to be a shrewd manipulator of the press. "She could lie very easily to reporters," recalled Bell. "It was fun for her—a game." On one typical occasion, Bell and Madonna drove to the Hamptons for the weekend with James Truman of Britain's *The Face* magazine. "He was going to do the first major piece about Madonna for a British publication," Bell said. "She called me up beforehand and said, 'Whatever you do, don't say a thing. Just play along.' Then on the ride out, she made up stuff, all these outrageous stories—how she grew up next to the slums, how her best friend was black, about these fights she got into and how she was arrested during a race riot and spent a week in jail. All untrue. We laughed our heads off when the piece came out. Madonna used to do that sort of thing *all* the time."

Her new management in place, Madonna then turned her attention to her next album. Reggie Lucas, flush with the success of her first LP, had made plans to go back into the recording studio with her when word came from Warner that he, too, had been dumped. Moving up the ladder, Madonna now set her sights on Nile Rodgers, who had produced records for such artists as Sister Sledge, Chic, and Diana Ross and was the brains behind David Bowie's pivotal "Let's Dance."

"Reggie was about one thing," Madonna explained. "He did R and B. He's a good producer, very open and sensitive. But Nile has worked with so many kinds of musicians, and every record he's made is a great one as far as I'm concerned. He has the pop thing in him really strong . . . and I identify with him. He's a real street person, and we hung out at the same clubs."

The song that would eventually wind up as the title cut on her second LP almost didn't make it into the album at all. Although it sounds as if it were tailor-made for Madonna, the salaciously camp "Like a Virgin" had actually been written years earlier. Nile Rodgers felt strongly that "Like a Virgin" was not right for Madonna, but changed his mind when, in his own words, "I couldn't get the hook out of my head."

Still, "Like a Virgin" was originally conceived of as a ballad. For Madonna, Nile Rodgers transformed it into an upbeat dance tune by concocting a driving rhythm track that made the tune sound more than faintly reminiscent of Michael Jackson's "Billie Jean." Similarly, the other songs on the album were given a relentless beat that evoked the danceable hits of the early 1960s—albeit this time magnified with synthesizers, amplified with drum machines, and clarified through state-of-the-art digital recording techniques.

Overriding such musical and technical considerations, however, was the album's recurrent theme of playful eroticism. On the title cut, true love supposedly makes a girl feel "all shiny and new, like a virgin touched for the very first time." Similarly, in "Dress You Up," Madonna implores a man to "feel the silky touch of my caresses. They will keep you looking so brand-new."

"You're an Angel" was, if anything, a breathless throwback to the carefree, saccharine days of Lesley Gore and Shelley Fabares ("You're an angel in disguise, I can see it in your eyes"). But far and away the most revealing and controversial tune on the album would be "Material Girl," Madonna's tongue-in-cheek tribute to eighties materialism and the gold digger's time-honored profession ("The boy with the cold hard cash/is always Mr. Right").

After finishing up the *Virgin* album in the spring of 1984, Madonna focused her prodigious energies on putting together a band for her first major tour. She then headed for Italy to film the video for "Like a Virgin" in Venice. Directed by Mary Lambert, the video alternately features a tarted-up Madonna writhing in a gondola and in a traditional white lace wedding gown. The palazzi, piazzas, and glistening waterways provide a lushly romantic backdrop for the song, although producers felt compelled to include two faintly erotic symbols—a lion that prowls a narrow side street and a mysterious stranger in a carnival mask.

Back in New York, director Susan Seidelman was casting her next film, a contemporary urban comedy-mystery called *Desperately Seeking Susan*. The script deals with a bored New Jersey housewife who vicariously tracks the life of a street urchin named

Susan through the personals—until she is struck in the head, winds up with a case of amnesia, and is left to assume that *she* is Susan. What she soon comes to realize is that Susan is the unwitting target of a murderer.

Desperately Seeking Susan had been floating around Hollywood for four years before it was optioned by Orion Pictures. Originally, the part of Susan had been conceived as sort of an aging hippie, to be played by Diane Keaton. Then the producers decided to go for a more modest movie featuring an up-and-coming star, allowing producers to trim the budget down to a bargain-basement $5 million. Early on, Seidelman, who had received critical acclaim for *Smithereens* (a film she brought in for $80,000, some of which she had inherited from her grandmother), had been brought aboard. The project really gained momentum in June of 1984, however, when Rosanna Arquette signed up for the starring role of Roberta, the bored New Jersey housewife. At twenty-four, Arquette had already racked up impressive credentials on the big screen (*Baby It's You, Silverado, After Hours*) and in television (*The Executioner's Song*).

"Madonna was someone I knew about from the local club scene," Seidelman recalled. "I'd go to Danceteria and Paradise Garage occasionally, and I'd see her there—I knew who she was, what she looked like." When mutual friend Seymour Stein told Seidelman of Madonna's interest in the role, she agreed to meet with the singer.

The trouble was, some two hundred actresses had already read or been videotaped for the part. Among them: Rebecca De Mornay, Melanie Griffith, Jennifer Jason Leigh, Ellen Barkin, and Kelly McGillis. "The executives at Orion had never heard of Madonna," Seidelman said. "Fortunately, one of the executive's sons had. So they said, if you're interested in this girl, why don't you give her a screen test?"

Seidelman did. When Madonna arrived for the audition, Seidelman recalled, "she got out of the cab but she didn't have enough money to pay. So here she is meeting with a bunch of movie people for a job, and the first thing she does is hit us up for cab fare. It was exactly what Susan would have done!"

During their first meeting, Madonna came across to Seidelman as "vulnerable, sweet, even a little bit nervous. There was none of the arrogance for which she was already becoming famous. And she had a sense of humor. Given what I'd been told about her, I wasn't at all sure she'd have one."

Seidelman admitted that "even when I was testing the other actresses—people like Melanie Griffith and Kelly McGillis—I just couldn't get Madonna out of my mind. She had a sense of self, of supreme confidence. She seemed more secure about who she was than anyone I'd seen. She was somebody who thought she was special and made *you* feel special."

One of the film's producers, Midge Sanford, shared Seidelman's enthusiasm for Madonna. "She had this presence you couldn't get rid of," Sanford said. "No matter how good the other people were, we kept going back to that screen test."

The intangible quality that came across to Sanford and Seidelman on screen was the essence of Susan. "It wasn't her crazy clothes or her jewelry or her gum-chewing or anything like that," Seidelman said. "It wasn't even her looks. It's something about her persona. She gives off a tremendous feeling of sex. The key to the character of Susan was that she had to be so magnetic that people were irrevocably drawn to her. Madonna has that quality—it leaps out at you."

Seidelman hired Madonna that July, although her decision to go with this relative unknown was not met with applause at the home office. "There was a definite lack of enthusiasm at first," she said, "but I was willing to take the risk." For her sizable role in the film, which required four months' shooting, Madonna was paid $80,000. Her costar, Rosanna Arquette, would be paid five times that amount.

Money was not a consideration for Madonna. She had already been given a shot at respectability on Broadway when Tony Award–winning dancer-director-choreographer Tommy Tune offered her the lead in his new musical *My One and Only*. She turned it down not because she would be earning a comparatively slim $20,000 a week, but because the show required a proficiency in tap dancing that Madonna felt she didn't have.

Seidelman's *Smithereens*, which dealt with a punk rock groupie struggling against the bleak and unforgiving backdrop of the Lower East Side, held an obvious appeal for Madonna. In many ways, she had lived the part. The character of Susan, however, was an even closer match. "My background was to take what a person has and mold them into the part," Seidelman observed. "Madonna layered over the basic character with elements of her own personality. It is very hard to do, but when it works, the results are magical. There is a lot of Madonna in Susan."

Self-absorbed and oblivious to convention, Susan sashays through life snapping gum, bumming handouts, and washing down Cheetos with Dom Pérignon. "Susan is conniving, an opportunist," Madonna said of the role. "But she really did care about people. Anybody who goes around acting like nobody matters obviously is protecting themselves and hiding what they really feel."

Seidelman had feared that, in the bargain, Madonna might turn out to be as difficult and unpredictable as her character. Instead, she was surprised to find her to be "incredibly disciplined. When there was a six A.M. call, the rest of us would have to be rousted out of bed. The driver assigned to Madonna would pick her up at a health club every morning where she'd already done fifty laps by six A.M."

As for any signs of temperament, Madonna was, according to Seidelman, "very down-to-earth, really eager to please. She was not a prima donna at all. She was very open to criticism, very willing to cooperate. Madonna wanted to do a good job, and she had no hesitation about taking direction. She'd do a scene over and over and over without complaint if that's what it took to get it right."

One such scene required Madonna as Susan to stroll through the ruins of the old Audubon Ballroom, lead the actor playing her boyfriend (Robert Joy) to a rear storage room, then hop on top of a pinball machine. "Got a quarter?" asks Susan. "Wanna play?" With that, he puts a quarter in the machine, then kisses Susan and starts to play. She falls backward as the pinball machine rings to the accompaniment of flashing lights.

124

This simple scene had to be shot ten times. Between takes, Madonna laughed at all the obvious wisecracks about scoring and pinball machines. When a rent-a-stripper showed up on the set for a crew member's fortieth birthday, Madonna was an enthusiastic participant in the gag. "You're going to take your clothes off, right?" the chagrined crew member asked the stripper. "No," cracked Madonna, "you take *your* clothes off." When the dancer stopped at her black underwear, Madonna was indignant. "She didn't really strip," she complained.

Madonna did a superb job of concealing her own insecurities during filming. "I had a few scenes where I was really shittin' bricks," she said later. "A few times I was so nervous I opened my mouth and nothing came out." But to everyone else on the set, Madonna appeared totally calm, even while those around her at times seemed to be indulging in a collective nervous breakdown.

"Madonna and I had an instant rapport," Seidelman said. "I can't say the same for everyone else on the set." The director, who admitted to being candid in her opinions, clashed loudly and repeatedly with Arquette and costars Aidan Quinn and Laurie Metcalf. "I had a *terrible* time with Rosanna," Seidelman recalled. "Neither one of us was happy and we fought constantly." At one point, after a bitter argument with Seidelman over the extent of her character's memory loss, Arquette wept. Seidelman followed suit. Madonna looked on in wonderment.

Ironically, although spared any direct involvement in these battles, Madonna was the indirect cause for the mounting turmoil on the set. No one, least of all Rosanna Arquette, could have anticipated Madonna's meteoric rise to superstardom that fall. "During that four-month span of shooting from September through December," Seidelman said, "she made a quantum leap from rock star to icon."

The transformation was helped by the approach of her second album and her first live stage appearance before a national audience. On Friday, September 14, rock royalty gathered at Radio City Music Hall for the Annual MTV Music Awards. For the show's opening number, Madonna made her entrance wearing a white wedding dress atop a twenty-foot-high wedding cake with a life-size mannequin for a groom. Awash in tulle and lace, dripping with strands of beads, and flashing her bold Boy Toy belt, she climbed down off the cake, then proceeded to wriggle, prance, and otherwise cavort through a pounding rendition of "Like a Virgin" while even jaded members of the cutthroat music industry sat dumbstruck. The performance, which went on to rank as one of her most-watched videos, set a standard for calculated tasteless-ness that Madonna would spend years attempting to transcend.

For some of those who knew her then, Madonna was already soaring out of reach. On November 7 she and Benitez attended a party at Private Eyes and were promptly escorted inside and up to the deejay's platform by Scott, the club's all-powerful doorman. When her old lover Jean-Michel Basquiat arrived with his mentor– father figure Andy Warhol, he made his way up the stairs to greet her, but was pushed back by a bouncer assigned to Madonna. "Make way for Mr. Warhol," he said, shoving aside the young black artist. "It's okay," Warhol protested, "he's with me." Humil-iated, Basquiat went up to Madonna, who kissed him passionately on the mouth. Benitez was too distracted by Warhol's presence to notice, busy thanking him for running a picture of him in *Inter-view* that made him look six inches taller than he actually was.

Basquiat, who had managed to kick his dependence on heroin for a time, was upset by this encounter. "Jean-Michel was moody," Warhol recalled, "because Madonna got so big and he lost her." Within weeks, Madonna's former lover would be back on heroin —the drug that would ultimately kill him.

For Seidelman and Arquette, the first inkling that Madonna's celebrity status had been radically upgraded occurred shortly after her picture appeared on the cover of *Rolling Stone* for the first time, just after the new album's release in mid-November. When cast and crew tried to shoot a key scene at New York's Magic Club, they were mobbed. "There were hundreds of kids there just to catch a glimpse of Madonna," recalled a crew member. "For the first time we needed police barricades, crowd control, the whole bit."

Instant fame brought with it the usual flood of rumors. While she was being driven to the set one morning, Madonna's driver said to her, "I have this bet going with my friend. He told me that all the music you do was done by someone else, and they picked the songs and did it all, and all they needed was a girl singer and you auditioned and they picked you. And Madonna isn't your real name, and all of it is fabricated."

"WHAAAATT?" Madonna screamed, ordering him to stop the car. "Are you out of your mind!" It was then, Madonna recalled, that it "suddenly hit me that that's probably what a lot of people think."

"It was hard on Madonna," Seidelman said. "I think she was as unprepared for the mayhem as we were." But it was Arquette who suffered the most. "Rosanna was very upset. Imagine how awful it is to be hired as the star, and then to be eclipsed by a novice. It made Rosanna crazy."

Arquette and Madonna made a concerted effort to appear friendly on the set—including snapshots of the two hamming it up in identical black leather porkpie hats. They did have the world of pop music in common; the onetime girlfriend of Toto drummer Steve Porcaro, Arquette was immortalized in the group's hit song "Rosanna." Publicly, Arquette praised Madonna's "focus" and described their relationship as "really tight." But one of the other actors remembered that Arquette "alternately fumed and sobbed" at all the attention being paid her suddenly superfamous costar.

Madonna's own pressures during filming were of a more personal nature. Jellybean Benitez's infrequent visits to her trailer invariably ended with his storming out in a door-slamming rage. Benitez's anger was understandable. Between scenes, Bobby Martinez was also paying visits to her trailer. "We did it in the trailer, man," Martinez said, "with everybody standing around outside. They'd call her, she'd run out to do a scene. Then she'd come back and we'd do it again." A worker on the set claimed Madonna's dalliances were no secret: "Her trailer would be rocking back and forth like there was an earthquake or something. Sometimes, you'd hear groaning inside. Afterwards a guy would come out— sometimes two different guys in the same day. *Like a Virgin* had just come out, so we all had a good laugh. But when it came to work," he added, "she was a total professional. She got along with everybody."

Madonna's turbulent relationship with Benitez in some ways

mirrored Seidelman's own domestic situation. "Madonna was fighting with Jellybean at the same time I was having similar problems," she said. "There's nothing like boyfriend trouble to bring two girls together."

Coincidentally, Madonna and Seidelman also lived on the same SoHo block, so they bumped into one another even when they weren't working together. "Once she was sitting on the steps in front of her building reading a book of Sam Shepard plays," Seidelman recalled. Later, over coffee, Madonna confided to Seidelman that the stars she admired most and wanted to emulate were Carole Lombard and Judy Holliday. "She sees herself as a comedienne, and while she is driven, she still has that sense of mischief that they had. Funny," Seidelman reflected, "she never mentioned Marilyn Monroe."

The wrap party for *Desperately Seeking Susan* was held that December at the Kamikaze Klub, a downtown spot popular with struggling actors and New Wave musicians. The most entertaining thing there, cast members recalled, was the fast-talking, bottle-juggling bartender who wore an earring and called himself Bruno. The bartender's real name: Bruce Willis. "He served Madonna and the rest of us," marveled Seidelman, "and six months later he was the star of 'Moonlighting.' Things can move awfully fast in this business."

Another prescient encounter occurred while Seidelman was editing *Desperately Seeking Susan*. Warren Beatty called her up unexpectedly and asked to look at the dailies, film from each day's shooting. "He came to the editing room and watched some scenes," she recalled. "He was obviously intrigued by Madonna. Watching his face watching hers, I knew he wanted her. From that point on, I had a premonition that someday they would be together."

Madonna Louise Ciccone, at age five in 1963 (the year her mother died), at nine when she shamed her father with a near-naked talent-show performance, and at twelve when she went out on her first date. "Even as a child I flirted with everyone," she said.

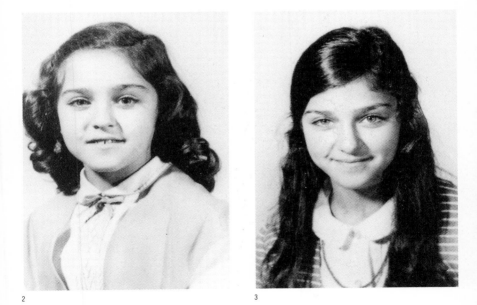

4

Madonna (second from left) was a star cheerleader at Rochester Adams High in her sophomore year in 1973. Vaulting to the upper-right corner of the pyramid, she liked to shock the crowd with her flesh-colored panties.

5

In 1975, sixteen-year-old Madonna acted and danced in school productions. Nights were spent cruising Detroit's gay discos with her dance teacher and mentor, Christopher Flynn.

7

A straight-A student, Madonna was described by her teachers variously as "dynamic," "dedicated," "sensitive," and "creative" when she graduated from Rochester Adams in 1976. She was determined to be a dancer —and a star.

9

8

Madonna played a rape victim who seeks revenge on her attacker in the low-budget film A Certain Sacrifice *in 1979. To attract attention to herself even between takes, she swung on the monkey bars.*

10

OPPOSITE—*Struggling to make it as a dancer in New York, twenty-year-old Madonna moonlighted as a nude model. Both* Playboy *and* Penthouse *would later publish the photographs.*

Madonna in A Certain Sacrifice, *an oddball underground film that quickly vanished only to reappear when she became famous. She tried unsuccessfully to halt its release on video.*

Clad in tattered denim and lace, Madonna struck this uncharacteristically calm pose in 1983, the year her high-voltage career as a rock star began to take off.

11

Cast in a small part in 1984 as a club singer in Vision Quest, *Madonna had yet to prove herself as an actress, but her new album, which included "Like a Virgin" and "Material Girl," was propelling her to stardom.*

Madonna in her "Boy Toy" belt and crucifixes, with deejay "Jelly-bean" Benitez in 1984. Their affair led to jealous rows, death threats, abortions—and very nearly to marriage.

13

A blond Madonna performing "Like a Virgin." By the fall of 1984, her records and tunes were selling at the rate of 80,000 copies a day.

15

With Rosanna Arquette in Desperately Seeking Susan, *the 1985 film that proved Madonna could act too. Arquette bitterly resented being eclipsed by her costar's sudden fame.*

Eager fans reach out to touch Madonna at a Madison Square Garden concert in June 1985. She had once lived in a flophouse directly across the street.

16

17

Madonna's enthusiastic performance at Live Aid benefit in 1985 coincided with the publication of her nude photographs in both Playboy *and* Penthouse. *"I ain't takin' shit off today," she told her audience. "You might hold it against me in ten years."*

The bride and groom appeared on a balcony after the ceremony on August 16, 1985, to begin what was later described as a marriage made in hell.

OPPOSITE—*Beseiged by press helicopters hovering over the site of his wedding to Madonna, Sean Penn fired a gun into the air and scrawled an obscene warning in the sand.*

20

Between arguing with the director and battling the press, Penn and Madonna snuggled on the Macao set of Shanghai Surprise.

Starring Madonna as a 1930s missionary and Penn as a drifter, Shanghai Surprise was an unmitigated critical and commercial disaster. It was the first and last time the two would work together in a film.

21

In a failed attempt to mend fences with the press, Madonna faced reporters in London with Shanghai Surprise *producer (and ex-Beatle) George Harrison on March 6, 1986. She would later disown the picture.*

23

Penn and Madonna share a midnight supper at New York's Columbus Cafe, a favorite hangout and the scene of several spats.

Sean Penn in action outside Madonna's Manhattan apartment on August 29, 1986, when he spat at Anthony Savignano, then attacked him and fellow photographer Vinny Zuffante. His temper would later land Penn in jail.

24

25

Madonna was a celebrity model at an AIDS benefit fashion show in 1986. Having lost many of her closest friends to the disease, she was deeply committed to the cause.

The American Music Award for Favorite Video Artist, 1987, tangible proof that Madonna, despite her flair for controversy, was the decade's most popular female performer.

Madonna's first "Tonight Show," June 6, 1987. She told host Johnny Carson she was "just a Midwestern girl in a bustier."

At the Who's That Girl? *premiere, more than ten thousand fans jammed Times Square for a glimpse of their idol.*

In 1987 Madonna was teamed with a cougar for her next Hollywood effort, Who's That Girl?

Sean and Madonna jog near their Malibu home following her triumphal Who's That Girl? world tour and his release from jail.

Madonna is congratulated by costars Ron Silver (left) and Joe Mantegna after making her Broadway debut in David Mamet's Speed-the-Plow. "No, She Can't Act" was the headline for one critic's scathing review.

It was the Spinks-Tyson heavyweight title bout, but backstage all eyes were on the battling "Poison Penns."

Madonna and Jennifer Grey as speakeasy showgirls in Damon Runyon's Bloodhounds of Broadway, *which aired on television in 1989.*

Madonna and Sandra Bernhard set tongues wagging at the Don't Bungle the Jungle benefit concert. Artist Keith Haring, left, would be among Madonna's many friends to die of AIDS.

A bitter feud between Madonna and Arsenio Hall began with remarks she made on his talk show in May 1990.

Madonna was at her most outrageous onstage during her Blond Ambition tour (above). Offstage, she became involved with the show's only heterosexual male dancer, Oliver Crumes (right). "I'm a very sexual person," she said. "What's the problem?"

Always seeking her father's approval, Madonna sang "Happy Birthday" to Tony Ciccone before twenty thousand screaming fans in Michigan when he turned fifty-nine in 1990.

41

OPPOSITE—*She borrowed her controversial crotch-grabbing gesture from Michael Jackson, her only rival as a rock superstar.*

In the wake of her divorce from Penn, Madonna's affair with Warren Beatty steamed up the set of Dick Tracy. *She called him Old Man, he called her Buzzbomb.*

Madonna as Breathless Mahoney and Warren Beatty as Dick Tracy in the 1990 summer blockbuster. This time critics applauded her as both a singer and an actress.

43

By way of introduction, Madonna (with her new collagen-enhanced lips) walked up to future boyfriend Tony Ward at a party and put a cigarette out on his bare back.

In her controversial 1990 "Rock the Vote" video for MTV, Madonna threatened nonvoters with a "spankie."

44

Madonna, a serious collector of modern art, attended a museum show with brother Christopher, a set designer and the only family member on her payroll.

45

46

Madonna with dance legend Martha Graham, whom she visited just months before her death in 1990. She has talked about portraying Graham in a film biography.

A scene from "Justify My Love." Too racy even for MTV, it still grossed millions. In another daring scene from "Justify My Love," Madonna kisses both a woman and her lover Tony Ward.

The Oddest Couple: Madonna and her date, Michael Jackson, leave Swifty Lazar's post-Oscar bash at Spago.

In March 1991, dripping with $20 million worth of diamonds, Madonna stole the Academy Awards show with her performance of "Sooner or Later" from Dick Tracy. Stephen Sondheim's torchy ballad won the Oscar.

"Condoms saved my life," said Madonna, here dancing up a sweat at an AIDS fund-raiser in Los Angeles in April of 1991.

At another AIDS benefit, Madonna was reunited with Tony Ward. She had dumped him when she learned he had secretly married another woman.

Madonna bared body and soul in Truth or Dare, *the film documentary of her Blond Ambition tour.*

BELOW—*She is shown with her* Truth or Dare *"family," and flirting with admirers in a publicity shot for the controversial film.*

Researching her next screen role, Madonna takes to the field in preparation for the baseball movie A League of Their Own.

56

OPPOSITE—*Flanked by* Truth or Dare *director Alek Keshishian (right) and producer Dino De Laurentiis, Madonna unveiled her documentary —and herself—at the Cannes Film Festival in May 1991.*

57

Madonna Ciccone, at the wheel of her car, alone but in absolute control of her career and her multimillion-dollar business empire.

12

"Sean is the perfect American male to me. I'm inspired and shocked by him at the same time."

The second half of the 1980s would herald the emergence of a new breed of female singer—"Rock's New Women," *Newsweek* would call them in a March 1985 cover story. These women with strong images, the mainstream press now noticed, were not only dominating the pop music charts but videos as well. As 1985 dawned, there was little doubt about who would have the most impact: Cyndi Lauper. After all, her triumphant debut album, the aptly titled *She's So Unusual*, scored an unprecedented four Top Five singles. And her motto—"Girls just wanna have fun"—was being eagerly embraced by a generation of rule-weary teens coming of age in the button-down eighties. Paired with Lauper in the forefront of this movement was Madonna, although, if anything, she sought to redefine what might constitute "fun" for the average red-blooded American female.

Sharing this newfound "woman power" were such performers as Chaka Khan, the Pointer Sisters, Pat Benatar, Joan Jett, the Go-Gos, the Bangles, Sheena Easton, Laura Branigan, Chrissie Hynde, Annie Lennox, and Sheila E. And threatening to eclipse

"I can be a sex symbol, but I don't have to be a victim."

them all was the veteran rocker whose miniskirt Madonna had tried to look up—Tina Turner. At forty-five, Turner had staged a phenomenal comeback with her triple-platinum *Private Dancer* album, which included the Grammy-winning single "What's Love Got to Do With It?"

Although the competition was keen, the focus was unquestionably on Madonna and Lauper. The similarities were obvious: outrageous thrift-shop duds, wild, multicolored coifs, and an attitude. Both women seemed to be thumbing their nose at convention and at the opposite sex—but there was a difference. Although one of Lauper's hits, "She Bop," is a barely disguised ode to female masturbation, the gist of her act was harmless, antic—an oddball urban urchin in an orange fright wig and lime green tights. Madonna's image was overtly salacious and unapologetically crass—an updated Mae West to Lauper's Betty Boop.

At first, most critics made it clear that they preferred the wacky, nonthreatening Lauper to her libidinous counterpart. Madonna's voice was dismissed as "Minnie Mouse on helium." Pointing to the dangling crucifixes and rosaries, the winking navel, the Boy Toy belt, an article in *Time* in late February of 1985 said that Madonna seemed "to be advertising some unholy sacrament." The writer, Dave Marsh, branded her "the product of the shopping-mall culture." There were even swipes that combined Madonna's phenomenal commercial appeal with her already notorious private life: "McDonna—Over 1 Billion Served."

Conversely, Lauper was hailed as "playful," "cheerful," and "loony." *Newsweek*'s Bill Barol found her "positively inspiring . . . [her] message: even in the age of Madonna, you don't have to be crass to sell records." Veteran rockers such as Mick Jagger derided what he viewed as a "central dumbness" to Madonna. Paul Grein, an editor at *Billboard*, predicted "Madonna will be out of the music business in six months. Her image has completely over-shadowed her music."

Publicly, Madonna did not respond to such criticism of her work. She did not, however, take it well. She called her old friend Christopher Flynn and told him she was deeply hurt. "Madonna would get very upset," recalled Erica Bell. "She'd always be wailing, 'Why are they saying these awful things about me?' "

Madonna was especially rankled by the unfavorable comparisons to Cyndi Lauper. According to one acquaintance, she responded to the *Newsweek* cover of Lauper by tearing it to shreds.
"For a while," recalled another acquaintance from this period,
"Madonna was incredibly jealous of the attention Lauper was getting." Erica Bell said: "Madonna really hated Lauper and would
do this really mean imitation of Cyndi. Underneath it all, Madonna was really hurt by all the sniping."

Most hurtful were the comments from feminists who claimed
Madonna was single-handedly sabotaging the women's movement. "Madonna set us back," said Loraine Segato, lead singer of
the group Parachute Club. "If we do not wear tremendously ex-
aggerated costumes or come up with phrases like 'Boy Toy,' we
pale beside her."

Madonna did respond to that criticism. "I get so much bad press
for being overtly sexual," she told *Newsweek*. "When someone like
Prince, Elvis, or Jagger does the same thing, they are being honest,
sensual human beings. But when I do it: 'Oh, please. Madonna,
you're setting the women's movement back a million years.' "

By this time, of course, Madonna was crying all the way to the
bank. When DeMann called to inform her that her first six-figure
royalty check would be arriving from Warner, she replied, "Great!
Now I don't have to take the subway anymore."

Before journeying to Osaka, Japan, on a sort of way-out-of-town
tryout for her upcoming American tour, Madonna faced an unexpected crisis. "Madonna was pregnant with Jellybean's baby,"
remembered DeMann's assistant Melinda Cooper, who like
DeMann was unaware at the time that Madonna had already had
at least one abortion. "She came to Freddy and me and she was
very upset—just this scared young girl who didn't want her family
to know. Madonna loved Jellybean very much, but she wanted a
career and so did he. So we arranged for Madonna to have the
abortion, drove her to the doctor's office, everything. She seemed
so innocent at the time; it wasn't until much later that I learned
she had others. But Madonna wasn't about to let something like a
baby interfere with the tour."

Once she got to Osaka two weeks later, Madonna was "desperately lonely and upset," Cooper recalled. She nearly suffered a nervous breakdown when someone called to tell her that her father had died. It was a hoax, but enough to push Madonna to the brink. "She would call me at four A.M. from Japan crying, begging me to fly Jellybean to Japan. Which we did. She was very much in love with Jellybean at the time, and heartbroken that things weren't working out. If Jellybean had gone along, she would have married him in a flash."

By the time Madonna headed for Los Angeles to make her "Material Girl" video in February 1985, the *Like a Virgin* album had sold 3.5 million copies in just twelve weeks and had toppled Bruce Springsteen from the top spot. The title song was firmly entrenched at No. 1, and her first ballad, "Crazy for You" from the newly released film *Vision Quest*, was also on its way to becoming the country's top single. To the amazement of Warner executives, her records and tapes were selling at the staggering rate of 80,000 a day.

Even when she was recording the "Material Girl" single—months before shooting the video—Madonna had a clear idea of the visual statement she wanted to make. One of her favorite movie scenes had always been Marilyn Monroe's trademark "Diamonds Are a Girl's Best Friend" number from the film *Gentlemen Prefer Blondes*. "I can just redo the whole scene and it'll be perfect," she told Freddy DeMann, as well as her producer, her director, and everybody involved with the video.

No one listened. Instead, Madonna received an avalanche of proposals, ranging from her standard writhing-on-the-floor concert footage to a high-tech Orwellian nightmare, elements of which would be absorbed into her controversial "Express Yourself" video years later. "Everybody was submitting their ideas and I kept mentioning mine," Madonna remembered. "Nobody seemed to pick up on it."

Frustrated by the ease with which the men around her brushed aside her ideas, she finally put her foot down. "This is what I want to do," she told them, "and this is what I'm gonna do."

The result was a classic video satire that marked a turning point in the way much of the public viewed Madonna. The tongue-in-cheek opening scene of the video, which takes place in a studio mogul's screening room, reveals much of what Madonna had in mind for her career. "She's fantastic," says the cigar-chomping mogul (played by Keith Carradine). "I knew she could be a star."

"She could be a major star," agrees the mogul's toady.

"She *is* a star," replies the mogul.

"The biggest star in the universe," concurs the toady without missing a beat. "Right now, as we speak."

For the video, Madonna is sheathed in a copy of Monroe's slinky strapless red satin gown. Bill Travilla, who also designed all the costumes for the television series "Dallas" and "Knots Landing," resented the fact he received no credit from Madonna as the creator of the original dress worn by Monroe. "Like a virgin," he cracked, "I've been knocked off for the very first time."

Gowned and coiffed like Monroe, Madonna, dripping with diamond bracelets, prances over a platoon of panting tuxedo-clad suitors while she sings her unrepentant paean to greed. Lost amidst the glamour is the video's final antimaterialist message, when Madonna gives in to the mogul's advances only after he shows up carrying daisies instead of roses and driving a battered pickup.

As personal assistant to both Freddy DeMann and later Madonna, Melinda Cooper remembered the Madonna of this period as "a fairly civil person. Actually she was pretty cool, pretty nice. She really needed protection, somebody to watch out for her. I used to have to tell her not to walk the few blocks from her hotel to Freddy DeMann's office in Century City at night, but Madonna was very much her own person. Since she didn't have a license at the time, I wound up driving her all over the place."

On the way to the Hollywood soundstage where "Material Girl" was to be filmed, Cooper asked Madonna if she was prepared for the loss in privacy that celebrity would bring. "Madonna didn't have a clue about how much her life was going to change. I finally said, 'You don't have any idea what's about to happen to you, do you, Madonna?' She got all indignant and said 'Yeah, I do.' But she didn't. It was going to come as one huge shock to her, and it would change Madonna for good."

The filming of the "Material Girl" video marked another milestone for Madonna, this time of a more personal nature. One morning the video's director, Mary Lambert, brought her friend Sean Penn along to watch from the sidelines. Penn, the son of television director Leo Penn and former actress Eileen Ryan, had grown up in the pampered and privileged environs of Beverly Hills. Yet at twenty-four, his churlish demeanor had made him Hollywood's favorite bad boy both on-screen (in such films as *Fast Times at Ridgemont High*, *Racing with the Moon*, and *The Falcon and the Snowman*) and off.

Press-shy and given to jealous tantrums, he had flown into a rage when he was told that his then-fiancée Elizabeth McGovern was being interviewed inside her trailer by a male reporter on the set of *Racing with the Moon*. While McGovern and the hapless reporter talked inside, Penn rocked the trailer violently from side to side, throwing her to the floor. In addition to McGovern, Penn had already conducted highly publicized romances with the likes of actress Susan Sarandon and Bruce Springsteen's younger sister Pam.

Penn brought the same fanatical approach to his craft that he did to his relationships. Cast in the role of a teen gangster in the film *Bad Boys*, he grew his hair shoulder length and had a wolf's head tattooed on his forearm. "I remember we went out on a raid with some Chicago cops so Sean could get the feel of it all," recalled the movie's director, Richard Rosenthal. "During the raid some more cops arrived who thought we were criminals and told us to raise our hands. I complied, but for Sean it was a chance to see what it's like for a gang member to take on a cop. He turned to a cop who was the size of an apartment block and said, 'Fuck you!' "

Then, Rosenthal continued, "the cop picked up Sean and threw him into a wall. His nose was almost broken, but later he told me that it was at that moment he finally became his character in the film."

On the morning of their fateful first encounter, Madonna was standing at the top of the staircase on the set, waiting for some adjustments to be made in the lighting, when she looked down and "noticed this guy in a leather jacket and sunglasses kind of standing in the corner, looking at me." Realizing the stranger was Sean Penn, she claimed she "immediately had this fantasy that we were going to meet and fall in love and get married."

This premonition aside, Madonna had a decidedly unorthodox way of expressing her interest. She walked down the stairs and past the five-foot-six-inch-tall Penn, tossing an icy glare in his direction. Hours later, when she spotted him still lingering in the shadows, she began haranguing Penn. "Get out!" she yelled. "Get out! Get *out!*" Madonna, who had given flowers to everybody on the cast and crew of the video, realized she had one left. "So when Sean was leaving, I said, 'Wait, I have something for you.' And I ran upstairs and I got this rose for him."

That evening, Penn was visiting a friend's house when his host picked up a book of quotations and selected a passage at random: "She had the innocence of a child and the wit of a man." "I just looked at my friend," Penn recalled, and he said, 'Go get her.' "

If Madonna was so profoundly affected by her first meeting with Sean Penn, she did not let on to friends. "She called me from L.A. late one night like some schoolgirl, giggling about all the famous people she'd met that day," Erica Bell recalled. "She said, 'Guess what? Today I met Elizabeth Taylor, Sean Penn, *and* Frank Perdue!' I'll never forget that—she gave equal emphasis to each name. Madonna was just as thrilled about meeting the chicken tycoon Frank Perdue as she was about meeting Sean Penn."

Madonna was more intent on becoming friendly with another powerhouse in the rock cosmos, Prince, whose purple reign had begun in 1984, just as Michael Jackson's phenomenal *Thriller* album began to cool. At one point, Prince Rogers Nelson boasted the top single in the country ("When Doves Cry"), the top album (*Purple Rain*), and the top movie (*Purple Rain*, which grossed over $70 million). In 1985, he won an Academy Award for his *Purple Rain* score, and several Grammys.

Prince and Madonna had more in common than their record label. He, too, was a product of a Midwestern upbringing (born and raised in Minneapolis). Prince worshiped Marilyn Monroe, (his purple-walled Minneapolis house was filled with posters of

Monroe), and while he professed to be shy, he writhed around onstage clad only in bikini briefs, stiletto heels, and sweat.

Despite his diminutive size (five feet three inches tall, 120 pounds) and his sexually ambiguous appearance, Prince had earned a reputation for womanizing that exceeded even Penn's. He played Svengali to a jazz percussionist and transformed her from plain Sheila Escovedo to sexpot singer Sheila (*Glamorous Life*) E., turned Pearl Drops toothpaste model Denise Matthews into the hit-making Vanity, and engineered the rise to stardom of protégée and *Purple Rain* love interest Apollonia.

Prince first spotted Madonna backstage at the American Music Awards in Los Angeles on January 28, 1985, and rather than introduce himself he instructed his manager to get her telephone number after the show. Madonna, meanwhile, was evidently too self-involved to notice. "She kept talking about her career, her records, her videos," recalled a staffer on the show.

She also ranted about Daryl Hall and John Oates, known as Hall and Oates and then the most successful duo in popular music. They performed on the program, and Madonna did not attempt to disguise her disapproval—in part because their number cut into her time. "She went around telling everybody how much she *hated* Hall and Oates," another staff member recalled. "It was very embarrassing. She had nothing—good or bad—to say about anybody."

The next day, Madonna received a phone call from Prince asking for a date. She assumed at first that it was Bobby Martinez or Jellybean Benitez or one of her other boyfriends playing a trick on her and was ready to launch into a stream of obscenities when it dawned on her that the voice on the other end of the line really belonged to Prince. She was scheduled to return to New York to rehearse for her upcoming tour, but she accepted Prince's invitation to attend his concert at the Los Angeles Forum. Once she hung up, recalled a friend, Madonna "squealed with delight."

For his part, Prince was equally excited. For the next three weeks leading up to their date, he talked about the Material Girl incessantly. The night of the concert, Prince had a white stretch limousine pick Madonna up at her hotel and whisk her off to the

Forum. And at the end of the show, he invited her to join him onstage, and she did.

After the concert, they piled into Prince's trademark purple limo and sped to the Westwood Marquis, where Prince and his entourage occupied the entire ninth floor. Madonna was instantly struck by the way Prince smelled of lavender. ("He reeks of it," she told Erica Bell). The party at the hotel turned raucous—at one point Prince ripped off his shirt and invited Madonna to dance with him on a tabletop—before finally breaking up at five A.M.

Madonna came back for Prince's final show, and the two made a date two days later for a late supper following the Grammy Awards, where they were both scheduled to perform. This time, Prince's purple limo wended its way to Yamashiro, an elegant Japanese restaurant overlooking Los Angeles. Once there, Madonna and Prince had Yamashiro's entire Skyview Room, which normally seats seventy-five, to themselves. The dinner lasted three hours; the rest of the evening was spent at a chic new disco called Facade.

Madonna was impressed with what she later described as Prince's "spiritualist" side. "He seems to understand what I'm thinking even before I say anything," she gushed. He also surprised her by being as soft-spoken and almost self-effacing in private as he was flamboyant in public. As for Prince, he told friends that he was impressed with Madonna's keen intelligence. "She has exactly what I've been looking for," he reportedly proclaimed, "beauty *and* brains."

Both were smart enough, certainly, to ascertain the obvious publicity value inherent in a relationship. And for the next few months, Prince squired Madonna around Los Angeles whenever she was in town. They dined at Spago, hit the trendiest clubs— and did nothing to discourage stories in the tabloid press that they were carrying on a "red-hot romance."

Throughout this high-profile "romance," Madonna pursued a serious relationship with Sean Penn. Despite her own public philanderings, she was unwilling to share Penn with other women. In late February while dining together at New York's Cafe Central, the couple was joined unexpectedly by Penn's former fiancée, Elizabeth McGovern. She sat close to Penn as they chatted, and after a few seemingly amiable moments Madonna erupted, letting fly a string of epithets before storming out of the restaurant in a jealous rage.

A week later, on March 2, Madonna and Penn had another violent row, this time at her Los Angeles apartment. Penn was enraged over press reports that she was having an affair with Prince. In the middle of the argument, he stomped out of the apartment and she slammed the door behind him. Still furious, Penn spun around and punched a hole through the wall. The next day, a delighted Madonna showed the hole off to Melinda Cooper. "She thought it was great," Cooper said. "Sean's violent streak appealed to her back then, and she likes pushing men's buttons."

Several days later, Prince arrived with some plaster, and he and Madonna repaired the wall. "They thought," says Erica Bell, "that it was all pretty hysterical."

From the outset, Bell understood Madonna's fascination with Penn: "He was playing at being the James Dean bad boy just like she was playing at being this tough girl from the streets. Penn talked like a rebel, but he was just this rich kid from Beverly Hills. And of course he was a movie star and she wanted to be a movie star, so the attraction there was pretty obvious, too."

Madonna was sufficiently impressed with what she perceived to be Penn's intellectual prowess that she began devouring the works of Rainer Maria Rilke, James Agee, Jack Kerouac, Charles Bukowski, Milan Kundera, Balzac, De Maupassant, J. D. Salinger, and V. S. Naipaul. "One day she'd never heard of these writers," recalled Bell, "and the next she was dropping Rilke's name in an interview as if she'd been studying him for years. Madonna wanted to be taken seriously."

Whatever their intellectual pretensions, Madonna's chums felt that she and Penn were a temperamental mismatch. "It never seemed to us that what they had was very serious," Bell said.

Contrary to her later statements of love at first sight, Madonna was not exactly swept off her feet by Penn—even though it was his idea to take her on a date to Marilyn Monroe's gravesite. "Sean is somebody whose work I have admired for a long time," she told writer Carl Arrington. "He's wild, though. He'll probably die young." Madonna claimed to be taken with Penn's resemblance to her father in his youth, and she saw some significance in the fact that her birthday and Penn's were a day apart.

Once back in New York, Madonna focused on preparing for her all-important first tour. She was soon interrupted by Susan Seidelman, who informed her that Orion, the producers of *Desperately Seeking Susan*, were eager to capitalize on Madonna's rising fame. The release date of the film was being pushed up two months to coincide with Madonna's tour. "I was shooting a sequence where I needed a song with a really good dance beat," said Seidelman, who asked Madonna to bring in a tape of a new song she had been working on with Steve Bray.

"Actually," recalled Madonna, "I wanted to test it out on all the extras who were dancing to it, to see if it was any good." As they neared a final cut, Seidelman pleaded with Madonna to let her use the new song in the film. Madonna sent Seidelman the original eight-track demo tape of "Into the Groove," and the director rightly deduced that it had the makings of a huge hit—the kind of hit that could only serve to boost the film's box office potential.

The sound track was not even close to completion, but MTV agreed to air a hastily assembled clip from the movie showing Madonna dancing wildly to "Into the Groove." It quickly became one of MTV's most requested videos and a hit on radio airwaves —even though the song itself would not be available in record stores for over a month. This was, as industry expert Kal Rudman said at the time, "virtually unprecedented."

The sudden insertion of "Into the Groove" into *Desperately Seeking Susan* had other, more serious repercussions. Madonna had written "Into the Groove" for Cheyne, and the promising black singer had already recorded a version for her own album. Mark Kamins was Cheyne's producer. "Cheyne saw that Madonna was doing "Into the Groove" and she freaked," recalled Kamins. "Cheyne screamed, 'I won't be the black Madonna!' It was a betrayal of Cheyne and as a young singer trying to make it, she was devastated, but Madonna couldn't have cared less."

She had other things on her mind. *Desperately Seeking Susan* was released that April, and Madonna was being praised as "a trampy, indolent goddess" by no less a critic than the *New Yorker*'s Pauline Kael. "Nobody in this movie comes through except Madonna, who comes through as Madonna. She has dumbfounding aplomb." Chimed in *New York* magazine's David Denby: "Madonna looks confident enough to crunch boulders."

Much to the chagrin of costar Rosanna Arquette, Orion was going after the huge youth market by focusing on Madonna's performance in the movie. With "Into the Groove" pulsating in the background, commercials for *Desperately Seeking Susan* looked less like a trailer and more like a Madonna video.

To counter the Madonnification of the movie, Arquette launched a publicity blitzkrieg of her own. She admitted that she felt overwhelmed by Madonna's instant megastardom. "I've never been like this," she told Fred Schruers for *Rolling Stone*'s "Madonna and Rosanna" cover story. "I'm a wreck. I get hurt very easily. I don't have a tough shell. That's why I'm so freaked out. I'm so insecure. I'm really insecure."

In print, Madonna appeared every bit as confident as David Denby had suggested. "Yeah, really? Who's it become an issue with—besides Rosanna?" Madonna harbored some reservations about being used as a shill—*Desperately Seeking Susan* was going to be a way for her to establish herself as an actress—but she realized how important it was that the film be commercially successful: "I have a big audience of kids for my music, and you know how they use sound tracks to push movies." Likening the film to the screwball comedies of the 1930s, she praised *Susan* for offering "a taste of real life—none of that adolescent-fantasy bullshit."

The studio's gambit paid off handsomely. Pulling in a far younger audience than they had anticipated, the film became one of the top moneymakers of the season.

Madonna's personality was already undergoing a not-so-subtle change as a result of all this heady success. The turning point for Melinda Cooper came when she received a late-night call from Madonna in Los Angeles. "I had arranged for a Dav-El limousine to pick Madonna up at the airport, but there was some sort of mixup and it wasn't there when she arrived in L.A.," Cooper recalled. "She screamed profanities at me, calling me a cunt and all sorts of other terrible things. It was the first time she made me cry."

After what seemed an eternity of rehearsals in Los Angeles and New York, Madonna kicked off her much ballyhooed Virgin Tour in early April in Seattle. Her handpicked opening act: the Beastie Boys, a group of white rappers whose shock value—they had already been widely castigated for glorifying sex and violence—strongly appealed to Madonna's rebellious nature. Over the next two months, the Madonna juggernaut would roll through twenty-eight cities, creating the kind of hysteria not seen since the onslaught of Beatlemania in the mid-1960s.

Sporting a series of costumes designed for the tour by Marlene Stewart—including her famous white lace wedding dress and a "Material Girl" *bustier* and pink hoop skirt encrusted with plastic fruit, ashtrays, coins, and toy watches—Madonna pranced, gyrated, and sang through a dozen songs. She was flanked by a six-member band, two male dancers, and prerecorded background vocals that bolstered her thin voice.

From the opening number, when she strutted down a staircase to the bouncing beat of "Dress You Up" in a boldly colored neo-psychedelic jacket, the show maintained a heart-pounding pace for its full seventy minutes—punctuated only by the star's naughty come-ons. "Hello, Miami," she shouted, "Watcha lookin' at? . . . I thought so." Another, delivered while straddling an enormous speaker: "Every lady has a box, only mine plays music." After she had whipped the crowd into an erotic frenzy with her writhing, campy version of "Like a Virgin," she yelled at the audience, "Will you marry me?" The predictable response: a thunderous "Yes!" Each show ended with the God-like voice of a father figure sternly telling Madonna that she's played long enough and it's time to come home.

Indeed, it was the unbridled, unabashed enthusiasm of her audiences that was elevating Madonna from mere rock star to bona fide phenomenon. They came by the thousands, wearing Merry Widows, leopard-print miniskirts, gold lamé *bustiers*, stretch lace leotards, and fingerless black evening gloves. To the untrained eye, it appeared as if most of these young women were merely wearing their underwear on the outside—and in truth, many of them were.

They were the "wannabes"—an army of females from ten to twenty-one who yearned to be exactly like their rule-breaking, tradition-smashing idol. Defiantly thumbing their nose at convention —and not incidentally, at parental authority—these young ladies spent millions on the official Madonna merchandise that was now part of her celebrity package: T-shirts, tour books, earrings, gloves, posters, sweatshirts, buttons. "If Madonna's face is on it," one wag observed, "it's for sale." Madonna herself was jubilant. Cash registers across America had barely started jangling when she celebrated her Seattle debut with a champagne toast. "To we," she said after her very first show, "who rule the universe!"

When Madonna stopped in San Francisco, it was Prince's turn to pay homage. He stood with his hulking bodyguards in the photographers' pit at the lip of the stage, looking up as Madonna strutted her stuff before five thousand screaming fans. Afterward, she accepted Prince's invitation to drop by his hotel suite. Stepping out of the elevator with her bodyguard Clay Tave, she sighed, "Well, time to go visit the midget."

Madonna was becoming increasingly impatient with Prince. She had flirted outrageously with him, but he consistently rejected her sexual overtures. "His outfits say touch me, lick me, love me, *lust me*" she complained, "but then he pretends he's wearing a monk's outfit." Besides, Madonna confided to friends that Prince was "too delicate for my taste. I went to hug him good-bye and he's so fragile I thought he'd shatter in my arms."

Sean Penn, meanwhile, was proving himself a durable lover. More important, he was pursuing Madonna in a way that no other boyfriend had, showing up at her concerts in Miami, San Diego, and Detroit. After her show at Detroit's Cobo Hall, she took him to meet her parents. (Penn introduced his parents to Madonna not long after, following her performance at Los Angeles' Universal Amphitheater). "Sean really paid attention to her," Melinda

Cooper said. "He really loved her in a way Jellybean never could. I mean, Jellybean was in love with Jellybean. But she was slow to come around."

Madonna had other things on her mind when she made her triumphant return to hometown Detroit. Sitting in the audience were friends, family, teachers. Stopping midway through "Holiday," she greeted her grandmother in the audience and delivered a tearful five-minute speech that reduced several band members to tears. In the front row sat her first mentor, Christopher Flynn, beaming, his hands folded neatly in his lap. "I was overwhelmed," he said. "When I looked up at her, I still saw this little fourteen-year-old girl clutching her doll. Now she had everything she wanted—everything I told her she deserved when I kicked her butt out of Michigan and told her to go to New York."

The audience member Madonna most wanted to please was Tony Ciccone. Still seeking her father's approval, she cut much of the potently suggestive material out of her show. "The show she gave for the hometown audience was squeaky-clean compared to what people in other parts of the country saw," said a former employee of Madonna's. "She was adamant that her father not be embarrassed." Nancy Ryan Mitchell, Madonna's high school counselor, said, "She did not use the language she uses elsewhere. Madonna was not about to risk her father's love and approval."

Madonna herself would confess that she was embarrassed to perform the more salacious portions of her show knowing her father was in the audience. This reticence did not manifest itself, however, when she looked out on thousands of twelve-year-old girls, many of whom were chaperoned by their understandably wary parents.

As part of an obvious attempt to reconcile with her father, Madonna invited Tony Ciccone to deliver the famous final lines of the show. "Dad," she told him, "I want you to come on and act like you did when I was little. You want me to get off that stage because you think I'm being naughty." For motivation, she reminded him of her scandalous go-go-girl performance in the fourth grade. "Now, really yank me," she told him, "because I'm going to give you a fight."

Tony Ciccone took his daughter's direction almost too well.

When he came on, he pulled Madonna's arm so hard that, in her words, "he almost dismembered me." At the end of the show, she beckoned him back onstage to take a bow.

Madonna had also taken care to invite a small group of family, ex-schoolmates, and teachers to join her at a small party at her suite in Detroit's St. Regis Hotel. Wearing a baseball cap, she moved around the room, greeting guests and asking repeatedly, "Hey, everybody, wasn't my dad great tonight?"

"It was really heartwarming, and a little tense at the same time," Nancy Ryan Mitchell recalled. "There was a lot of hugging and kissing, and Madonna was wonderful and affectionate toward everybody." Particularly toward Marilyn Fallows, the high school teacher who had nurtured her dreams a decade earlier. "There was Madonna in this baseball cap, taking this little old lady around and introducing her to people," Mitchell said. "It was very sweet." Throughout the evening, however, Tony Ciccone appeared uncomfortable. "When Madonna kept praising him, he just rolled with it," Mitchell said. "I mean, here he was trying to make conversation with the Beastie Boys. It wasn't really his crowd."

As usual, Madonna was disappointed in her father's less-than-enthusiastic reaction. "He's not a very demonstrative person," she said at the time. "It isn't realistic for me to think he'll change. But yes, I'm feeling a little rejected."

Completing the rest of the tour without Penn, Madonna had time to reflect on the nature of their relationship. "She called me up from Cleveland at two in the morning," Erica Bell recalled, "to talk about Sean and the audiences and how boring it was on the road. Sean was on her mind, but it didn't seem to me that she was as passionate when she spoke about him as she had been with Jellybean, for example."

Riding the crest of her triumphant tour, Madonna was in reality as flirtatious as ever. When she invited David Lee Roth to her opening night party in Los Angeles, she did little to disguise her interest in the libidinous former lead singer of Van Halen. "Should I bring a date or will I be busy later?" he asked her. "Sure, bring a date," Madonna replied. "We can *all* do something later."

She was equally faithful to Penn once she was back on the

eastern seaboard. With Penn on location in Mexico working on his film *At Close Range*, Madonna took standby lover Bobby Martinez and eight other men to the Palladium disco on the eve of her sold-out, five-day New York City debut. Fans had bought 17,000 tickets in just thirty minutes, setting a record for the fastest sellout in Radio City Music Hall history. When she was spotted by two photographers, Martinez and Madonna's bodyguard Clay Tave sprang to her defense. As the wiry Martinez chased after AP photographer Felice Quinto, Tave slammed *Daily News* photographer Dick Corkery against a wall. Madonna giggled as she watched the melee, then pulled a camouflage hat over her face and male retinue in tow, fled the club.

Once on the street, Tave and Martinez again attacked photographer Corkery, mauling and pummeling him. Corkery later pressed charges that resulted in an apology from Tave, but it was Martinez who threw most of the punches. "It was all over the papers, but I was the one who slugged the guy," Martinez admitted. "Clay took the rap." Why? "Because Madonna didn't want my name in the papers. She didn't want Sean to know she was still seeing me."

In city after city, critics assailed Madonna's amateurishness as a performer, then conceded it was that very quality which made her, in the words of *Rolling Stone* reviewer Michael Goldberg, "likable." When Madonna arrived in New York June 5 for her final performances at Radio City Music Hall and Madison Square Garden, *The New York Times* published the most scathing review of all. "The fact of the matter," wrote the *Times*'s Robert Palmer, "was that Madonna . . . simply didn't sing very well. Her intonation was atrocious; she sang sharp and she sang flat, and the combination of her unsure pitch and thin, quavery vocal timbre made the held notes at the end of her phrases sound like they were crawling off somewhere to die." He also pointed out, somewhat ungallantly, that "she should learn not to toss tambourines into the air unless she's going to be able to catch them."

Throughout the tour, Madonna had gradually been gaining a reputation as a prima donna—barking orders at her band members and dancers, throwing tantrums during sound checks, shouting profanities at everyone from crew members to limo drivers at the slightest provocation. "Overnight she became maniacal, demanding," Melinda Cooper said. "You never knew from one minute to the next what was going to happen. Suddenly it was, 'Do it. Do it now. And don't ask me why, or you're fired.'" Boasted Madonna: "Yes, I am a bitch. I am also the *boss*."

The final performance at Madison Square Garden was an emotional one for Madonna. She had once lived in a grimy apartment nearby, and old friend Steve Bray shook his head in wonder as she told the crowd, "There's a place across the street . . . I used to look out the window at the Garden and say, 'I wonder if I'll ever get in there.'"

After the performance, famed palimony lawyer Marvin Mitchelson went backstage to pay the star a compliment. "I've heard all about you," she told the attorney best known for obtaining enormous divorce settlements for his female clients. "I want to congratulate you for the work you've done for women's rights." Mitchelson replied: "If women continue to be as successful and affluent as you, you can bet I'll be representing more men in the future."

That night there was an official "Homecoming" party for Madonna at the Palladium. More than five thousand people showed up. Anyone with the $15 admission fee was allowed inside the club, but only VIPs were allowed past the velvet rope and a solid wall of hired muscle to the Mike Todd Room. The room was draped with white lace, as were the bartenders, waiters, and waitresses. Here Madonna, wearing a strapless black minidress and layers of gold necklaces, held court. Among those paying tribute were rocker Billy Idol, Matt Dillon, and Rob Lowe, who had ditched his fiancée Melissa Gilbert in hopes of starting up a serious relationship with Madonna. Lowe would land in considerable trouble several years later after videotaping himself and another man having sex with a teenage girl in an Atlanta hotel room.

Around one-thirty A.M., Madonna walked into the main room, stepped onstage, and accepted an armful of white roses from club owner-entrepreneur Steve Rubell. The crowd, which had waited for hours to see her, began booing when she said good-night. By way of appeasement, she did a few quick dance steps with a group of go-go boys fruging in the background. Then she departed, leaving five thousand disillusioned fans grumbling in her wake.

One close aide of Madonna's had seen her undergo a profound change as the tour progressed. "Once we had reached New York, she really believed her own publicity," she said. "She had already had number one records and been in a hit movie, but it wasn't until she got out there and felt that surge of power from big live audiences that she changed. You look out at thousands of people every night and they're screaming your name and dressing just like you—it's bound to give you a distorted view of your own importance."

According to Melinda Cooper, Madonna's newfound sense of power manifested itself in a "cruel streak. She became more maniacal, more demanding." During her New York stay, the tour had taken a floor at the Westbury Hotel on Madison Avenue. "Two little girls, maybe four and six years old, sat up all day long waiting in the lobby," Cooper recalled. "We'd see them as we passed. Finally I said, 'They've been waiting here all day, Madonna. Why don't you sign an autograph for them?' " Madonna walked up to the two little girls and pointedly refused to sign their books. "If I do it for you, then I'll have to do it for everybody," she told them. "You're *nothing*. You don't mean anything to me." Madonna then turned and left. "One little girl was in tears," Cooper said. "I apologized to the mother, who was standing there in disbelief."

It was not the only display of cruelty toward children witnessed by Cooper. "During her shows, she often has it arranged so these kids are down there on the stage and she gives them a hug. But on her own time, she doesn't want anybody bothering her. I got the impression she hated kids." It was an impression shared by many who knew Madonna. "She had enough of kids when she was growing up," said one of her closest advisers. "Madonna doesn't have a maternal bone in her body."

Teenage boys were another matter. According to several sources, when the tour brought Madonna to New York's Radio City Music Hall, America's newest superstar took to the streets to indulge her taste for young Latin men. "We'd get all dressed up and drive in her limousine to Avenue D," Bell recalled. "When she spotted some good-looking Puerto Rican boy, she'd order the driver to stop the car, then roll down the window and call out, 'Hey, cutie, want a ride?'

"She'd invite the boy to join us, and they always obliged. Sometimes she just kissed him, and that was all. But if she really liked the kid, she'd just rip off his clothes and do whatever she wanted with him while we drove around New York. The windows were blacked out—nobody could see what was going on inside the car. We'd end up driving around with two or three guys at a time." Then, Bell said, "we'd drop them off right where we found them." According to Bell, the boys were "really young, the way she likes them."

On occasion Madonna brought her street-tough "banji boys," as they were known, home to her new apartment on the Upper West Side. "She ran a Puerto Rican stud farm up there," former lover and mentor Mark Kamins said. "There were parties at her apartment where Madonna slept with three or four guys at once," says a close friend of some of the participants.

Madonna also continued to plumb the depths of her bisexual nature. She would talk about inviting her gay dancers to engage in homosexual acts while she watched, or about making love to a woman while one of her straight lovers watched. "I am aroused by two men kissing," she later admitted. "I am aroused by the idea of a woman making love to me while either a man or another woman watches. Is that kinky?"

Young Bobby Martinez was a frequent guest. During one of her "parties," Madonna, Martinez, and another couple took off all their clothes and repaired to the steam room she had installed in her apartment. Martinez described the scene: "Madonna and this other girlfriend of hers fooled around while me and the other guy watched, then we all had a really good time. I think she likes women as much as she likes men."

Madonna's practice of cruising the Lower East Side of New York would continue for years, with the exception of a brief period during her marriage to Sean Penn. Amazingly, she did not worry that she would be recognized. "Of course she was recognized," Bell said. "You could go down to Avenue D and find dozens of guys who'll tell you they were picked up by Madonna. And they'd be telling the truth." She wasn't concerned that the stories of wild sex with strangers might result in scandal. "These were just banji boys, downtown kids," explained Johnny Dynell, a close-hand observer of Madonna's sex life. "Madonna was smart. She knew nobody would believe them."

Ironically, Madonna would soon be swept up in controversy— over issues so comparatively tame that it had those who knew her scratching their heads in disbelief.

13

> "I've been called a tramp, a harlot, a slut, and the kind of girl that always ends up in the backseat of a car. If people can't get past that superficial level of what I'm about, fine."

"**N**ow then, parents," began *Time*'s May 27, 1985, cover story, "the important thing is to stay calm." In two cover stories spaced barely a month apart, *People* struck a similar note. "She's tart but delicious, she's campy but coy, she's the pop world embodiment of personality-as-art," declared *People* in its cover story, appropriately titled "That Man-Smasher Madonna on Tour."

Less than three months after she set foot on the stage of a major arena for the first time, Madonna was now regarded as a sociocultural force that could not be denied. "Everyone seems to agree there is something puzzling and inscrutable about Madonna," wrote College of William and Mary government professor Joel D. Schwartz in *The New Republic*. "It is this quality that goes a long way toward explaining her cult appeal."

Madonna played the press like a virtuoso, making the kinds of provocative pronouncements that were certain to keep her in the public eye. One of the most hotly debated topics was what *Time* called Madonna's "Hi-there" belly button: "I have the most perfect belly button—an inny, and there's no lint in it. When I stick my finger in my belly button, I feel a nerve in the center of my body shoot up my spine. If one hundred belly buttons were lined up against a wall, I could definitely pick out which one is mine."

Madonna's harshest critics only served her purposes by fueling public debate. Sam Janus, associate professor of psychiatry at New York Medical College and author of *The Death of Innocence*, condemned Madonna as "a corrupting Pied Piper, leading impressionable young girls down the primrose path to a depraved and degrading lifestyle." Dr. Danilo Ponce, professor of psychiatry at the University of Hawaii agreed: "The whole image that Madonna projects is that of a tramp—a streetwalker eager to sell her favors to the highest bidder." As for sporting crucifixes with black lingerie, Ponce denounced it as "a bizarre combination, mixing sex and religion in a way that ridicules spirituality."

Madonna reveled in the controversy. So long as the public was debating the image she had so finely crafted, she could only bask in the resulting publicity. "I will be a symbol of something," she predicted. "Like Marilyn Monroe stands for something. It's not always something you can put a name on, but she became an adjective."

Toward that end, Hollywood beckoned. The Goldwyn Studios approached her with an offer to star in a remake of *Ball of Fire*, the 1941 film in which Barbara Stanwyck played a stripper. Director Herb Ross, who three years earlier had turned her down for the Lori Singer part in the hit *Footloose*, sought her out for his next film. Touchstone Pictures was also hot on Madonna's heels, coming close to signing her for *Ruthless People*.

Madonna was also considering a Ray Stark production, a film biography of Libby Holman, the 1930s torch singer who was accused and acquitted of murdering her husband, then spent years battling alcoholism. "It's a very exciting role," Madonna said coyly. "It seems to be working out in Hollywood for me, but I'd like to make my own movies." In fact, she was already collaborating with the husband and wife team of Ashford and Simpson on a $15-million movie musical for Warner Brothers called *Street Smart*.

That June, Madonna divided her time between Bobby Martinez

in New York and Penn, who was spending two months in Tennessee filming *At Close Range* with his brother Chris Penn and Christopher Walken. On weekends, she flew down to Nashville incognito and went straight to Penn's room at the Maxwell House Hotel. And it was during one of these trysts that she made up Penn's mind that they should be married.

On the morning of Sunday, June 17, a nude Madonna was jumping up and down on the hotel bed—presumably part of her morning exercise routine—when, she recalled, "all of a sudden he got this look in his eyes. He was asking me to marry him, but he didn't say it out loud. I felt like I knew what he was thinking and I read his mind."

She stopped jumping up and down on the bed. "Whatever you're thinking," she told Penn, "I'll say yes to."

Taking his cue, Penn asked her to marry him. As promised, she said yes. They then got dressed, dashed across the street to a 7-Eleven, and celebrated their engagement with a "brunch" of jawbreakers. Later it would always be a matter of debate between the two of them about just who had proposed to whom.

Madonna then jetted back to Los Angeles and her five-room, $1,350-a-month apartment beneath the fabled Hollywood sign. Now that she had a California driver's license—Madonna had not owned a car since moving to New York—she treated herself to a $44,000 midnight blue Mercedes sports coupe.

At a beach party given by record tycoon David Geffen at his Malibu mansion, Madonna informed her host that she was altarbound with Sean Penn. "Madonna," the bisexual Geffen quipped, "I was going to go straight for you!"

Within a week, news of the engagement was leaked to the press. Publicist Liz Rosenberg, who would ride Madonna's coattails to the position of vice president at Warner Records, confirmed that the most contentious couple since Elizabeth Taylor and Richard Burton were planning to wed the following month.

The news caught even those closest to Madonna off guard. Martin Burgoyne heard it over the radio and called Erica Bell. "When Martin told me, all I could manage to get out of my mouth was '*What?*' I was stunned," recalled Bell. "She told *no one* that she was going to marry Penn. Even his family didn't know about it until they saw the news on TV."

Madonna's ex-boyfriends were also taken by surprise. "When Jellybean and I saw that Madonna was marrying Penn, we laughed," said Mark Kamins. "I mean, it's something that you'd expect from her—she goes to Hollywood and marries a Brat Packer. But we had to laugh because we also knew he was genuine psycho."

The press hammered away at their obvious differences. While publicity was only slightly less necessary for Madonna's survival than oxygen, Penn shunned the press; he had once gleefully threatened to squirt a female reporter with a urine-filled water pistol. But Madonna's oldest friends were genuinely concerned for her welfare. The outspokenly homophobic Penn had earned the undying enmity of nearly all Madonna's New York acquaintances —gay and straight. "He would come up and say, 'Hi, homo,' to Martin," Johnny Dynell recalled. "Or she'd be talking to someone and he'd yell out, 'Who the fuck is that *faggot?*' You never went near her when he was around. He was a jerk, a real jerk." Ed Steinberg concurred: "I'm not gay, but I can tell you it was sickening to hear him call her friends queers and fags. Everybody hated him."

Bell believed that envy was at the heart of Penn's homophobia. "Sean was jealous of Madonna's gay friends, especially Martin. He had a special relationship with her that in a sense was deeper than anything she could have with a straight man." Years later, Madonna herself would admit she had "the most camaraderie" with homosexual men. "They are looked at as outsiders, so I relate to that. On the other hand, I feel that most gay men are so much more in touch with a certain sensitivity that heterosexual men aren't allowed to be in touch with, their feminine side. To me they're whole human beings, more so than most of the straight men I know."

Of more concern to Bell was Madonna's sudden fascination with Penn's highly publicized penchant for violence. "I feel Sean is like my brothers," Madonna said in her fiancé's defense. "They were wild and rebellious, starting fires in the basement, throwing rocks at the windows." Penn's wild streak could be traced to high school, where, reportedly wearing a ski mask, he and a buddy had tied another student to a tree, poured a gas can full of water over him, and tossed a lit match at the terrified teenager. "That guy," Penn boasted to Madonna, "has never been the same since!"

Penn frequently carried a gun when he was out on the town in Los Angeles and New York; now Madonna was joining him for target practice. When Penn bragged to her that he had once shot the watch off Elizabeth McGovern's wrist during an argument, she phoned Bell to tell her the story. "She thought it was funny," Bell recalled. "I said, 'Girl, are you crazy? He is *cracked.*' We all told her to drop him, that he was insane, that he was nuts." In addition, Bell recalled that Penn "drove like a complete maniac. If somebody didn't get shot, I was afraid he was going to drive her off a cliff."

Her fears were borne out only days later in Nashville, where Madonna was spending another steamy weekend with Penn at the Maxwell House Hotel. Vexed by rumors that Madonna was pregnant, Penn exploded when someone sent the couple a bouquet of balloons with a card reading, "Sean and Madonna, Congratulations Mom and Pop." The next morning as she left the hotel on her customary jog around the grounds, Penn looked out his window and spotted a suspicious-looking car and went down to investigate. Inside were two free-lance journalists, Ian Markham-Smith and Laurence Cottrell, on assignment for *The Sun* of London.

When Madonna returned to the hotel, the two reporters emerged from their car and tried to snap a picture of her. Penn picked up a large rock and started toward them. "No pictures!" he yelled. "You take my picture and I'll break your fucking back with this rock!" Recalled eyewitness Lori Mulrenin: "He was screaming and his face was turning beet red. He looked like a bomb ready to explode."

Cottrell described what happened next: "We asked what's the problem. Then he came after us and threw the rock at me and hit me in the middle of the back with great force. He also ruined my camera when he grabbed it and started hitting me with it. I was in tremendous pain. He just kept on and on. It wasn't a quick assault.

Penn was acting like a madman—as if he was crazy. I've never seen such a look of pure evil on anyone's face."

With Cottrell on the ground, Penn then went after Markham-Smith, punching him repeatedly in the face. "He just went for us straight off," Markham-Smith recalled. "He went berserk, like a whirlwind." Cottrell managed to snap a few more photos of Penn pummeling his colleague before the actor turned and threw yet another rock at him full force, aiming for Cottrell's head. The reporter spun around, ducked, and was struck in the back a second time. Penn resumed smashing their cameras on the ground.

Madonna shielded her face from the photographers with a base-ball cap, but watched the melee through her fingers. "Throughout the whole thing," remembered Cottrell, "she never said a word. She just stood there and watched as he did his thing with the rock."

Limping back to the safety of their car, the reporters drove to the police station and swore out a complaint. That evening, Nash-ville police officer Thomas Nelson arrested Penn at his hotel and took him to be booked on two misdemeanor counts of assault and battery. The penalty if convicted: a $500 fine and/or a year in jail on each count. He was arraigned before Night Court commis-sioner Bill Norris, who asked him if he understood the charges. "Yeah," replied Penn. Norris then released him on $1,000 bail. Ironically, Cottrell and Markham-Smith had intended to ask Ma-donna and Penn for a single quote on their impending marriage, and to snap "just one picture of the happy couple."

Publicly, Madonna offered no comment on her fiancé's hair-trigger temper. Privately, she defended him enthusiastically. As far as the beaten and bruised British newsmen were concerned, she told her hairdresser-confidante Debi M. the attack was totally jus-tified. "They'll live," she added with a sneer.

Two days after the Nashville fracas, Penn and Madonna were at it again—this time trying to elude photographers in New York. He led them on a high-speed chase through city streets that topped ninety miles an hour, stopping once to position a garbage can in the path of a pursuing car.

During the first two weeks of their engagement, the notorious couple was scarcely ever out of the news as Penn rampaged, with Madonna looking demurely on. Yet she was about to be thrust center stage in a public furor over something she had done six years before. In the bargain, she would also touch off a multimillion-dollar feud between the nation's two most powerful publishers of men's magazines.

On July 7, *Penthouse* magazine announced with much fanfare that it was going to publish photographs taken in 1979 and 1980 during Madonna's brief career as a nude model. The pictures were to be featured in a seventeen-page layout in the magazine's sixteenth anniversary September issue. "A great number of Madonna nudes surfaced all at once, and we had first choice," said *Penthouse* publisher Bob Guccione, whose decision to publish sexually explicit photographs of Vanessa Williams in 1984 had forced her to resign as the first black Miss America. "They came from many different sources—photography teachers and their students, amateurs and professionals—and we had the opportunity to select the very best." In the end, Guccione had paid an estimated $100,000 for the photos taken by Bill Stone.

Catching Guccione by surprise, spokesmen for Hugh Hefner's *Playboy* announced that they had their own set of Madonna nudes, and that theirs would beat *Penthouse*'s Madonna issue to the newsstands. *Playboy*'s photographs were those taken by Martin Schreiber and Lee Freidlander. Each pocketed $100,000 for his efforts.

Following the *Playboy* bombshell, Guccione fired off a salvo of his own. He now conceded that the quality of the black-and-white photos he had left something to be desired—"She wasn't well groomed, there was lots of hair on her arms and hair sticking out of her armpits"—and offered Madonna $1 million to pose for "Scavullo, Avedon, any photographer she wanted." The offer was declined.

The race between the two magazines was being called a "navel battle" and ended with *Playboy* hitting the stands on July 11—a day before its rival. Madonna remained above the fray, and with good reason. In exchange for her $25 modeling fee, she had signed releases that gave the photographers complete control. Powerless to act, she issued a terse statement through Liz Rosenberg. "I'm not," she declared, "ashamed of anything."

Some of Madonna's family members were. Back in Bay City, Michigan, Grandma Elsie Fortin first learned of the photographs while watching the *Donahue* show. "I was shocked," she recalled. "I was all alone and I started to cry. I didn't like what I was seeing. It bothered me." It also bothered local officials, who withdrew their offer to present Madonna with the key to Bay City after the nude pictures surfaced.

Madonna did, according to Erica Bell, "laugh hysterically," recalling the day three years before when they sat on the floor of her bare room and joked about the day when these photos would be published. Yet she was upset over the fact that, for the first time in her career, she was not in control of the situation. "I can't say I wasn't devastated by the experience," Madonna later admitted. "It took me by surprise." She also fretted about her father's reaction. The lurid manner in which both *Playboy* and *Penthouse* went about promoting their respective Madonna nudes could hardly be considered flattering. Back when she was posing for them, Madonna later explained, "it didn't really occur to me that I was setting myself up for scandal for years to come."

Madonna's attorneys would use the same argument only weeks later to try to derail Stephen Jon Lewicki's planned release of *A Certain Sacrifice* on home video. At Lewicki's invitation, she had attended a private screening with her entourage and with the exception of when she was on-screen, had talked loudly the entire time. When she got up to leave, she turned to Lewicki and said, "Well, fuck you, Steve." She then explained, "We've always had an adversarial relationship. I just thought I'd keep it that way."

A woman of her word, she offered Lewicki a meager $10,000 to keep *A Certain Sacrifice* out of circulation. Predictably, Lewicki declined. With 60,000 advance orders at $59.95 apiece, he expected to gross at least $3.5 million for a film that had cost $20,000 to make. "Her lawyer actually said to me," recalled Lewicki, "that 'poor Madonna' is out in Hollywood trying to make a living, and this film could have serious consequences for her career. It really broke my heart."

Madonna then ordered the attorneys for her Boy Toy corporation to file suit thwarting distribution of *A Certain Sacrifice*. In an affidavit she conceded that she had signed a release on September 20, 1980, authorizing commercial depiction of her performance. Yet she stated that she "did not consent to the use of my name." She went on to say that release of the low-budget, soft-core film containing several nude scenes would make it impossible to "maintain the image and the aura I have created." Although she lambasted the movie as "mediocre" with a "dreadful" story line, what bothered her most was that "my performance was second-rate."

Lewicki defended his film as "New Wave, Lower East Side, post-punk, and sexy," adding that "Madonna's image is hardly saintly. She can be a demanding bitch," he later observed, "but she's honest. She put a lot of herself into this role—a strong woman, but without anger, without a chip on her shoulder. In that sense, I think she really exemplifies her generation of women." The courts would eventually side with Lewicki on the matter, making him an overnight millionaire.

All the pressures came to a head on July 11, when Madonna took the stage before a live audience of 90,000 and a global television audience as part of Live Aid. Humiliated by the events of the previous two weeks, she had said nothing to coworkers about the scandalous nude photos and video during rehearsals. But she confessed later that inside she actually felt "small." All of which made her determined to "get out there and kick ass."

Bette Midler did not make it easy, introducing Madonna as "a woman who pulled herself up by her bra straps and who has been known to let them down occasionally." Temperatures were hovering in the nineties, but as she belted out "Holiday," "Into the Groove," and "Love Makes the World Go Round," Madonna remained covered up in a long white brocade coat. "I ain't takin' shit off today," she told the sweltering crowd. "You might hold it against me in ten years."

Having "kicked ass," Madonna returned to the business of planning her wedding and looking for a new apartment. When film producer Bill Gerber put his sprawling twelve-room cooperative apartment in the exclusive San Remo up for sale, Madonna snapped it up for $1.2 million. All that remained for the sale to go through was approval by the co-op board, a delegation of apartment owners.

Like all other prospective tenants, Madonna had to be screened personally by the board. She opted to dress demurely for the occasion, wearing a simple black dress with several strands of pearls, her customary slash of fire-engine-red lipstick—and a number of huge gold crucifixes. Several older board members were visibly taken aback by her appearance, but in view of the fact that such celebrities as Dustin Hoffman, Paul Simon, and Diane Keaton owned co-ops in the San Remo, approval appeared to be little more than a formality.

Confident that she would soon be moving into her dream apartment with the wraparound terraces and breathtaking views of Central Park, Madonna put on another black dress and headed for her bridal shower. Held at the East Eightieth Street apartment of producer Nile Rodgers's wealthy girlfriend Nancy Huang, the party was attended by twenty-five of Madonna's friends, including Alannah Currie of the rock group The Thompson Twins, actress Mariel Hemingway, and such longtime pals as Erica Bell, Debi M., and Maripol. Men were barred, but following Madonna's decree that males wearing women's clothing would be allowed to attend, a half dozen showed up in drag. Among them: Madonna's best friend, Martin Burgoyne, and ex-lover Jellybean Benitez. "I loaned them my clothes," said Bell, "and I'm *still* waiting to get a couple of dresses back." Cameras snapped as Madonna opened her presents, which included such standard items as jewelry, lingerie, and a quilt. The only flashy gift: a push-button phone covered with sequins.

At the height of the festivities, Madonna was dealt another blow. She was told that the San Remo co-op board had turned her down flat, ostensibly on grounds that her presence would result in an invasion of paparazzi that would disrupt the lives of other tenants and compromise security. Diane Keaton was Madonna's only supporter on the board. Off the record, other board members confessed that the nude photos in *Playboy* and *Penthouse* had tipped the scales. "Hers," sniffed one matron, "is not the kind of image we wish to project. If we let her in, we'd have to let everybody in."

As she left Huang's apartment and stepped out onto East Eightieth Street, Madonna was, as usual, besieged by waiting reporters. This time, following her fiancé's lead, she confronted them. "Why don't you go back to hell," she screamed, "where you came from?" She then piled into a limousine with her friends—including men in full makeup and evening gowns—and headed for the Palladium to dance away the rest of the night.

It was during this short drive that Madonna complained about another problem. She was being sued by her former manager Camille Barbone for $5 million on grounds that she had never legally dissolved their manager-client relationship. The $5-million figure presumably represented 20 percent of Madonna's $25-million fortune at the time. Erica Bell seized the opportunity to ask if Madonna and Penn had signed a prenuptial agreement. "Of course," Madonna replied guilelessly. "I have much more money than he does—and I plan to keep it."

If she was harboring any serious doubts about marrying Penn, Madonna kept them to herself. She was, like any twenty-six-year-old bride-to-be, soon swept up in the excitement of planning her wedding. Not to forgo tradition, she registered her china patterns at Tiffany's: Monet's Giverny at $260 a place setting, and Coeur de Fleur at $660 per place setting.

Back at Freddy DeMann's offices in Los Angeles, Madonna, Melinda Cooper, and two secretaries worked the phones, trying to find the addresses of the biggest names in town to add to the guest list. For weeks, the world's press was in a frenzy not unlike the one that had preceded the state wedding of Prince Charles to Lady Diana Spencer. When would the nuptials take place, and where? Who was invited? What would the gown look like; would she dare to wear white? All these issues were debated endlessly in print and over the airwaves. Anticipation grew to a fever pitch on August 12 when Madonna, who had let her hair return to its natural dark brown color, was spotted with Penn taking out a marriage license at the Los Angeles County Courthouse.

Only a chosen few—for the moment, at least—were privy to the fact that Madonna and Penn would be wed August 16 (the mutual birthday) at multimillionaire developer Dan Unger's clifftop Malibu estate. There was still time for these symbols of youthful rebellion to cut loose. Penn's actor-brother Chris and friends Tom Cruise, Robert Duvall, and David Keith threw a raucous bachelor party for the groom, complete with nonstop drinking and stripper Kitten Natividad, who took it all off to the strains of "Material Girl." When actor Harry Dean Stanton showed up an hour late, Penn called Natividad over, lifted up her blouse, and then shoved Stanton's face into her breasts. "See what you missed?" cracked Penn.

Not to be outdone, Madonna whooped it up at a bachelorette party of her own. With a dozen friends, the blushing bride-to-be cheered on competitors at the Tropicana, a mud-wrestling club in one of Hollywood's seediest districts.

On the day of the ceremony, even as reporters donned camouflage gear and fueled up helicopters for a full-scale invasion of the wedding site, serious questions about the wisdom of this union remained. Madonna courted the limelight. Penn eschewed it. She was, as Mark Kamins had pointed out, accustomed to juggling three lovers or more at a time. He was obsessively, even violently possessive. Added to this were the career pressures, titanic egos, and long separations inherent in any show business marriage, and one wondered why the two most celebrated iconoclasts of their generation were plunging headlong into the respectability of marriage. Certainly not to have children. While Penn wanted to start a family, Madonna had already confided to her closest friends that she would "never" have a child with Penn.

There were other signs that Madonna was having trouble with commitment. Just days before her wedding day, according to Bobby Martinez, the two had rendezvoused secretly. "The trouble from the beginning," reflected one friend of the couple's, "is that he loved her more than she loved him."

Over the course of the next four acrimony-filled years, the hot-headed groom and his hot-blooded bride would make the Battling Burtons look like Dwight and Mamie Eisenhower. But at this moment, Madonna was guardedly optimistic. "We have so much in common that he's almost like my brother," she explained. "His temperament is also similar to mine. That doesn't always make for ideal relationships, but I don't know what will happen. . . ."

14

"Every time they jump out to take pictures, it's like they're raping me. . . . They might just as well take a gun and shoot me."

"Sean wants to protect me. He has . . . an integrity, and he sticks with what he believes in, no matter what. There's not many people who do that."

The chaos of their wedding day behind them, Sean took the wheel of Madonna's new Mercedes and the couple drove at breakneck speed up the serpentine Pacific Coast Highway toward the picturesque oceanside hamlet of Carmel. The spot they had chosen for their honeymoon could scarcely have been more conspicuous. The Highlands Inn, perched on a craggy bluff high above the rugged Pacific coastline, had been popular with newlyweds in the San Francisco Bay Area for decades. Erica Bell, who happened to be house-sitting for friends in Carmel, invited the Penns to stay at the secluded hilltop mansion instead. "When Madonna told me they were going to the Highlands Inn for their honeymoon, I told her she was crazy—that they were sure to be hounded by reporters if they went there," Bell said. "But they insisted."

Reservations for a $250-a-night suite had been made under the name of Madonna's friend Michael Ochs, but the travel agency that made them tipped management off to the fact that their guests would actually be VIPs. When the couple arrived exhausted at around eleven that night, the bellhop tried to open the car door for the female passenger. Hiding her face, she refused to unlock the door. "At first I didn't know who she was, so I thought she was a real snob," recalled the bellhop. "Then I realized it was Madonna, so I took her and Sean to their suite."

With its mirrored walls and ceilings, a hot tub adjacent to the king-size bed, and the only private room secluded enough for nude sunbathing, No. 429 was understandably one of the Highlands Inn's most requested suites. Once there, the Penns, already swigging out of beer cans, offered one to the delighted bellhop.

The next morning, waiters at the Highlands Inn drew straws for the privilege of carrying up Madonna's room service order of fresh raspberries and cream. The waiter who won arrived to find Madonna sitting in a corner, concealing her face behind the covers of a book. "I congratulated her on getting married," recalled the waiter. "She put the book down, grinned, and said, 'Thank you.'"

For two days, the couple holed up in their room, sneaking out only to pick up candy, popcorn, and orange juice in the hotel food shop. One evening, the hotel restaurant remained open after hours just for the Penns, both of whom ate only salad and fruit. Highlands Inn staff members were impressed with how down-to-earth the couple seemed—until another room service waiter arrived to find the Penns romping fully clothed in a hot tub full of water.

Apparently growing bored outside the spotlight, the new Mrs. Penn made a reservation under the name Madonna at Clint Eastwood's restaurant, the Hog's Breath Inn. Dinner there was followed by drinks at a popular Carmel watering hole, Toots Lagoon. Having alerted the immediate world to their presence, Sean and Madonna then returned to the Highlands Inn where, said a staffer, "the phones never stopped ringing. Fans rushed to the inn with flowers and notes, and their quiet honeymoon was over."

It was not long before a rowdy group of surfers gathered outside Suite 429 and pleaded noisily for Madonna to smoke pot with them

—apparently unaware of her well-publicized aversion to drugs. After a half hour of this, she threw open the door to her room and showered the surfers with a torrent of expletives. Hours later Sean and Madonna, wearing the same black sweat suits for the third straight day, cut short their honeymoon and returned to Los Angeles.

The Penns purchased a Spanish-style villa on fifty acres in the rugged canyons of Malibu, with a huge gate, sweeping views of the ocean, and mountains looming in the back. Shielded from prying eyes, Madonna realized that snooping fans and intrusive reporters weren't the only pressures she faced as a new wife. Penn's excessive drinking and violent mood swings were already putting strains on their life behind closed doors. According to close associates of both Penns, Madonna began seeing a psychiatrist barely six weeks after the wedding and urged her husband to do the same. He refused.

Thwarted in her efforts to confront their personal difficulties head-on, Madonna turned her attention back to her film career. During their engagement, she and Sean had considered a number of properties in which they could act together. But it was not until they were personally approached by ex-Beatle George Harrison to costar in a film for his Handmade Films studio that the couple found a project to their mutual liking. Combining elements of Marlene Dietrich's 1932 classic *Shanghai Express* and John Huston's *The African Queen*, *Shanghai Surprise* dealt with a Yankee missionary escaping the boredom of a safe marriage back home and the scruffy American drifter she encounters in China during the Sino-Japanese War.

Another project that intrigued the newlyweds was *Blind Date*, a Tri-Star film dealing with a businessman whose blind date gets drunk and wreaks havoc on his career. After months of negotiations, both would bow out of the film, leaving Bruce Willis and Kim Basinger to star in the comedy.

Filming on *Shanghai Surprise* was to begin in early January of 1986, so Penn studied Mandarin for his part while Madonna, who had no Chinese dialogue in the movie, worked with old lover Steve Bray on songs for her next album. There were the infrequent forays to Helena's, the Los Angeles celebrity haunt co-owned by their friend Jack Nicholson, but for the most part Sean and Madonna tried to maintain a low profile.

On October 17, as rumors persisted that the couple was expecting a child, Penn flew to Nashville to face assault charges stemming from his attack on British journalists Laurence Cottrell and Ian Markham-Smith the previous June. Given a $150 fine and a ninety-day suspended sentence, he turned around the same day and flew to Los Angeles—but not before verbally accosting another photographer at the airport. "I wish I had AIDS," he said menacingly (if not altogether coherently), "so I could shoot you. I wouldn't do it fast, but slow, from the toes up."

Penn returned to Malibu determined to make good his wedding day promise to build an impenetrable fortress for himself and his bride. Dissatisfied with the mountains that shielded the estate from prying camera lenses, he ordered some changes. He stopped short of erecting a gun tower, but he did hire contractors to build a high wall around the property, topped with steel spikes.

Since the Penns had given the public precious little to laugh about of late, Madonna was intent on proving that she had a sense of humor. Toward that end, she arrived in Manhattan on November 9 to host the season opener of NBC's "Saturday Night Live." The program, which had created such comedy stars as Gilda Radner, Chevy Chase, John Belushi, Dan Aykroyd, Billy Crystal, Jane Curtin, and Eddie Murphy since its debut in 1975, gave Madonna a rare opportunity to spoof her own celebrity before a national audience—and to disarm her critics.

Before a live audience that included Cher, actress Jennifer Beals, and *Superman*'s Christopher Reeve, Madonna parodied Marilyn Monroe and Princess Di in the course of the ninety-minute program. But the biggest laughs came from her opening monologue narration of "home movies" taken during her own Malibu wedding—complete with a recreation of the helicopter invasion to the accompaniment of Wagner. She ended the monologue with, "We have a great show. We have Simple Minds, we have Penn and Teller. I'm not pregnant, and we'll be right back."

After the show, Sean and Madonna reverted to type, avoiding the packed post-taping party at the Palladium that included "Saturday Night Live" alumnus-turned-top-box-office-draw Eddie

Murphy. Madonna's "Saturday Night Live" appearance aside, the Penns showed no sign of becoming more accessible to the media or their fans. At the Columbus Cafe on the city's Upper West Side, Madonna was followed to the ladies' room by an admirer who, after apologizing profusely for bothering her, showered her with compliments. Madonna responded with stony silence, and the disappointed fan returned to her husband. On the way out of the restaurant, Penn walked over to the woman's table and let fly with a torrent of blistering obscenities that left other diners stunned and upset. Madonna looked on approvingly.

This incident contrasted sharply with the scene a few weeks later at the Pediatric Wing of New York Hospital–Cornell Medical Center. Loaded down with scores of brightly wrapped presents, the Penns visited the children's wards, dispensing gifts to youngsters who would not be home for the holidays. They had agreed to play Mr. and Mrs. Claus only when the hospital pledged that there would be no advance publicity. Afterward, in a gesture of devotion, Penn tattooed his wife's current nickname—Daisy (after Daisy Miller)—on his toe.

Still smarting from her rejection at the hands of the San Remo board of directors, Madonna was overjoyed when tenants at 41 Central Park West approved her purchase of a sprawling apartment in that building for $900,000. Adhering to the terms of their prenuptial agreement, Madonna purchased the co-op with her own funds. Unlike the Malibu house, which they owned jointly, the co-op belonged solely to her. Once she had given her decorators their marching orders, she joined her husband on a flight ultimately bound for Shanghai—and a filmmaking experience she would not soon forget.

Madonna and Penn arrived in Shanghai in the predawn hours of January 8, 1986, after an exhausting flight from Los Angeles. Too excited to sleep, they walked through the city and were at once greeted by a surreal sight: thousands of Chinese going through the deliberate, slow-motion movements of t'ai chi in the parks and on the streets, their hands slicing gracefully through the air.

Madonna was watched, as she was everywhere, only this time with a major difference. She was being stared at not because of who she was, but what she looked like. Her hair, now dyed platinum blond for her missionary role, made her look as weird and otherworldly to the Chinese as a creature from another planet. "I'm like from outer space to them," she said. "A Martian. I loved that. That was great."

From dreary Shanghai, cast and crew moved on to the comparative orgy of sight and sound known as Hong Kong. Here they could come closer to recreating the anything-goes atmosphere of Shanghai in the 1930s. Everyone had expected to face challenges during the filming of *Shanghai Surprise*, but no one, least of all Madonna, anticipated just how daunting those challenges would be. Jim Goddard had directed television miniseries before, but never a feature film. He was caught off guard by local mobsters who sought huge payoffs in exchange for access to certain seamy parts of the city. At one point, Madonna and Penn were trapped when a street was blocked off by someone demanding $50,000 just to move his car. Another time, the local mob killed the production's generator, forcing Goddard to close down the set.

The climate presented other difficulties. *Shanghai Surprise* was set in the summer, but this was the dead of winter, and while Penn could wear long underwear under his baggy 1930s suits, his wife shivered in her filmy summer dresses. To make matters worse, parts of Hong Kong where they filmed were teeming with vermin and huge black rats—some of which made a home beneath Madonna's trailer. These conditions, coupled with Madonna's own sizable insecurities about her acting ("I'll be a terrible actress, he won't love me anymore, all that stuff"), caused her to worry that her marriage might not survive the experience. "Strangely enough," she said later, "we never got along better. We took turns being strong. . . . I was so overtaken by it, and I was crying, and he said, 'Don't worry, baby, we'll make it work.' " Two weeks later, it would be her turn to bolster her husband's morale as he contemplated throwing in the towel.

Even in a country where Madonna was viewed by most people as "a Martian," as she put it, the Penns eventually encountered their nemeses. In its search for the elusive couple, the *Hongkong Standard*, an English-language tabloid, went so far as to offer a $500 reward for any tips on Madonna's whereabouts. The full-page "Wanted" poster asked for any information concerning "Madonna Louise Ciccone, rock singer and film star. Last reported strolling on the Choung Chau waterfront Saturday, January 11. If you can identify where she will be at a given time, or if you can take a shot of her in Hongkong, you can pick up $500 by contacting the *Hongkong Standard* news desk. Madonna is in town with actor husband Sean Penn for a film called *Shanghai Surprise*. But in a week here, she has so far avoided contact with her fans and the news media. The offer expires at midnight tonight!"

Moving on to the colorful port city of Macao, the Penns managed to avoid the small army of fans in the lobby of the luxurious Oriental Hotel. Retinue in tow, they were rushed to an elevator and whisked to their suite on the eighteenth floor. But when the elevator doors opened, Leonel Borralho, owner of the *Hongkong Standard*, leapt out from behind a door and started snapping pictures. Apparently Borralho, frustrated that his $500 offer had produced no information in Hong Kong, had taken matters into his own hands.

"What are you doing here?" screamed Penn. "Can't you see my wife is trembling?"

Borralho certainly had more reason to tremble. Penn was held back by one of his own burly bodyguards, but a camera strap managed to get wrapped around the journalist's neck in the ensuing struggle. The bodyguards refused to let Borralho leave until he turned over the film to them, which he did—in exchange for the promise of an exclusive interview with the Penns. When it became obvious that they had no intention of sitting for an interview, Borralho filed assault charges against Penn and sued for damages in the amount of $1 million.

Madonna again stood foursquare behind her husband. Claiming she had no idea the paparazzi would pursue them to China ("We thought we'd be safe here"), she branded Borralho a "jerk" and dismissed her fans as people "who lead such boring lives" that fantasizing about stars is their only escape. The next morning, a small crowd of reporters waiting for Penn to be booked at Macao police headquarters was greeted by the familiar sight of the saturnine star emerging from his car, his leather jacket pulled up over his head to conceal his face from photographers.

At a time when the producers could ill afford hard feelings on the part of their Chinese hosts, Penn was being pilloried in the press as "The Ugly American." Chris Nixon, the veteran Hollywood publicist assigned to the film, had a simple solution. He asked Penn and Madonna to defuse the situation merely by posing briefly for photographers. "Once they had what they wanted," said a studio official, "Chris figured they'd just go away. Photographers hunt down celebrities who play hard to get. Once they've got what they want, they move on."

Penn would have none of it. "Your job is not to cater to the photographers," he bellowed at Nixon, "but to the film and me!" Nixon returned the fire. "My job is to promote the film," he shouted back, "and right now it needs the publicity!" Accustomed to getting his own way, Penn demanded that the impudent Nixon be fired. He was. The director was feeling only slightly more secure. The Penns had been given script approval, and they overruled Goddard on scene after scene. "It was," said a crew member, "basically hell for everyone involved."

In London, meanwhile, George Harrison was monitoring the situation carefully. The former Beatle was uniquely qualified to appreciate his stars' awkward position and the pressures they were subject to. In his early twenties, Harrison along with his colleagues had created havoc on the sets of their films A *Hard Day's Night* and *Help!* "We were really a handful then," he later confessed. "We'd get the lines wrong and fool around on the set; it must have been hell working with us."

The Beatles, however, had a surplus of one resource that the Penns sorely lacked: charm. And they got along with the press. Paul McCartney, John Lennon, Ringo Starr, and Harrison held frequent press conferences during which they sparred playfully with reporters and poked fun at their own fame.

Harrison flew to the set of *Shanghai Surprise* to give his feisty stars a stern talking-to, and to suggest that they call a truce with the press. Neither Penn nor Madonna could bring themselves to charm reporters, but Penn grudgingly consented to take off the gloves and concentrate on the movie.

Peace prevailed, but only for the remaining four weeks of their China sojourn. Before flying to London to resume work on *Shanghai Surprise,* the Penns hoped to fare better with the press on the Continent. They appeared at the Berlin Film Festival for the world premier of *At Close Range.* Associated Press photographs flashed over newswires around the world showed the familiar sight of Penn and Madonna in dark glasses, pulling their jackets over their heads. "Why in the world do these two seek the 'sanctuary' of such public events," lamented one columnist, "remains a mystery." During a press conference hastily called by festival officials, Penn reportedly held a cigarillo, a joint, and a bottle of beer as he mumbled barely intelligible answers to foreign reporters.

No sooner did they touch down at Heathrow on February 24 than reporters who had been waiting in the driving rain for the famous couple swarmed over their motorcade. In the crush, Dave Hogen, a photographer for *The Sun,* fell beneath the tires of Madonna's Mercedes limousine, badly injuring his foot. Not exactly chastened by the episode, Penn sought to dissuade another aggressive photographer by spitting on him.

The next day, the cast and crew of *Shanghai Surprise* were assembled at London's Park Lane Hotel to film a ballroom scene. Susan Crimp, a reporter for Britain's largest independent radio network, Capital Radio, was determined to get on the set by masquerading as an extra. "I went to the costume designer for the film," she recalled, "and had them make up a 1930s costume for me so I would blend right in." Once at the hotel, Crimp went to a basement-level rest room where she checked to make sure the tape recorder she had hidden in her evening bag was in proper working order.

As she left the bathroom, a burly man in a leather jacket and jeans grabbed her arm and demanded to know who she was. "I was really frightened," Crimp said. "Here I was standing alone in the basement of this hotel, and I didn't know if this was a rape or a robbery or what. I screamed, but more of these strange men came, grabbing me and pushing me around. They were really roughing me up, and I was struggling to free myself. Finally, someone from hotel management called the men off and brought me brandy. I'm a little embarrassed to admit it, but I started to cry."

The strange men were, according to Crimp, "Madonna's bouncers—local thugs who were hired for protection." The Park Lane management apologized to Crimp, admitting that this was not the only incident at the hotel involving the Penns' hired muscle. "He told me that these bodyguards were out of control," she remembered, "and that Sean and Madonna apparently didn't give a damn."

Over the next three weeks, the tense standoff between the "Poison Penns," as they now had come to be called, and the implacable British press repeatedly flared into violence. Reporters were being shoved, beaten, and even had fire hoses turned on them when they got too close for the Penns' comfort. When several Polaroid shots of Penn and Madonna taken for director Jim Goddard's use were purloined, the stars exploded, refusing to go back before the cameras until the thief was identified and the stolen pictures destroyed. Handmade Films' American cofounder, Denis O'Brien, pleaded with the temperamental pair for several costly hours before they finally agreed to resume shooting.

Strangely, the press seemed to concentrate its wrath not on Sean Penn but on his wife. The next day, tabloid headlines denounced Madonna for trying to "push her way around England." *The Sun* was more evenhanded in assigning blame. "Spoilt Brat Who Rules Madonna," screamed its headline. Madonna soon chalked up another distinction, becoming the first pop star whose conduct was heatedly debated on the floor of the House of Commons. And to add insult to injury, British papers gleefully carried the story that Madonna was on American designer Mr. Blackwell's annual Worst Dressed List. Blackwell described her as "Skid Row's nomination for a poverty party centerpiece contest."

Penn remained resolutely unapologetic. In an article in *Vanity Fair*, which carried his picture on the cover, he confessed to writer James Wolcott, "I prefer the bar to the gym any day. I like to drink and I like to brawl." On the subject of Mrs. Penn, he mused, "No whale, no nuclear war, no starving country, is more important."

Harrison, growing increasingly impatient with his stars' truculent behavior and the expensive delays they were causing on the set, decided to attack the Penns' public relations problem head-on. With the platinum-coiffed Madonna at his side, he held a press conference at London's exclusive private club Roof Gardens on March 6. Penn chose not to show.

Seated side by side at a small table, Madonna and Harrison faced seventy-five clamoring print journalists; all radio and TV reporters had been barred. She wore black; he chewed gum incessantly. A dozen bodyguards—known as "minders" in England—hovered around the perimeter of the room.

Things started off cordially enough. To the question of whether or not Madonna had been a Beatles fan, she replied coolly that, since she was barely six when Harrison and his friends invaded the United States, she was too young for Beatlemania. Yet, as the *Observer*'s John Peel noted, there was a "palpable hostility in the room that became increasingly obvious as the press conference went on."

Ironically, it was Harrison—not Madonna—who then threw down the gauntlet, calmly asking if members of the press were "capable of recognizing the truth. You're all so busy creating a fuss, then writing about it as if we've created it for the publicity."

"And what did you expect?" asked a nonplussed reporter.

"We expect nonanimals," answered Harrison.

Without missing a beat, a voice from the back of the room responded, "Speaking of animals, is it true that Sean Penn was giving orders to everybody on the set?"

Harrison responded with an observation on the nature of celebrity: "Stars are people who become famous. They are just human beings. After a while, the only thing left is to knock them."

When another reporter pointedly asked Madonna if she and her husband fought, Harrison jumped in again: "What kind of question is that? Do you have fights with your wife?"

How did Madonna feel about all the criticism being leveled at her? "I have nothing to apologize for," she said, shrugging. When asked what she thought of England, she smiled sweetly. "It must be lovely," she sighed, "somewhere." Her final comment: "We're not such a bad bunch of people, are we?"

The next morning, Madonna turned on her radio to hear her "I have nothing to apologize for" statement played over and over again. If her words had come back to haunt her, it hardly mattered. Harrison's gambit had worked; the tabloid press moved on to other prey, leaving the Penns free to dine out at restaurants and even go jogging (accompanied by bodyguards, of course) without being accosted.

As soon as shooting on *Shanghai Surprise* was completed in late March at a total cost of $17 million, cast and crew returned to the United States, leaving an embittered British public behind them. "People in England hated Madonna then," Susan Crimp said, "because she and Sean Penn acted like bullies, pure and simple. Madonna could stand up at any time and say to her bodyguards, 'Stop it!' But she doesn't because any altercation is a headline. It's all manipulation."

Madonna realized that the true master of manipulation was George Harrison. Although she would describe him to one journalist as "a sweet sort of hapless character without a mean bone in his body," the fact remained that he accomplished what he intended with his *Shanghai Surprise* press conference. Moreover, the conference yielded a publicity dividend. It was for all intents and purposes covered as a major news event by the world media; *People* magazine carried the forty-three-year-old Beatle-turned-movie-mogul and his controversial blond star on its cover. Not bad publicity for a film that was months away from release, and about which Madonna was already having serious doubts.

Taking what they learned from this experience, Madonna and Penn did an abrupt about-face once they were on home turf in Los Angeles. The battling couple now went to Orion Pictures personally and without prodding offered to promote Penn's forthcoming film *At Close Range*.

Madonna had already made a significant contribution to her husband's movie. After screening some dailies and reading the script, she wrote and recorded "Live to Tell," a moving ballad that would serve as the movie's theme song and be the first single released on her next album. Some Warner executives fretted that the moody, almost dirgelike song would flop miserably with fans accustomed to Madonna's sassy, bouncy repertoire.

They needn't have worried. "Live to Tell" was an enormous hit, helped along by a video that interspersed gut-wrenching scenes from the father-son drama of *At Close Range* with film of an unadorned Madonna singing directly to the camera. Wearing a simple short-sleeved blue-and-orange flowered dress, her hair its natural dark brown color and free flowing, Madonna looked the very essence of a fresh-scrubbed farm girl.

Unmistakably, she was consciously overhauling her image. Gone was the sleazy, scruffy Boy Toy. The brassy, trashy Material Girl was also history. Her hair now clipped short and blond, she had scraped off a layer of mascara, chucked the clunky jewelry, and traded in her lace teddys and ripped fishnets for hip-hugging miniskirts or jeans worn with off-the-shoulder tops. What remained were the blazing red lips, the hypnotic ice-blue eyes, and of course, Madonna's trademark beauty spot.

The star's legion of wannabes followed suit, exchanging their Material Girl uniforms for the gamine getup that their idol now favored. Unfortunately for Madonna's French friend Maripol, whose jewelry business marketed the Madonna paraphernalia of yesteryear (giant crucifixes, oversize Boy Toy belts, rubber bracelets, etc.), demand began dropping off in mid-1986. By fall, the business was forced to declare bankruptcy, a victim of Madonna's changeability.

Madonna's new look also sent a strong message to Seventh Avenue. Mr. Blackwell's Worst Dressed List or no, this young woman from the suburbs of Detroit was showing unmistakable signs of exerting a powerful, long-term influence on American fashion. Her demographics were superb. Those ubiquitous music videos (she was already the most-watched performer on MTV) were giving Madonna unprecedented visual exposure before a vast audience of young women aged twelve to twenty-five who accounted for a sizable chunk of the billions spent each year on clothing in the United States. And as she changed, it was becoming apparent that they were changing with her. "I wanted to clean myself off," Madonna said of her new look. "I see my new image as very innocent and feminine and unadorned. It makes me feel good."

Holed up in a cramped Burbank studio with Patrick Leonard, the musical director on the Virgin Tour, engineer Michael Verdick, and Steve Bray, Madonna spent much of April remixing her third album, *True Blue*. A tough and unforgiving taskmaster, she presided over their exhausting sessions with an iron hand—shouting orders, insults, and ultimatums to her colleagues. "The musicians yell at me," she allowed, "because when they take a meal break, I'm looking at my watch the whole time. 'Okay, thirty minutes is up, get back in the room.' I hate taking breaks; people come back lethargic, the energy's down."

"Pat Leonard will tell you she's sweet and wonderful," recalled a witness to this bizarre work process. "But there were lots of Fuck You's emanating from that building. Madonna steps on people's feelings very easily, and regardless of what they tell you, there were lots of bruised egos. Madonna's wasn't one of them."

"It's delicate," allowed Bray. "There's a single-mindedness to her . . . you can read it the wrong way if you're expecting her to give you something she really doesn't have time to."

Madonna and Penn did have time to party nightly with Jack Nicholson, Cher, et al at Helena's, and it was there on April 12 that she was dealt a rude awakening. When songwriter David Wolinski, an old friend dating back to Madonna's early days in New York, approached her table, she embraced him enthusiastically. "David is exactly Madonna's type," said Camille Barbone, who knew them both in Manhattan, "and she can't help flirting." Her fatal mistake was miscalculating the depth of her husband's jealous streak. Penn spotted Wolinski kissing his wife and attacked him, viciously beating and kicking him before picking up a chair and threatening to slam it into Wolinski's bleeding forehead. The mayhem ended only when shocked onlookers managed to pull the crazed, profanity-spouting Penn off his dazed victim.

With the help of the club's proprietor and namesake, Helena Kallianiotes, Madonna dragged her husband from the club. One acquaintance described the incident as "the first really traumatic episode for her. Wolinski was someone she knew, and it really shook her up." A former member of Madonna's staff concurred: "I don't think she cared about photographers getting beaten up. Maybe she even got a little charge out of watching Sean go to it. But when it was a close friend of hers, and she actually saw blood spilled, she got scared. He'd threatened her before, but now she saw he was capable of doing real harm to people who weren't just members of the press." In addition, said Melinda Cooper, "Madonna loves guys, but even more she loves to be in control. When he drank, Sean was too violent for her to control, and this was her first real glimpse of that."

Perhaps to prove to herself and the world that she was still the mistress of her own destiny, Madonna showed up the next night at Helena's with Penn in tow—"acting," said a patron "as if absolutely nothing had happened."

At the star-studded U.S. premiere of *At Close Range* at Los Angeles' Bruin Theater, the couple—he in a pricey suit but tieless, she wearing her new short haircut and a stylish short black cocktail dress—beamed and nuzzled for the cameras. After the lights came up and the audience applauded, she gushed for reporters, "I'm so proud of him."

They again repaired to the celebrity carousel at Helena's. Don Johnson approached Madonna and asked if she would do a duet with him for his new album (she hedged, but later declined). Michelle Phillips, formerly of The Mamas and Papas and now a star of television's "Knot's Landing," gave her new friend Madonna an approving wink. "Pretty little bad girl," she said, summing up Madonna's sophisticated new image. Throughout the evening, however, there was an almost palpable fear that Penn might erupt again. Thankfully, he did not. He even managed to keep his drinking in check for a few days, until the critics took aim at *At Close Range*. Blasted by reviewers, the movie quickly sank from sight.

As Penn tended to his bruised ego, producer Robert Stigwood was on the verge of signing his wife to star in the film version of the Tony Award–winning Broadway hit musical *Evita*. Barbra Streisand was another candidate, as was Patti LuPone, who had starred on stage in the original production. But Madonna was clearly Stigwood's first choice, and for good reason. As symbols of blond ambition, Madonna and Argentine director Juan Perón's notoriously power-hungry wife, Eva, seemed perfectly matched temperamentally. Both women were driven, shrewd, sexy, and after revamping their images with the help of peroxide, ultimately worshiped by millions. Nor could the marquee value of Madonna's name be easily overlooked—particularly in a role that would require her to sing and dance.

The saga of *Evita* would in fact drag on for years, as custody of the project ricocheted from one studio to the next like an unwelcome stepchild. With each new producer would come a new director, and with that new director a preference for a specific star. Madonna's chief competition over that period was destined to be neither Streisand (deemed too old for the part) or LuPone (too obscure) but the versatile Meryl Streep. Their tug-of-war over the movie would last for years. Yet for now, Madonna seemed all but guaranteed the coveted role.

Looking very much like an updated version of the 1950s screen star Jean Seberg, Madonna appeared on the cover of *Rolling Stone*'s June 5 issue—all blond hair and pale white shoulders, daintily touching a large flower tucked in her cleavage. The cover line screamed, "The New Madonna," and the woman portrayed inside was indeed not the pop tart of old. The piece portrayed Madonna as cool, collected, and in control of both her private and personal lives.

Not for long. On June 6, Penn and Madonna got into a heated public argument at a Manhattan nightclub called The Pyramid. There a fight erupted into violence as an obviously inebriated Penn shoved his wife up against a wall, then carried their shouting match out into the street. As Pyramid employee Michael Gregor and club patrons looked on in stunned disbelief, the couple screamed at each other before she hailed a taxi and sped away alone into the night.

The main bones of contention between them were Penn's violence, and what he perceived to be Madonna's infidelity. She did not stop seeing her old friends and lovers. One night a jealous and intoxicated Penn stalked Bobby Martinez with a gun. "I was at the Palladium," Martinez said, "and I heard that Sean was looking for me. He walked up to the deejay and I was right behind him, but it was dark and there were a lot of people and he didn't see me. When he pulled back his jacket, I could see he had a gun. And he looked really nuts, man. So I got the hell out of there."

With "Live to Tell" still riding high on the charts, Madonna's third album was released at the end of June to almost universal praise—and a predictable dose of controversy. *True Blue*, its title taken from a favorite expression of Penn's, was dedicated to him, "the coolest guy in the universe." The album was, said Madonna, a reflection of "my husband's very pure vision of love." That sets the tone of the album, a swing away from driving, oversynthesized dance rhythms toward the more wholesome, optimistic sounds of the early 1960s. "The songs," wrote Stephen Holden in *The New York Times*, "are shrewdly crafted teenage and preteenage ditties that reveal Madonna's unfailing commercial instincts. And her singing, which has been harshly criticized as a thin imitation of the '60s girl-group sound, has strengthened."

The record was as sleek and polished as the newly revamped Madonna herself. "She's pop music, impure and simple," wrote Vince Aletti in the *Village Voice*," with all its contradictions, limitations, and delights. Madonna's got pop's knowing innocence and dumb fun down cold. She understands the allure of the pop surface, but she's even more savvy about pop's underlying spirit, energy, and emotion." *USA Today*'s Roy Trakin agreed: "With a newfound sophistication in looks and sound, Madonna should win over even her harshest critics."

The title track, written by Madonna and Bray, was as bouncy and exuberant as "Chapel of Love," or any number of other girl-group classics that had dominated pop music a quarter century earlier. "An extended sigh over Sean Penn," *Village Voice* reviewer Aletti called *True Blue*. "Madonna sinks into it gratefully as if it were a bed of cotton candy." David Hinckley rightly viewed this as part of Madonna's strategy to hold on to her original audience of wannabes while she upscaled her image. "Madonna knows that if you have a core group as loyal as Madonna's fourteen-year-olds," wrote Hinckley, "you take care to keep them loyal—while at the same time working on the hearts and minds of everyone else. To this end, *True Blue* is masterful."

Madonna called the sultry "La Isla Bonita" her heartfelt tribute to "the beauty and mystery of Latin American people." The more suggestive "Open Your Heart" ("I've got the lock, you've got the key") is a pleasingly plaintive attempt to change a potential lover's mind. And in "Where's the Party?" Madonna came closest to saying something directly about life in the eye of a media hurricane. "It's my ultimate statement," she said, "about what it's like to be in the middle of this press stuff with everybody on my back, my world about to cave in. Whenever I feel like that—and it does get to me sometimes—I say, 'Wait a minute, I'm supposed to be having a good time here, so where's the party? It doesn't have to be this way. I can still enjoy my life.'"

All of these songs would go on to become enormous hits over the next several months, along with the slick videos that accompanied the release of each as a single. The album also included a James Cagney tribute called "White Heat," another up-tempo tune titled "Jimmy Jimmy," and the socially conscious "Love Makes the World Go Round."

But none of the other songs on Madonna's third album would reap the whirlwind of publicity that accompanied the release of "Papa Don't Preach." Written by Brian Elliot, the song deals with a pregnant teenager who pleads with her father to approve of her decision to keep the baby. "When I first heard the song, I thought it was silly," Madonna claimed. "But then I thought, wait a minute, this song is really about a girl who is making decisions in her life. She has a very close relationship with her father and wants to maintain that closeness. To me it's a celebration of life." She was also delighted to point out that "Papa Don't Preach" is "a message song that everyone is going to take the wrong way. Immediately they're going to say I am advising every young girl to go out and get pregnant."

The "Papa Don't Preach" video, shot on location in a blue-collar section of Staten Island and directed by old friend Jamie Foley, was a slice-of-life departure for Madonna and was lauded by critics and audiences as a compelling domestic mini-melodrama. Featuring Danny Aiello as the father coping with his headstrong daughter's out-of-wedlock pregnancy, "Papa Don't Preach" also proved that at twenty-eight Madonna could look as fetchingly fragile as any working-class Lolita. There are tense moments toward the end as Madonna waits anxiously for her father's approval, and the heartwarming conclusion when the father embraces his daughter and presumably, her decision.

Not that Madonna was willing to bank solely on waifish innocence. To hedge her bets, the girl in the video unself-consciously wears a T-shirt emblazoned with the message Italians Do It Better. There were also cutaways to Madonna in a sexy black bodysuit, dancing and caressing herself as she sang the song's refrain.

Madonna's confident prediction that "Papa Don't Preach" would ignite a firestorm of controversy was quickly borne out. Abortion rights advocates were livid. "The message," said Alfred Moran, executive director of Planned Parenthood in New York City, "is that getting pregnant is cool and having a baby is the right thing and a good thing, and don't listen to your parents, the school, anybody who tells you otherwise—don't preach to me, Papa. The reality is that what Madonna is suggesting to teenagers is a path to permanent poverty."

For the first time, conservatives opposed to abortion found themselves singing Madonna's praises. "Abortion is readily available on every street corner for young women," said right-to-life advocate Susan Carpenter-McMillan. "What Madonna is telling them is, hey, there's an alternative."

Even Tipper Gore, whose Washington-based Parents Music Resource Center criticized the sexual content of Madonna's work, had praise for the song. "To me the song speaks to a serious subject with a sense of urgency and sensitivity in both the lyrics and Madonna's rendition," said Gore, "It also speaks to the fact that there's got to be more support and more communication in families about this problem, and anything that fosters that I applaud."

Gore's applause added to the clamor of ringing cash registers—not merely in the United States but globally. The world's top-selling album in 1986, *True Blue* hit No. 1 in Australia, Austria, Belgium, Brazil, Canada, Denmark, Finland, France, Germany, Hong Kong, Ireland, Israel, Italy, Japan, the Netherlands, New Zealand, Norway, the Philippines, Switzerland, the United Kingdom, and Venezuela. Where it failed to reach the top of the charts, the album nevertheless went gold. Ultimately, *True Blue* would sell an astonishing seventeen million copies.

No one was more pleased than Martin Burgoyne. Madonna's best friend, now working in New York as a graphic designer, was still a fixture on the club scene and often escorted Madonna when she was on the town without Penn. When the couple threw a small party at their Malibu house in June to celebrate the release of the "Papa Don't Preach" video, Penn, in an uncharacteristic gesture, flew Burgoyne and Erica Bell out to join the festivities. By this time, this tight group from the early days in Manhattan had a code name for their famous friend: Herself.

At the party, the normally indefatigable Burgoyne was unusually quiet. "It was obvious that something was wrong," Bell recalled. "Martin just wasn't his old energetic self." When he returned to Manhattan, he grew increasingly lethargic. "Martin was this wonderful imp—a beautiful human being inside and out," said Karen Bahari, who lived across the hall from Madonna in her early days downtown and was a close friend of Burgoyne's. "He was clearly sick. But nobody took it seriously at first," recalled Bahari, who claimed that Burgoyne was reluctant to seek medical attention.

In truth, Burgoyne did seek help at a free clinic, which failed to diagnose his deteriorating condition correctly. "He started having stomach pains, and he was tired all the time," Bell recalled. "The people at the clinic kept on giving him vitamin B shots and sending him home." In late June, Bahari was shocked when she bumped into Burgoyne on the street. "I saw him standing on the corner and his eyes were red," she remembered. "He was so weak he could hardly stand up."

A few days later, Burgoyne's stomach pains were so severe that he called Erica Bell to take him to the St. Vincent's Hospital emergency room. "The nurse took me aside and said she had no business telling me this, but that she'd seen young men like Martin with these symptoms before and it could be AIDS. I was stunned." Burgoyne returned to his family in Florida, and after further testing the nurse's suspicions were confirmed. Burgoyne was suffering from AIDS.

He called Madonna with the news. She was devastated. But it was only after she hung up that she burst into tears. "From then on, all you had to do was mention Martin's name," Melinda Cooper said, "and Madonna would get very emotional. It really ripped her up. She loved him."

It was then, as Bell put it, that "Madonna's pragmatic side took over." "Herself" sublet an apartment for Burgoyne on Twelfth Street, around the corner from St. Vincent's Hospital. She arranged to take care of all his extensive medical expenses, in addition to paying virtually all his bills. "He did everything for her when she was starting out," Bahari said, "so it was only right that she do what she could for him. The trouble was, it was too late." Over the remainder of 1986, Madonna would call Burgoyne daily, delivering pep talks, reassuring him that a cure for his deadly disease was around the corner.

Sean Penn was sympathetic at first. As much as he disapproved of her gay friends, he seemed determined to do what he could to keep Madonna happy and their marriage afloat. According to close associates of the two, Penn flew to Mexico at Madonna's urging and returned with an experimental AIDS drug not at the time available in the United States. It was a gamble—but one that he was willing to take if it offered him an opportunity to salvage their relationship.

Burgoyne was among the twenty guests Penn invited to Madonna's twenty-eighth birthday party at New York's Gotham Bar and Grill, but it failed to pull Madonna out of a darkening mood. As two beefy security men hovered in the wings, she stood up and modeled the green silk pants suit she had purchased in China during the making of *Shanghai Surprise*. "I like it," she told her guests, "because it's green, the color of envy. I envy all of you because you all have your privacy and I don't." Then she excused herself to go to the ladies' room, escorted—as she now was nearly everywhere—by one of her bodyguards.

Penn's unpredictable behavior had undoubtedly made her life much more difficult, but the fact remained that she was still in breathless awe of his talent. So it was not surprising when Madonna seized the opportunity to act with her husband on stage in David Rabe's seldom-seen caper comedy *Goose and Tom-Tom*. The production, also directed by Rabe, was not meant for the public, however. Madonna merely wished to learn from the experience, to hone her craft without worrying about the critics. But not everyone involved with Rabe's latest work-in-progress was thrilled with all the attention it got. "This is *not* a tryout," sniffed a Lincoln Center spokesman. "Nobody cared a hoot in hell when we had works-in-progress before. But because its Sean Penn and Madonna, everyone is interested."

There was, however, one by-invitation-only performance at Lincoln Center, on August 29. That night, a celebrity audience saw Penn and Harvey Keitel in the roles of two thieves named—what else?—Goose and Tom-Tom, with Madonna as Lorraine, their moll.

All of which paled in comparison to the fiery show Penn put on after the show. Walking the two blocks from Lincoln Center to their apartment building at Sixty-fourth Street and Central Park West, Penn and Madonna stopped in for a late supper at the popular Ginger Man restaurant. When they emerged, Anthony Savignano was one of several photographers waiting. "I followed them into the courtyard in front of their building," Savignano said, "and suddenly Penn spun around and swung at me. He missed. Then he spit at me." Savignano, still clicking away, captured that moment on film, head-on.

When Savignano shoved Penn away, Penn punched him. It was then, Savignano recalled, that Penn spotted another photographer. Mild-mannered if tenacious Vinnie Zuffante would eventually sell enough photographs of Madonna to hungry newspapers and magazines to warrant the vanity license on his Mercedes: 10-Q MADONNA. But right then, he was Sean Penn's target. "Vinnie is this slightly built guy," Savignano said, "and Penn went after him. Penn can be very brave when his bodyguards are around, but when he's alone, he likes to pick on people who won't put up much of a fight." Madonna stood in the shadows, again making no effort to restrain her husband. After pummeling Zuffante, Penn retreated inside his apartment building.

It was vintage Penn, who may have merely been venting pent-up frustration over the dismal failure of *Shanghai Surprise*. Released over the Labor Day weekend in those parts of the country where Madonna's record sales were strongest, the movie opened to empty houses. "Awareness in the film was there," said MGM marketing president Greg Morrison. "Interest in it wasn't."

The film's stars had already virtually disowned the film, dooming it at the box office and infuriating both George Harrison and MGM. Harrison had begged Madonna to do a video to support the movie, but she refused outright. After one more fruitless telephone conversation with Madonna, Harrison confessed that "the press was right about her." According to an associate at Harrison's Handmade Films, he was "deeply hurt by Sean and Madonna. He had defended them to the hilt before a very hostile press, but now they were turning their back on him. It was a major betrayal. George Harrison is a real gentleman, but he walked away from that experience hating Madonna."

"They were the essence of noncooperation from the outset of production," seethed MGM's Greg Morrison. "They have done nothing, absolutely nothing, to help sell the film." Morrison acknowledged that Madonna was riding high as a pop star, but added that she still hadn't "proven her draw as an actress. As for Penn, his behavior off-screen isn't helping. Stars like Marlon Brando and Frank Sinatra never had the greatest relationship with the press, but you had to bow to Sinatra's singing, to Brando's acting. What you've got today is a lot of young people like Sean and Madonna with fictional star power—who are basking in celebrityhood that's not translating into ticket sales."

The Penns weren't just ignoring *Shanghai Surprise*, they were actively bad-mouthing it. "The director turned out not to know what he was doing," said Madonna, "we were on a ship without a captain, and we were so miserable while we were working that I'm sure it shows . . . if it was *directed* poorly, you can't imagine how poorly it was *edited*. It was a great learning experience, that's all I can say."

Once the dust had settled, *Shanghai Surprise* was a bona fide catastrophe, grossing an embarrassing $2.2 million. To Madonna, this was only one more sign that she had made a serious mistake in marrying Sean Penn. If one of her main purposes was to learn from him while getting a boost up the ladder to movie stardom— and there was general agreement among her friends that this was a strong factor in her decision to become Mrs. Penn—the gambit was failing.

As for the couple's deteriorating relationship with the media—

their new nickname among battered members of the press was S&M—Madonna would continue to defend her man publicly. "I've been dealing with the media since the very beginning of my career," she explained, "and Sean never really had to. I wanted it, and I was sort of ready to deal with it, and he wasn't. That's all there is to it. I would rather see some sort of harmony taking place than all the violence, and when I say violence, I don't mean necessarily hitting, but people screaming and tugging at you. I don't like any of that."

Violence of the hitting kind and worse was also a concern for Madonna. She had been willing not only to overlook Penn's violent streak but to tacitly endorse it, so long as his fury was directed at strangers. Now that he was assaulting friends such as David Wolinski and abusing her in public as he had done at the Pyramid Club, she was becoming concerned for her own safety.

She was unaware that Penn had pursued her ex-boyfriend Bobby Martinez through a nightclub with a pistol tucked inside the waistband of his pants, but Madonna was also increasingly concerned about his growing fascination with guns. After watching in horror as he fired at the helicopters that intruded on their wedding day, she had convinced the firearms-loving Penn to lock his guns away in a strongbox. "She told him she'd leave him if he didn't," a friend said, "and he knew she meant it." That lasted for only a short while, however, and Madonna did not protest when Penn, having assembled a small arsenal that included rifles as well as handguns, built a target range in the soundproofed basement of their Malibu villa. There, donning a headset to protect his ears, he practiced his marksmanship. Depending on the focus of his anger, according to one acquaintance, he occasionally tacked up photographs over the targets. At various times, Penn riddled pictures of Prince, Jellybean Benitez, Madonna's singer friend Nick Kamen, John F. Kennedy, Jr., and other perceived lovers and would-be lovers of his wife with bullets from a .357 magnum. It would not be long before Penn started using a poster of his wife for target practice.

15

"I am afraid that in five years, all my friends will be dead."

AIDS. By the autumn of 1986, the mere mention of the acronym for acquired immune deficiency syndrome was enough to strike terror in the hearts of most Americans. Sean Penn was no exception. He had always disapproved of his wife's homosexual buddies, and now that Madonna's closest friend was dying of the disease, he was adamant that she get a blood test.

Madonna refused. She viewed Penn's concern that she might already be carrying the disease as a sign of outright paranoia. "Sean actually said he's scared I might pick up the virus or already be carrying it," she confided to a friend. "He keeps insisting that it's possible because not that much is known about AIDS. I told him to grow up."

Madonna had other reasons for not being tested. She told one of her dancers that, since there was no cure for AIDS, "she didn't want to know" if she was HIV positive. Besides, she viewed Penn's latest demand as just another manifestation of his deep-seated possessiveness. He had always been jealous of the attention Madonna paid her gay friends, and that only intensified now that she was calling Burgoyne every day and paying his bills.

These tensions erupted in public on the afternoon of September 26, 1986, when Penn and Madonna began arguing loudly at the offices of her newly formed film company on the Universal Studios lot. A witness recalled the scene: "Sean dragged the fight outside and started screaming, 'You're more concerned about your damn friends than you are about me! You spend more time worrying about your friends with AIDS!' Madonna told him, 'Stop acting like a child. Why don't you just run off somewhere and get it together?' " Penn fumed for a time, then followed her back inside.

In Penn's defense, his concern may have been justified. By her former manager's account, Madonna had had "at least one hundred lovers" between her arrival in New York in 1978 and her first hit record four years later. Madonna herself boasted of her prodigious sexual appetites and seemed to justify the public's perception of her by naming her publishing company Slutco.

Beyond her sexually promiscuous lifestyle, there were other factors that may have caused Penn's concern that Madonna could be at risk for contracting AIDS. Her beloved mentor Christopher Flynn, the ballet teacher she described as her "imaginative lover," was openly homosexual and would die of AIDS in late 1990 (although that was well over ten years after they had been intimate). Madonna had also, according to Erica Bell, seduced one of Martin Burgoyne's bisexual lovers.

Penn may have been equally disturbed by Madonna's penchant for picking up Latinos in "Alphabet City"—the name bestowed on the Lower East Side neighborhood where the avenues are lettered, not numbered. It was anybody's guess whether any of them were carrying the AIDS virus or had been intravenous drug users or sleeping with IV drug users. According to friends in whom she confided and at least one ex-lover, Madonna did not always practice safe sex prior to her marriage in August of 1985. Although a gnawing jealousy of her gay friends was undeniably at the core of Penn's insistence that she be tested for AIDS, he could have been concerned for other reasons as well.

Penn was also encountering some new heterosexual competition for Madonna's affections in the fall of 1986—this time in the tall, darkly handsome form of singer-model Nick Kamen. Madonna first noticed Kamen's photograph in the pages of Britain's

The Face magazine, but it was the television commercial for Levi's 501 jeans in which he strips down to his underpants before a dozen gaping women in a Laundromat that got the rest of the country buzzing about Kamen.

When a contact at Warner Records sent Madonna one of Kamen's demo tapes, she made up her mind to take him on as her protégé. "I said to myself," Madonna recalled, "this guy's got everything. He's got a beautiful voice and so much charm and charisma, and there's something in the eyes, and that inspired me to write for him." She telephoned the aspiring singer at the office of his record company in New York and told him she was going to compose a ballad for him. "She was so easy to talk to," recalled Kamen. "And all I could say was, 'Fantastic, get it over here.' It was only afterwards, when I put the phone down, that it hit me who I had been talking to."

Moments later, Madonna called him back—this time with an offer to produce the record as well. "I mean," she told him, "I feel like if I don't, then I might be sorry because they might change the character of it and then I'll be sorry I did it." Kamen flew to Los Angeles, and the two worked together in the studio for five straight days on the song "Each Time You Break My Heart."

Mentor and protégé soon discovered they had much in common. Kamen, who owed his exotic good looks to the fact that he was of Dutch, French, Irish, Burmese, and Javanese descent, had also been profoundly influenced by the early death of a beloved parent. His father died of cancer when Nick was just fifteen. "It was the worst thing that ever happened to me," he recalled. "Fifteen is not a good age. You think you know everything and you want to go your own way. There are so many things I wish now I could have talked about with him."

In Kamen, Madonna clearly saw a kindred spirit, as well as a talent she felt compelled to nurture. None of which escaped the attention of the relentlessly jealous Penn. Determined to hold on to his wife, he accompanied her to a rally in Los Angeles for Amnesty International and in a very dramatic public gesture, lifted Madonna up and carried her offstage. At an AIDS benefit in Los Angeles in September, it was quite a different story. Penn refused to accompany his wife to the celebrity-packed event. The emcee, apparently confident that Madonna would not be offended by his remarks, asked the crowd if anyone had seen Sean Penn. "Sean," he said, "come up and hit me and I'll never have to work again." Far from being offended by the wisecrack, Madonna laughed.

For the rest of 1986, relations between the Penns seesawed violently as they veered from love to hate and coast to coast. While Sean was in Los Angeles shooting *Colors*, Dennis Hopper's graphic film about gang warfare, Madonna had begun work in New York on a comedy tentatively titled *Slammer*. She was still chafing over her *Blind Date* experience six months later. Although she had publicly given overwork as her reason for pulling out of the film, Madonna had angrily quit the project because of what she viewed as an outright betrayal by the producers. Her contract with Warner's stipulated that she would have script, costar, and director approval. But while she was in New York, the producers had unilaterally hired Blake Edwards as the director ("Too old and boring," she told one friend) and then cast Bruce Willis ("*Him?* Ugh") in the film. She had wanted her friend Jamie (*At Close Range*) Foley to direct and planned to push Penn for the male lead.

That was before the release of *Shanghai Surprise*. Once the incredibly low box office figures were in, Madonna put on hold any further plans to work with her husband. She promptly pulled out of *Dead End Street*, which was also to have been directed by Penn's father, Leo. Meanwhile, the planned screen biography of torch singer Libby Holman also slipped through her fingers; producer Ray Stark promised the role to Debra Winger.

Madonna also expressed a keen desire to repeat Judy Holliday's triumph in *Born Yesterday*, but at that stage the producers preferred to go after Whoopi Goldberg. She seemed to have a better shot at landing the Marlene Dietrich role in a remake of the 1930 classic *The Blue Angel*, which her pal Diane Keaton was working on with producer Joe Kelly at Fox. Alan Parker was tapped to direct the updated version, which was to be set in the 1950s, and Madonna was courting Robert De Niro for the role of the tormented professor. When the eighty-five-year-old Dietrich got word of talk that Madonna had arranged a meeting with her to discuss the upcoming project, the reclusive screen legend broke her silence to make her position known. "I have no intention," she stated from her home in Paris, "nor have I been contacted, to meet this Miss Madonna." To acquaintances she was less equivocal: "That woman play *my* part?" she reportedly snapped. "Who does she think is?"

Evita was still on Madonna's mind. When she met with producer Robert Stigwood, she arrived wearing a 1940s evening gown and her hair styled up in an Eva Perón twist. Later, when Academy Award–winning director Oliver Stone took over the long-gestating project, she met with him and suggested writing some new songs for the musical with composer Andrew Lloyd Webber. The abject effrontery of that proposition ended their meeting after only fifteen minutes. "Oliver just thought," she believed, "I was going to be a huge pain in the butt."

Now, Madonna was more determined than ever to showcase her comedic talents in a highly physical screwball comedy à la Carole Lombard. A few months earlier, she had set up her own production company, housed in a bungalow on the Universal lot in Burbank. There was no mistaking who was in charge. Amidst the purple-and-pink leopard-print decor, Madonna and her adviser Carol Lees pored over scripts in search of the screwball comedy that would give her a clear shot at becoming her generation's Lombard or Holliday.

Instead, the script she had been searching for was literally dropped in her lap by the best man at her wedding, the Penns' old friend Jamie Foley. Written by Andrew Smith and developed by producer Rosilyn Heller at the Guber-Peters Entertainment Company, *Slammer* begins with a yuppie lawyer (played by Griffin Dunne) assigned to pick up paroled murderer Nikki Finn (Madonna) outside a prison and put her on a bus to Philadelphia. She would rather track down the rat who framed her. What ensues is the predictable twenty-four hours of mayhem that includes chase scenes, mobsters, a society wedding, and a 160-pound cougar named Murray. Any resemblance to *Bringing Up Baby*, the 1938 classic in which Cary Grant and Katharine Hepburn pursued a leopard, was strictly intentional.

Despite Madonna's enthusiasm for the project, the producers

were initially hesitant. Foley, whose last film was Penn's somber *At Close Range*, had never directed a comedy. Madonna, meantime, was coming off one of the most highly publicized screen bombs in recent memory. To allay any fears, Foley and Madonna met with Warner executives personally to reassure them that they were up to the task. For these sessions, Madonna wore the same businesslike uniform: a navy blue suit. At the star's urging, new writers were called in to give the story more focus and to strengthen the romance between Dunne's uptight character and his free-spirited charge.

Originally, Foley had his friend Penn in mind for the male lead, but Madonna was still less than enthusiastic about pairing up with her husband so soon after the *Shanghai Surprise* fiasco. Still basking in the success of the surprise comedy hit *After Hours*, in which he played opposite Madonna's old pal Rosanna Arquette, Dunne was all but immune to such doubts; he had already proven his aptitude at playing hapless straight men. He had also wanted to work with Madonna ever since seeing her onstage at Lincoln Center in *Goose and Tom-Tom*. "She seemed to be very inside herself," he recalled of her performance in the limited-run David Rabe play. "When she came out with a cigarette that needed to be lit, all you were concerned about was who was going to light it. She was fantastic in the play. I knew she could act."

What Dunne didn't know was that wherever she went Madonna drew enthusiastic crowds. When they took to the streets of New York or Los Angeles to shoot a scene, cast and crew would be mobbed by curious onlookers. Dunne recalled that during the first few days of shooting he thought to himself, "God, this is really out of control. I always thought something terrible was going to happen, but nothing ever did."

Once again, her colleagues marveled at Madonna's uncanny ability to shut out all distractions and focus on the task at hand. She may have been the reason thousands of gawking onlookers showed up to watch filming, but she was also the person seemingly least affected by it. "Her concentration was unshakable," said director Foley. "She would never stop and become Madonna the pop star dealing with boisterous fans."

"Madonna's under a lot of pressure for this movie to do well,"

Dunne told a reporter, "but she doesn't wear the pressure on her sleeve." Foley concurred: "She's sort of a combination den mother and prom queen." When she didn't have her nose buried in a book between takes, Madonna defused tensions by joking with the crew, climbing up on ladders, mock-threatening to fix the lights herself. When one technician flew into a rage at an extra, demanding that someone "get that woman out of here," Madonna launched into her own tongue-in-cheek tantrum. "That woman! That *woman!*" Everyone, including the actress and the technician, laughed.

There were times, however, when she got on coworkers' nerves. Although Madonna was nearly always satisfied with her first take, Dunne, like most actors, preferred to do four or more before he was satisfied. "She always says, 'You got it, you got it,' and she was driving me crazy, just the way her character would," Dunne observed. "I mean, she's a very noisy girl. If you're having lunch or something, she's not at all like that, but on the set she'd use this talent she has for grating on my character's nerves—talking nonstop between takes—and I'd look at her and I really would go: Who *is* this girl?'

That was a question that Penn may well have been asking himself. By all accounts, there was nothing romantic between Dunne and his costar. But Madonna did confide some of her personal troubles to him, and Dunne felt obliged to lend a sympathetic ear. Predictably, Penn suspected that he was being made the cuckold once again and accused his wife of carrying on yet another alleged affair with her leading man. No sooner did Madonna return to Los Angeles to film some interior scenes for *Slammer* on a Warner soundstage than Penn left their Malibu house and moved in briefly with his actor-brother Chris.

For a time, both Penns doffed their wedding bands and hit the town separately—each bound and determined to make the other jealous. Penn returned with Chris to Helena's, the scene of his attack on Madonna's friend David Wolinski, and there the two brothers proclaimed loudly that they were "emancipated men." But within days, Penn apparently had a change of heart. During a rare appearance on "The Tonight Show," Penn, constantly criticized by Madonna for his shoddy footwear, proudly showed

Johnny Carson his new pair of leather boots. He told the camera he was wearing them "for Madonna—wherever you are."

A few days later in New York, they seemed to have patched things up. Madonna always found time in her schedule for an hour-long jog through Central Park, clad in a parachute running suit, baseball cap, and dark glasses. During one such run, Penn came along with her, and they once again clashed on the familiar topics—namely, Madonna's devotion to the AIDS-stricken Martin Burgoyne, and her continuing interest in Nick Kamen's career. The two stopped to shout accusations at each other in front of disbelieving passers-by—a confrontation captured on film by one enterprising photographer who had trailed them from the apartment building. The next morning, a contrite Penn picked out a $5,000 outfit at a pricey boutique and presented it to Madonna as a peace offering.

The ploy worked, for a time. Penn returned to Los Angeles to meet with his lawyers about criminal assault charges stemming from his savage attack on David Wolinski at Helena's. Madonna remained behind, working on *Slammer* and despite Penn's disapproval, still seeing Nick Kamen. When she invited Kamen to join her at a Band Aid gala in London the day after Thanksgiving, Madonna must have anticipated Penn's reaction.

It came at Helena's when the disc jockey played "Papa Don't Preach" and Penn leaped onto the dance floor, imitating his wife's wild gyrations in a less-than-flattering way. Was Madonna around? asked a patron. "Madonna?" boomed Penn, hoisting another beer. "Madonna who? I don't know anyone named Madonna!" Chris Penn then reportedly confronted his brother with the fact that he would either have to get a divorce or annul the marriage. "No," Penn replied, who still walked around Los Angeles with a loaded .22-caliber pistol tucked into the back of his pants. "I'm going to annul her!"

Given Penn's penchant for violence, that statement had a decidedly ominous ring to it. Living together again with Penn in Malibu, Madonna discovered that the guns that were once packed away were now scattered about the house—in dresser drawers, desk drawers, the nightstand next to their king-size four-poster bed. While Madonna exercised in their home gym, Penn spent hours sitting on his office windowsill, swigging beer and randomly firing off shots into their backyard pool.

It may have been one of the side effects of being married to the world's leading sex symbol, but Penn had amassed a sizable collection of X-rated videos and left pornographic magazines scattered about the house. Madonna, offended by the graphic photographs and still somewhat bruised by her overexposure in *Penthouse* and *Playboy*, ordered the housekeeper to toss them out.

Madonna viewed her husband's bizarre behavior as a cumulative cry for help. She was determined to take the next step to save their marriage, but first she had to keep her promise to show up for an AIDS benefit. On November 10, she joined Debbie Harry, Paloma Picasso, and Peter Allen as a surprise celebrity model at a fashion show to raise money for a hospice in New York. Of the eighty-three denim jackets to be auctioned off—each emblazoned with the designs of such artists as Andy Warhol and Robert Rauschenberg—Madonna strutted down the runway modeling several, including a jacket adorned with the work of her AIDS-stricken friend Martin Burgoyne.

On her return trip to Los Angeles, she was the one bearing a peace offering: a large box containing thousands of dollars' worth of designer shoes for Penn. This time the reconciliation lasted for less than a day, and Madonna checked into a hotel in the San Fernando Valley under the name Daisy Miller. Drinking even more heavily than usual, Penn spent hours alone in the Malibu house. There, he watched the private home videos he and Madonna reportedly shot of themselves making love, and stared at Polaroids they snapped of themselves *en flagrante* that he kept stashed in a metal box.

Given the tempestuous nature of their marriage, it could hardly have come as a shock to Penn when the Cable News Network reported that Madonna had asked her lawyers to draw up divorce papers. But it did. The CNN report was later retracted for lack of corroboration, but not soon enough for Penn. When he saw the TV report, he broke down sobbing. "I love her," he screamed at the set. "Doesn't she know I love her?" His parents, fearing that their anguished son might do something irrational, asked Chris to cancel his schedule for the day and stay with his brother. Alternately melancholic and hysterical, Penn talked incessantly about his undying love for Madonna until dawn. Chris would tell friends that he had never seen his brother so shaken.

Meanwhile, back in New York, Madonna turned her laserlike focus on the completion of *Slammer*. On the set, her easy, kidding manner had made her a favorite of normally hard-bitten crew members. As temperatures dipped to below freezing, they constructed a small, heated booth where Madonna could wait between takes. "She'd sit in there like a princess and love it," recalled the director, Jamie Foley. "She's the greatest flirt of all time."

Not that Madonna was all sweetness and light during the making of the film. During so-called looping sessions at which actors are required to overdub unclear lines, she continually refused, insisting that her first takes were the best. She relented only after her director, imploring her to overdub a single line of dialogue, literally knelt down and kissed her feet.

Madonna's take-charge attitude was also in evidence off the set, where she now plotted the world tour that would coincide with the release of her film the following summer. A savvy strategist, she was not about to leave the success of either to chance.

As Penn and his lawyers conferred on how best to avoid a jail sentence on assault charges stemming from his attack on David Wolinski, wary Warner executives decided that the title *Slammer* might now carry unfortunate connotations. The new working title for the film: *Who's That Girl?* On that score, Madonna was determined to keep her public informed. She, more than anyone, appreciated the value of the promotional drumroll. "She could be terribly impatient on a personal level—it was always 'Give me this now,' " said a former staffer. "But when it came to her career, she thought months, years, in advance."

Her chameleonlike transformation from voluptuous Boy Toy to svelte, soignée beauty complete, Madonna now set out to sell the movie- and concert-going public on her new, more sophisticated image with a series of cover stories and photo layouts in several of America's most widely read magazines. In his *Vanity Fair* cover piece, Michael Gross breathlessly chronicled her striking metamorphosis. Pointing to her strict vegetarian diet ("Vegetarians are paler"), her daily three-mile runs and grueling workouts under the watchful gaze of trainer *terrible* Rob Parr, Gross noted that Madonna had shed ten pounds of pubescent "puppy fat" and replaced it with muscle and sinew.

"All makeovers should be like this," he wrote. "The gooey girl has become a glamour queen. . . . The swelling belly is flat as a board. The tarty look has softened to a cinematic siren's. . . . And there is a message in all this shiny newness." Coining a phrase that years later would become Madonna's anthem, Gross proclaimed her to be "the rightful inheritor to the long-vacant throne of blonde ambition." Madonna herself waxed less poetic. "When you've got a product," she said, shrugging, "you promote it."

With the same beauty spot and platinum coiffure, Madonna still invited comparisons with Monroe—provided that the public understood the crucial difference: unlike Monroe, this sex symbol was in total control, the mistress of her own fate. She made that crystal clear during the *Vanity Fair* photo shoot with her old friend Herb Ritts. Overruling stylist Joe McKenna, she refused to wear a 1964 Chanel suit once worn by Catherine Deneuve ("It's not me"). Instead, she instructed her assistant to have one of Sophia Loren's old gowns flown in from California for the session.

When the editors of *Life* approached her to work with photographer Bruce Weber on a layout, she jumped at the opportunity. Weber, best known for his elegant photographs of movie legends, had taken one of Madonna's favorite shots—a sultry portrait of her onetime idol Jessica Lange. His work, she declared, was imbued with a "sexual energy."

So was their first meeting. "I want this to be a collaboration," she told the captivated Weber. "I want us to create this together." Then she crumpled up the script that had been meticulously mapped out by *Life*'s hapless editors and began to improvise.

Taking to the narrow, teeming streets of Manhattan's Little Italy, photographer and subject drew a crowd as she began to flirt with chisel-jawed, leather-jacketed male models for the camera. "She ain't no Madonna," smirked one skeptical onlooker. "She ain't nasty enough to be Madonna."

The stylist, hairdresser, and makeup artist for the shoot might well have disagreed with that assessment. "Her favorite phrases seem to be 'Get over here' and 'Do it *now*,' " said one *Life* staffer, who also claimed that Madonna "hollered orders nonstop" and "literally shoved people who got in her way." The exhausting day-long shoot behind her, Madonna returned to Los Angeles and more work on *Who's That Girl?*

The result of her collaboration with Weber was another striking homage to Marilyn Monroe. The headline on *Life*'s cover read, "That Fabulous Couple: Madonna and the Camera," but the bare-shouldered, peroxide-crowned femme fatale gazing up off the cover could have stepped straight off the set of *The Seven Year Itch*. Infinitely more revealing was the spread that kicked off the story inside the magazine. It showed an unself-conscious Madonna leaning across a makeup table to kiss her own reflection.

On her return to Los Angeles, Madonna overcame her own avowed hatred of dogs—"They pee in the house, and they get dog hair on your clothes. It's like having a kid, only kids wear diapers"—and brought home a puppy, half Akita, half wolf, for her husband. "When he saw this dog, he looked like he was going to start crying," she remembered. They named him Hank. "It was like I'd just had a baby. . . . He took it everywhere with him, he wanted to sleep with it, and I was like, uh, what have I done?"

Her stay was brief. On Thanksgiving weekend, Erica Bell telephoned from New York with the news that Martin Burgoyne's condition was deteriorating at an alarming rate. "He was very weak and in terrible, terrible pain," said neighbor and friend Karen Bahari, who stopped by Burgoyne's apartment nearly every day for six months to make breakfast for him. His AIDS-weakened body ravaged by infections, the once-robust Burgoyne now weighed less than one hundred pounds.

Racing the clock, Madonna flew from California to see her closest male friend one last time. He was slipping in and out of a coma, but friends and family gathered at Burgoyne's bedside whispered reassurances in his ear that Madonna would soon be there. As soon as she arrived, she kissed his cheek and told him she loved him. She sat holding his hand until he died. Burgoyne was twenty-three. It was the Sunday after Thanksgiving.

"Martin worshipped Madonna," said old friend Johnny Dynell. "He waited to die until she got there." Erica Bell, who was one of those at Burgoyne's deathbed, concurred that "they loved each other deeply." Yet while everyone else sobbed, Madonna remained, in Bell's words, "typically unemotional." No stranger to untimely death, she had developed a mechanism of her own for coping with grief. "When you know someone's dying," she said, "you have to make your peace with it before they die. I make my peace with it before it happens, so I don't get really hurt. And then when it happens, I don't feel anything."

There had been plans for a modest memorial service for Burgoyne, but Madonna insisted that something grander be done. "Hire a big hall," she told her old comrade and Danceteria denizen Johnny Dynell. "I'll spend anything you want. Just do it." Five days later scores of mourners—many who had also been close to Madonna in the early days of her career—waited in the rain outside the landmark Puck Building on Manhattan's Houston Street to pay their respects. Inside, hundreds more packed the entire ninth floor—including club impresario Steve Rubell and artist Keith Haring, both of whom would also succumb to AIDS. Much of the assembled crowd wept openly as Bahari delivered a soulful rendition of "Over the Rainbow." In accordance with Burgoyne's wishes, the raucous party that followed lasted into the early morning hours.

Notably absent from all the proceedings was Madonna herself. Immediately after Burgoyne's death, she had spun around and jetted back to Los Angeles. "A lot of us wanted to know where the hell she was," remembered Dynell. "She said later that she didn't want to cause a riot, but I think she just didn't want to take any more time out of her schedule."

Yet it was Madonna who had picked up Burgoyne's medical and other expenses exceeding $100,000. Which made her reaction when she received the bill for the memorial service all the more inexplicable. She initially balked at paying the $4,000 tab. "She didn't want to pay for it," said a friend. "There is no question that Madonna loved Martin and was deeply shaken by his death. But when it comes to business, she can be very hard-nosed. And I

230

guess she felt that they were being charged too much." But after complaining bitterly about the cost, she finally wrote out the check.

Martin Burgoyne's tragic death marked an end to one phase of Madonna's life at the same time that her new glamorous image was aborning. It was the Christmas season and her "Open Your Heart" video was completing its climb to the top of the MTV charts. The song had been inspired by her futile attempts years earlier to befriend ghetto-hardened kids in the Lower East Side neighborhood where she lived. This would have made the perfect scenario for a video during her street-urchin period, but no longer.

In keeping with Madonna's provocative new persona, this time she was cast as the writhing star of a sleazy peep show. Directed by Jean-Baptiste Mondino and photographed by Pascal Lebegue, "Open Your Heart" also boasted a slick production design by Hollywood veteran Dick Sylbert. Surrounded by a Felliniesque assortment of voyeurs gazing at her from windowed booths, the *bustier*-clad Madonna struts, prances, and slithers her way through a sufficiently suggestive routine. For added measure, the video ends with her kissing a twelve-year-old boy full on the mouth, then happily skipping off with him into the sunset. "Extraordinarily provocative," rhapsodized film critic Vincent Canby of *The New York Times*. "In a brisk, haikulike 4 minutes and 22 seconds, [it] presents Madonna as every adolescent boy's wildest, sweetest fantasy. It's a tiny, comic, sexy classic."

Madonna had intended for this "tiny classic" to ignite another debate over decency, and it did—thereby ensuring its success. What she had not anticipated was the turmoil it would create on the home front. Still angered by her friendship with Nick Kamen and her refusal to be tested for AIDS, Penn now fumed over a video that portrayed his wife as every pervert's fantasy. Moreover, he was, in the words of one cohort, "sickened" by the sight of her kissing a child in a more-than-sisterly fashion. Another door-slamming, name-calling row ensued and Madonna once again returned to New York. There, comforted by Nick Kamen, she would spend the holiday season without her husband.

16

"His bark is worse than his bite."

"I think Sean will emerge from jail as a
better person, and an even
greater actor."

After months of plea bargaining, a somber Sean Penn stood
before Los Angeles Municipal Court commissioner Juelann
Cathey and pleaded no contest to assault and battery charges
stemming from his attack on David Wolinski at Helena's nightclub
ten months earlier. Commissioner Cathey opted for leniency, sen-
tencing Penn to a year's probation and fining him a modest $1,000
plus $700 in court costs.

He was hardly chastened by his run-in with the law. At the
Who's That Girl? wrap party held—where else—at Helena's, Penn
bickered with his wife over her friendship with costar Griffin
Dunne and her too-handsome protégé Nick Kamen.

Fueled by prodigious quantities of alcohol, Penn's obsession
with Madonna's extramarital affairs careened out of control. Their
daily rows grew more violent. He threw a chair through a closed
window and smashed a full tureen of soup on the floor; she hurled
a vase at his head and pummeled him with her fists. He stuck
her head in their gas oven. Once, he tossed her fully clothed into
the pool. He repeatedly threatened to seriously harm her—or
worse. For the first time, he was no longer suppressing his urge

to strike Madonna—although he later insisted, "I got most of the beatings."

None of these tactics of marital warfare frightened Madonna as much as Penn's predilection for venting his frustrations on the local fauna. After an argument, he would typically take one of the weapons from his arsenal and go out onto his property to hunt gophers, birds, rabbits—in the words of one former employee, "anything that moves." Then he stormed out, holing up in friends' desert hideaways for four and five days at a time.

By the end of February, Madonna was ready to move out. "I want to buy a house," she ordered a stunned real estate agent over the phone, "and I want to buy it now! I can go up to as much as two and a half million." She was subsequently chauffeured in a white Rolls-Royce to over a dozen available homes in Beverly Hills and Bel Air.

But then the volatile couple experienced another rapprochement. They dined at Beverly Hills' chic Le Bel Age, and at one of Sean's favorite hangouts, Patrick's Roadhouse in Santa Monica. He fondly called her Lou—"Lulu was my nickname because I was worshiping [silent screen star] Louise Brooks"—and they promised to call each other every day at exactly three A.M. eastern standard time. "No matter where you happen to sing," he declared, "or where I happen to be." Madonna was scheduled to return to New York to be photographed for *Cosmopolitan*'s anniversary issue (she was to become the first celebrity ever featured on the magazine's cover). Before she left, Penn bought her a sapphire bracelet. Symbolically, it would be stolen the first day she arrived in Manhattan.

Yet when they were not together, each gave the other ample ground for suspicion. As if to outdo his wife, Penn made a habit of picking up women—usually tall, leggy blondes or Asian beauties—taking them to the exclusive La Mondrian Hotel, then calling up friends the next morning to boastfully provide the lurid specifics regarding his sexual escapades. Aware of her husband's cheating, Madonna eavesdropped on his phone conversations and checked up with friends to see if he was really with them instead of cavorting with "some California bimbo." Her own conduct, however, could hardly be described as "true blue."

Following a glittering party at the Upper East Side triplex of a record producer, Madonna and Erica Bell piled into a black limousine and resumed their old practice of cruising Avenue A for pickups. "It was wild—just like the old days," she remembered. According to Bell, they sipped Louis Cristal champagne in the backseat, sizing up young Hispanics from behind the car's opaque smoked-glass windows. "When Madonna spotted some Puerto Rican guy she really liked, she ordered the driver to stop, opened the door, and we pulled the guy inside."

Madonna did not fear that she would be recognized. "Of course these guys recognized her once they got inside the car," Bell said. "But Madonna is fearless. She couldn't care less if these guys talked. Again, nobody would believe them."

With an eye to the impending release of *Who's That Girl?* Madonna made her debut as a presenter at the Academy Awards telecast on March 30. By now, her *True Blue* album was well on the way to selling a remarkable 17 million copies (up from the *Like a Virgin*'s 11 million copies). Thus the fact that she had yet to live up to her promise as a movie star hardly mattered to fans gathered outside the Shrine Auditorium; her arrival with Penn triggered the kind of hair-pulling frenzy reserved for a Lombard or a Monroe.

Two weeks later, Penn sparked some hysteria of his own on the set of *Colors*. Playing a volatile young Los Angeles cop, Penn was shooting a scene on the colorful Venice, California, boardwalk with costar Robert Duvall when he abruptly halted mid-dialogue. Jeffrie Klein, an Orange County scrap-metal dealer who with two hundred other nonunion extras was being paid $35 a day to stand in the background, had reached into his pants pocket, pulled out a camera, and started clicking away.

As director Dennis Hopper and Duvall looked on in disbelief, Penn bolted toward the stunned extra, shouting obscenities. "What are you doing taking pictures?" he screamed at Klein, who at five feet ten inches and 210 pounds dwarfed the surly young actor. Despite his decided size advantage, Klein politely explained that several others in the crowd were also taking snapshots. With that, Penn spit in Klein's face. "What," he said, grinning at the shocked extra, "are you going to do now?"

What the thirty-two-year-old Klein did was spit right back. Penn then punched him in the face and kept punching until bystanders separated them. In truth, security guards and crowd members pulled them apart three times. On each occasion, Penn managed to slip free and plow into Klein again.

The ruckus did not end there. Even after it seemed tempers had cooled, Penn attempted to jump over the heads of the security guards and strike Klein with a clenched fist. Once the dust had settled, Klein was nursing facial contusions and Penn faced charges of violating his probation. Hopper, who himself had conquered a longtime addiction to alcohol and drugs, urged his friend to check himself into a substance abuse clinic. Penn appreciated his friend's concern, but told him not to interfere.

New York *Daily News* columnist Liz Smith predicted that Penn would soon be "Sean with the Wind," but Madonna continued to defend her husband—publicly at any rate. "I think the longer we're together," she told writer Chris Chase, "the more we grow to love each other, the more stable we'll feel."

Penn was not her first priority, however. Realizing that her upcoming world tour could be used to promote her new movie, Madonna's manager Freddy DeMann suggested that they both be called Who's That Girl? To prepare for her Who's That Girl? tour, Madonna trained like a marathoner. In addition to her three-mile runs through Central Park and her workouts with weights, she now ended each day by sprinting up and down the stairs of her apartment building.

Her twelve-hour workdays began taking a toll. Tempers were frayed. Shouting matches with tour director Patrick Leonard became commonplace. During rehearsals, Madonna exploded over every technical glitch, sour note, and botched dance step. "Madonna whined and sulked and blew up a lot," one roadie said. "She would swear a blue streak at Patrick Leonard and push the dancers out of her way if they goofed up. She'd pace up and down and throw tantrums—literally stamp her foot like some spoiled little girl if everything wasn't exactly the way she wanted. Everybody was afraid of her."

The one man who wasn't afraid of Madonna was back in Los Angeles adding to his rap sheet. Stopped on Memorial Day for speeding and running a red light, Sean Penn was given a blood test that revealed an alcohol content of .11 percent, marginally above the legal limit of .1 percent. Initially charged with drunk driving (later reduced to reckless driving), Penn had now racked up his second probation violation. It seemed likely that he would go to jail.

Completely out of touch with Penn at this point, Madonna learned of her husband's arrest like millions of others—by reading about it in the newspapers. She was also reading rumors that she had actually filed for divorce. "They are having some problems," Madonna's harried publicist, Liz Rosenberg, told reporters, "and they're taking some time to think things through. But as of now, they have no intentions of getting a divorce."

Not while Madonna had pressing career matters to contend with —such as her debut on "The Tonight Show." It was, in fact, her first appearance on *any* television talk show. Scantily clad in black, she told a transfixed Johnny Carson that she was "just a Midwestern girl in a *bustier*" and confessed :o being an irrepressible flirt. When he admitted to being won over by Madonna's self-mocking wit, Carson probably echoed the sentiments of his enormous audience.

Her talk show debut behind her, Madonna now assayed more familiar territory, her "Who's That Girl? tour, which would begin in Japan. Not since Marilyn Monroe had anyone so thoroughly captivated the collective imagination of the Japanese public. Like other top American superstars who have refused to sully themselves by endorsing products in the United States, Madonna had no qualms about signing a $3-million deal to appear in commercials for Mitsubishi.

The tour logistics alone were daunting. It took a 747 cargo plane and a DC-7 to fly all the equipment across the Pacific, then twenty-three semi trucks to ferry the steel stage to each venue. Just to erect the set took Madonna's fifty-member technical crew a full three days.

When she arrived in Osaka, where she was to give the first of five concerts in Japan, 1,300 troops had been mobilized to handle

25,000 screaming fans—most of whom had paid $45 and up for tickets. Altogether, Madonna sold an estimated 150,000 tickets for the five concerts, but there were still nowhere near enough to meet the demand. Promoters returned more than $7 million in cash that had been sent in by fans the moment the concerts were announced.

Things turned ugly a week later in Tokyo, when rain and strong winds made it impossible to set up the stage at the Korakuen Baseball Stadium. More than 40,000 ticket holders were turned away, but some refused to accept the cancellation. Hundreds of angry fans, many young girls in tears, strained at police barriers, while fights broke out between fans and guards.

Those 110,000 Japanese who did get to see their idol were not disappointed. By the time she finished each ninety-five minute concert, Madonna had gone through no fewer than sixteen songs and eight full costume changes, each the brainchild of designer Marlene Stewart. Beginning with the "Open Your Heart" corselet with lamé pasties, Madonna shifted effortlessly from top-hatted Material Girl (in a *bustier* festooned with charms, rubber lobsters, fuzzy dice, and Slinkies), to the *True Blue* 1950s blue taffeta prom dress, to the flaming red hand-beaded flamenco outfit for "La Isla Bonita." The high-energy movements were choreographed by Jeffrey Hornaday, best known for choreographing the hit film *Flashdance*. For all this, Japanese scalpers were asking—and getting—$700 a ticket.

Madonna ended her clamorous Japanese tour and was en route to her next date in Miami when, on June 24, Penn was sentenced by Municipal Court commissioner Juelann Cathey to sixty days in the county jail. The sentence, which could be reduced to thirty days with good behavior, was to be followed by an additional two years' probation. The commissioner also ordered Penn to seek psychological counseling. Wearing a blue suit, dark glasses, and (for the first time in weeks) his gold wedding band, Penn appeared uncharacteristically contrite.

Since his sentence was not to begin until July 7, there was time for a passionate reunion in Miami. Promising Penn a "second honeymoon" before he reported for jail, Madonna checked the couple into a penthouse suite at the exclusive Turnberry Isle country club. Once again, he brought along a gift: a tiny carousel —in fact, a miniature of the full-scale merry-go-round he was having restored for her in Vermont at a cost of $100,000.

The couple remained secluded in their suite for the next four days—until Madonna kicked off the U.S. leg of her tour, performing in a torrential tropical downpour before 60,000 people crammed into Miami's Orange Bowl. Penn was seated in a roped-off section of the field. Midway through the concert Madonna, clad in her black corselet and fishnet stockings, gestured to her husband and said, "This one's for you." She then delivered a moving rendition of "Live to Tell," the song she had written for his film At Close Range.

The lovers' tender moment was broken when someone in the front row hurled his underwear onstage. "Stop throwing your pants up here," Madonna yelled angrily, halting the show. Minutes later, someone else tossed a sealed condom onto the stage. Incongruously, this met with her hearty approval. "Yeah," she hollered, holding the condom up to the crowd, "practice safe sex!"

A week later, Penn was due back in California to begin serving his jail term. Madonna was in Chicago for her next concert, and the couple rendezvoused there. Her parting words to him: "Goodbye, I love you, good-bye." It was a brief separation. Within five days, Penn was a free man—at least temporarily. Prison officials agreed to let him leave to make a film in West Germany, with the understanding that he would return afterward to resume serving his sentence. The authorities' decision to release Penn raised serious questions concerning preferential treatment afforded celebrities, but only briefly.

On July 13, Madonna gave what she considered to be the most significant performance of the tour—a $100-a-ticket AIDS benefit in New York dedicated to the memory of Martin Burgoyne. Penn was again on hand, and moments before the concert, he cornered her backstage, angrily accusing her of sleeping with Nick Kamen.

The show started right on schedule, with the star prancing onstage in her oversized man-tailored tuxedo jacket for the opening "Who's That Girl?" number. But when her face was flashed twenty feet high on screens above her head, the close-up revealed the stress of another bitter quarrel with Penn.

Still, Madonna managed to go through the show, and to get her intended message out. "I don't want to turn this into a morbid event," she told the audience, "but AIDS is a painful and myste-rious disease that continues to elude us." She said she hoped the $400,000 raised that evening for AMFAR (the American Founda-tion for AIDS Research) might speed a cure, then, somewhat jar-ringly, switched back to her good-time girl persona to belt out "Lucky Star." The show made its most overt statement during the "Papa Don't Preach" number, when the words SAFE SEX were flashed on the screen behind her.

At the trendy Gotham Bar and Grill, where Madonna hosted a postconcert party, the Poison Penns picked up where they'd left off. Ironically, a song by none other than Nick Kamen boomed over the restaurant's sound system as the Penns sparred acrimo-niously over her relationship with the young British singer. Penn stormed out.

Thanks to the aggressive marketing campaign masterminded by Freddy DeMann, throughout the summer of 1987 Madonna's image was everywhere as the tour thundered through sixteen North American cities—on billboards, in newspapers and maga-zine ads. In addition, the title song from the sound track had already soared to No. 1 on *Billboard*'s Hot 100. With her tumul-tuous personal life also fueling media coverage, Madonna was riding a publicity rocket that seemed almost certain to carry her new film into the box office stratosphere.

On August 6, 10,000 fans mobbed Times Square, hoping to catch a glimpse of their idol as she attended the world premiere of *Who's That Girl?* When her limousine pulled up in front of the National Theater one hour late, the throng went wild. Police struggled to push back the crowd as she stepped up to a platform that had been built on a traffic island. "Shut up," she said, "so I can talk." They did.

"I guess this is what you call making a spectacle of yourself," Madonna said, clutching a microphone emblazoned with the name of one of the area's most popular rock radio stations, Z-100. "This is real irony. Ten summers ago I made my first trip to New

York and I didn't know a soul here. I told the taxi driver to drop me off right here in the middle of Times Square. I was completely awestruck. And now here I am looking at all of you people and I'm completely awestruck. Thank you, and I hope you like the movie."

Unfortunately, it soon became clear why the film had been rushed into theaters without the customary press screenings. " 'Who's that girl?' isn't really the question," wrote USA Today critic Mike Clark. " 'What the hell happened?' is." The Los Angeles Times labeled the film a "rattling failure," while Variety minced no words in simply branding the film "a loser." The most charitable review came from Vincent Canby of The New York Times, who credited the film with almost nearly achieving "its fairly modest goals."

Commercially, Who's That Girl? was an even bigger calamity. At its first regularly scheduled performance at the 1,151-seat Ziegfeld Theater—just one day after the much-ballyhooed premiere—there were fewer than sixty people in the audience. The film, which had taken $20 million to make, grossed a disastrous $5.1 million in its first nine days in theaters. It was downhill from there. Who's That Girl? would make the transition to video in a record three months.

Vincent Canby lamented Hollywood's failure to tap what he regarded as a wellspring of acting talent. "You might even suspect," he suggested sardonically, "that there's a Cyndi Lauper 'mole' among her advisers, someone bent on wrecking a career before it's decently gotten started and gained any momentum. . . . In Madonna, Hollywood has a potent, pocket-sized sex bomb. So far, all it does is tick." Madonna was defiant. Unlike Shanghai Surprise, which she had acknowledged from the outset to be an unqualified mess, Who's That Girl? was, she insisted, "a good film. I'm proud of it."

Days after the movie's release, Madonna found herself embroiled in another controversy—this time over the aromatic attributes of her hometown. During a rare interview with the "Today" show's Jane Pauley to promote the film, she was asked about her background.

Madonna: "I came from Michigan."
Pauley: "Where from Michigan?"

Madonna: "Bay City."

Pauley: "Little town?"

Madonna: "Uh-huh. Little smelly town in northern Michigan."

By unhappy coincidence, the "Today" show interview aired the day her Who's That Girl? tour arrived at the Pontiac Silverdome outside Detroit. For this homecoming, Penn, once again on leave from California's Mono County Jail, was in the audience. Madonna paused midway through the concert to reminisce about riding her bicycle through the fields where the Silverdome now stood. "I was pissed off," she told 42,000 fans, "when they tore down the trees and built this place."

She then seized the opportunity to explain the unkind remarks she had made about her hometown. "I do not think Bay City is a stinky city," she told the audience. "I said it smells bad. I didn't say that about the people. I said it about the Dow chemical plant. It was near my grandma's house. I do mean to cause a commotion because that's where I was from. I think I'll shut up now," Appropriately, she then launched into her new hit, "Causing a Commotion."

Madonna was just about to embark on the European leg of her tour when *Penthouse* magazine put her on its cover once again. Inside were eight more pages of nude photographs from her art-model days—shots that Madonna's lawyers, faced with her signed releases, were powerless to suppress. To make matters worse, someone mailed copies to the Mono County Jail where Penn had resumed serving his sentence. Madonna blamed the magazine for sending the copies to her husband—a maneuver she then simply described as "really nasty."

That phrase might also have been used to describe her four-concert British tour. Well before Madonna's arrival on August 15, Fleet Street capitalized on the British public's fascination with the Material Girl. While she dominated the pop charts in England just as she did in much of the civilized world, Madonna still had to contend with residual ill feelings from the *Shanghai Surprise* fiasco eighteen months earlier. One who certainly did not count himself among Madonna's fans was the manager of London's swank Ritz

Hotel. When Madonna's assistant tried to book a suite for her at the Ritz, she was turned away. The hotel management merely explained that Madonna was "NOCD—not our crowd, dear."

Once again, the tabloid press whipped the public into a frenzy over her arrival. When her Concorde touched down at Heathrow ninety minutes late, two hundred frantic fans were there chanting, "We want Madonna, we want Madonna." She let the suspense build by exiting the plane last, then waved at the throng before climbing into a waiting Mercedes limousine. By announcing the details of Madonna's arrival, said the police, the press had acted in a "highly dangerous" manner.

There were other concerns. More than two thousand people living near Wembley Stadium in northwest London wrote to local authorities complaining that the noise level of Madonna's concerts would constitute a nuisance—although it was unclear how her show differed from all other rock concerts and events held at the stadium. To placate residents, decibel meters were installed on nearby rooftops to insure that the concert stayed within acceptable noise levels.

Noise would turn out to the least of Madonna's problems opening night. When she took the stage in her black "Open Your Heart" corselet, many in the crowd of 77,000 surged out of control. Fistfights broke out, and security men had to use water hoses to control rowdy teens. Scores of fans who fainted from the excitement were lifted over barricades to the sidelines so they would not be crushed underfoot. Amidst the chaos, underwear flew up from the audience and landed at Madonna's feet.

In France, she also encountered opposition—but this time with radically different results. Madonna wanted to give her concert in Sceaux Park south of Paris. The seventeenth-century park, famous throughout France for its manicured grounds, was the work of the celebrated architect André Le Nôtre, who also designed the gardens at Versailles. Convinced that 100,000 rock fans would destroy the park, Sceaux Mayor Pierre Ringenbach moved to block the concert. "I don't know very much about Madonna," said the mayor, "but I know the park is not the proper place for a concert like that. I've read some of the articles about Madonna, and I'm not very impressed with her."

But twenty-four-year-old Claude Chirac, whose father Jacques happened to be prime minister and mayor of Paris, was impressed with Madonna. She was such an ardent fan, in fact, that she waged a campaign to have her powerful father intervene. She sat the conservative Chirac down, all but forced him to listen to Madonna's records, then showed him a pile of news clips about the singer. Chirac responded by moving to have Mayor Ringenbach overruled. He then granted an interview for one of France's most popular teen magazines, *Podium*, explaining that he had taken on Madonna's cause because "this is a great and beautiful artist. She is superb." In the same article Prime Minister Chirac, whose wardrobe consisted mainly of impeccably tailored suits, was shown wearing a sweatshirt and jeans, listening to his daughter's Sony Walkman. Skeptics pointed out that Chirac, a candidate for the French presidency the following year, was doing all this simply to woo young voters. Not so, said Chirac, who promptly cut the value-added tax on records almost in half.

"Is he going to wear boots and an earring next?" quipped former French minister of culture Jack Lang. *Le Monde* ran the photograph of the jeans-clad prime minister accompanied by a one-line caption: "Who's That Boy?"

A grateful Madonna accepted Chirac's invitation to attend a reception at City Hall, where she spent nearly an hour with the prime minister and his family—much of that time recalling her early days in Paris as one of disco singer Patrick Hernandez's unknown backup singers. She then presented Chirac with an $83,000 check for AIDS research—for which she was rewarded, in typical French style, with kisses on both cheeks. Madonna responded by giving him what she called "an American bear hug."

That night, Madonna gave her concert at Sceaux Park before 130,000 fans. It was the largest crowd ever to attend a rock concert in France. Next stop: Turin, and an uneasy reunion with her Italian cousins.

Meanwhile back in his cell at the Mono County Jail, Penn was anticipating his mid-September release. "There's a fire storm out there," he told one visitor. "I'm just going to go about my business quietly and hope it all calms down."

The fire storm, he would soon discover, had only begun to rage.

17

"Let's just say I love Sean,
and I'm feeling hopeful."

With time off for good behavior, Sean Penn was released from jail after serving only thirty-three days of his sixty-day sentence—most of that tailored so as not to interfere with his film-making schedule. Back from her tour, Madonna was waiting for him in Malibu, and that same day, the couple learned of rumors sweeping Europe, Asia, and the United States that she had been killed in a California car crash. Before the rumor could be squelched, anxious fans flooded newspaper and television switchboards, as well as Madonna's record company, wanting to know the truth.

The real tragedy in Madonna's life was the public unraveling of her marriage. She hoped to see a more mellow Penn emerge from jail; instead, he started drinking again and wasted little time before accusing her of carrying on affairs while he was behind bars.

In fact, she had added soulful-looking model-turned-actor Sasha Mitchell, the star of a small film called *Spike of Bensonhurst* to her list of "protégés." She had even condescended to be Mitchell's stylist for a spread in Andy Warhol's *Interview* magazine. During a four-hour session, she spiked up his hair in a New Wave style, then, before startled onlookers, ordered him to remove his shirt while she knelt down and ripped huge holes in his pants. "It was pretty steamy," said a witness to the session "and very obvious that these two knew each other very, very well."

Adding fuel to the already blazing fire was a professional dispute between Madonna and Penn over her plans to star in the screen adaptation of *Evita*. Penn reportedly wanted a costarring role in the film, but Madonna agreed with the producers that he would only be suited for a supporting part. Her planned $1.6-million *Evita* salary—four times what Penn had been offered for his small role—constituted another sticking point. It was apparently hard enough on Penn's male ego that her records, concerts, and videos had now helped her amass a personal fortune already approaching $70 million. Although he had a proven track record as a film star and she decidedly did not, Madonna now threatened to outearn him on his turf as well.

Their contretemps again flared into violence, and Penn again left the Malibu house. A friend suggested that a separation might help. "We're separated all the time," Madonna sighed wearily, "and that doesn't make it any better."

The final straw for Madonna occurred November 25, 1987, when after four days incommunicado Penn showed up at their New York apartment expecting to share Thanksgiving dinner the following day. "You're not having Thanksgiving dinner here!" Madonna exploded. She told him that she had already instructed her lawyers to draw up divorce papers. Now she was going to tell them to file the documents. Their marriage was over. She then left for Brooklyn to celebrate Thanksgiving with her sister Melanie.

Hours later, Penn arrived at a favorite old haunt, the Columbus Cafe. He told friends that Madonna was divorcing him. Then he promised to "get pie-eyed," which he promptly did. When the news hit the papers, Penn's publicist rose to his defense. "I know the tendency in these matters is to always blame him," said Lois Smith, "but it really is too bad because these two people love each other."

On Thanksgiving Day, Penn flew back to Los Angeles, where he continued his binge. At Helena's he noticed Vinnie Zuffante, the New York paparazzo he had once attacked, chatting with rocker Billy Idol at the bar. Zuffante was not carrying a camera, but it hardly mattered to the soon-to-be-ex-Mr. Madonna. Penn loudly insisted that Zuffante be kicked out, and he was. Not long after, Penn, not willing to wait in line outside the men's room, walked outside and in full view of passers-by urinated on the side of the building.

Madonna wasted no time pursuing new interests. In New York, she went out with Penn's former *Bad Boys* costar Esai Morales, the young Latino actor who had scored a major success of his own in the hit film *La Bamba*. She was also photographed dancing into the wee hours with handsome British rocker Simon F.

Madonna's most intriguing liaison during this period was undeniably with John F. Kennedy, Jr., whom she had met briefly at a party years before. Madonna, who had read every Marilyn Monroe biography ever written, knew all the details of Monroe's starcrossed affair with the late president. As undisputed heiress to the Monroe persona, she confided to friends that she felt fated to consummate a relationship with Kennedy's only son. For his part, Kennedy was dazzled by the notion of "dating" Madonna, the most glamorous, celebrated, and by all accounts exciting woman of her generation.

They decided to keep their relationship as private as possible. Since they both worked out religiously at the same health club, it provided a convenient locale for their initial rendezvous. They jogged together in Central Park, and later, Kennedy took Madonna to meet his mother. At Jacqueline Kennedy Onassis's sprawling Fifth Avenue apartment, Madonna was greeted somewhat frostily by the former First Lady, who must have wondered what designs the unpredictable superstar might have on her son. Madonna coyly signed the guest register "Mrs. Sean Penn."

Jackie was not amused, according to a friend of her son's. Kennedy told him that after meeting Madonna, his mother "hit the roof. She warned her son to stay away from Madonna. She felt Madonna would exploit the Kennedy name for publicity, and basically, that she was a crass social climber, a tramp—and still married to Sean Penn." The single most important thing in Madonna's favor: "John didn't have to worry that she was after him for his fame or his money. She was twice as famous as him and ten times as rich."

The fact that Madonna was technically a Roman Catholic might have been a major plus for her in the eyes of the Kennedys, if it hadn't been for her habit of publicly thumbing her nose at Catholic rituals and symbols. "Jackie is a very devout Catholic," said another family acquaintance. "She thought Madonna's use of crucifixes and other Catholic imagery was incredibly sacrilegious. Jackie didn't want her son involved with a woman who was being widely condemned as a heretic."

Jackie's overriding objection may have had nothing at all to do with Madonna, but with the woman whose persona she sought to emulate. "Jackie was shocked when she picked up *Life* magazine and saw Madonna looking exactly like Marilyn," said her friend. "It must have been like Marilyn coming back from the grave, this time to steal her son instead of her husband. It was a nightmare for her."

Madonna and Kennedy managed to conceal their relationship from the press in New York, going to such lengths as attending plays and parties separately—only to get together in private afterward. Yet they let their guard down on Cape Cod, where, bundled in sweaters and jackets, they jogged along the beach near the Kennedy family compound in Hyannis Port.

For all the excitement provided by her various liaisons, Madonna told friends she still loved Penn and was waiting for him to come back to her and apologize as he had always done before. For three days following their breakup, she had refused to take his calls. When his calls abruptly stopped, she had started phoning him.

This time it was his turn to play hard to get. On December 4, Madonna's lawyer Michael Inglis filed her petition in Los Angeles Superior Court. In it, she asked for her maiden name of Madonna Ciccone to be restored and invoked the couple's prenuptial agreement calling for all their separate earnings to remain separate.

At this stage, it had become frighteningly clear to her that Penn was not about to come running back begging for forgiveness. No wonder. By all reports, he was spending every night partying with such movie star pals as Tim Hutton, Judd Nelson, and Michael J. Fox, then topping off each evening by picking up a different woman to take home.

A number of Penn's friends, Hutton and Dennis Hopper among them, tried to convince Penn to talk to Madonna. It took the intercession of director Jamie Foley, whom both Penn and Madonna had called their "best friend," to bring about a truce. Foley convinced Madonna that they still loved one another, and to give Penn another chance. Penn responded to the happy news by bombarding his wife with flowers, silver-balloon bouquets, and love notes. When a singing telegram arrived, Madonna collapsed with laughter—undone and charmed at the same time by the intentional corniness of the gesture.

The couple resumed phone contact and at one point talked on the telephone for nearly two hours straight, hammering out the conditions of a reconciliation. By the time these transcontinental negotiations were over, Penn had agreed to cut down on his drinking, curb his temper, and seek psychological counseling. For her part, Madonna would put less emphasis on her career and start a family in 1989.

Four days after filing for divorce, Madonna flew to Los Angeles for a reconciliation. Wearing a black wig and dark glasses, she checked into their most-frequented premarital trysting place, Malibu's secluded Hotel Shangri-La, and waited for Penn in their favorite room: Suite 607. For the next several days, they did not leave the $130-a-day suite. Twelve days after she filed for divorce, the papers were withdrawn "without prejudice"—meaning that Madonna had not relinquished any of her claims, and that the papers could be refiled at any time.

Why the hurried rush to recement the marriage? "Madonna has this thing about Christmas," said a friend. "Her mother died just before Christmas, and she's always very shaky emotionally during the holidays. She didn't want to have one more horrible memory to associate with the holiday. If this had all happened some other time of year, she might not have caved in so quickly."

. . .

Her marriage back on track—at least temporarily—Madonna embarked for New York to act in a television adaptation of Damon Runyon's *Bloodhounds of Broadway* costarring Jennifer Grey and Matt Dillon. One of the reasons she joined the cast was director Howard Brookner's passionate commitment to the project. She was also impressed with his courage. Brookner, who had earlier been diagnosed with AIDS, was in a race against time to finish the film.

"I knew something was wrong," recalled Madonna, "but I wasn't going to press him. He had the right to keep it private." Later, when Brookner phoned her and said, "I have to tell you something," he found it impossible to blurt out the truth. Madonna told him she already knew. "I think it was kind of a relief for him that I knew," she said, "and that my feelings about him weren't going to change."

Shooting started Christmas Eve outside the Knights of Columbus Hall in Union City, New Jersey, and Madonna rebuffed fans and press alike, refusing to give interviews or sign autographs. When Mayor Robert Menendez offered to present her with the key to the city in a small public ceremony, she turned him down flat. "Madonna," huffed a spokesman, "is not giving mayors free publicity." Day after day, scores of teenagers shivered in the cold for hours hoping that she would at least acknowledge their presence with a nod or smile. She did not. It appeared that, during her steamy marital reunion, much had rubbed off from Sean.

Bloodhounds of Broadway would bounce from Columbia to Vestron and back to Columbia before finally being released in November of 1989—nine months after Howard Brookner's death. He was buried on his thirty-fifth birthday. "Long before I knew anything," remembered Madonna, "Howard asked me if I had ever seen anybody die." She told him about Martin Burgoyne. "He wanted all the gory details." When Brookner was being treated at St. Vincent's Hospital in New York long after filming had stopped, Madonna paid a visit to the AIDS Ward. "It was like Judy Garland," said Brookner's friend Brad Gooch, "visiting another sort of Oz."

Prophetically, Madonna had accepted her first offer to star in a play on Broadway just as *Bloodhounds of Broadway* wrapped. In truth, she had been working on landing the part of the office temp in David Mamet's *Speed-the-Plow* for over a year, ever since Mike Nichols told her about the play. She asked the play's director, Gregory Mosher, with whom she had worked on *Goose and Tom-Tom* in 1986, to keep her in mind. Nonetheless, actress Elizabeth Perkins, who started her career with Chicago's Steppenwolf Company, got the part. It was only after she bowed out suddenly in January that Madonna phoned Mosher and asked to read for the part.

"I knew I was jumping into the fire," she later told *The New York Times*. "I knew that people were going to have all kinds of ideas of why I'm doing this—oh, I just got the part because I am who I am, or I'm doing this because I'm desperate to make people believe that I'm serious about acting. The fact of the matter is I loved Mamet's writing. . . . When the script came along I wanted the part. It's as simple as that."

Mosher and Mamet were sold after her first audition. "She was mesmerizing," exulted Mosher, who could not have been unaware that Madonna's name on a marquee could double box office receipts. "She was magnif! It was like nothing I've ever seen from her in the movies. We didn't hire a rock star; we hired an actress. She really earned this. It's not [us] seeking the biggest-name person for the show." Throughout six weeks of punishing rehearsals, Madonna did not falter. Marveled Mosher: "She's a rock."

In *Speed-the-Plow*—the title is never explained—Madonna played against type as a drab, bespectacled office temp who goes to work for two Hollywood sharks, portrayed by stage veterans Joe Mantegna and Ron Silver. While this sweet, guileless underling tries to convince the foulmouthed producers that a serious book she is reading might make a good movie, Silver bets Mantegna $500 he can't seduce her. After going to bed with Mantegna, she shows unexpected savvy in negotiating a deal with him but is ultimately outmaneuvered. "Karen," Madonna said of her character, "is honest and sincere and naive, and hungry for power, like everybody else."

It had not dawned on Madonna until midway through rehearsals that her character was not an altogether benign one. "It was a real mind-fuck of a script," she told writer Kevin Sessums. "Little did I know that . . . everybody else involved saw me as a vixen, a dark, evil spirit."

The nature of her character took an emotional toll on Madonna. She felt "defeated—and that actually influenced everything I did, because it made me very sad." Each night during rehearsals and then during the run of the play, she prepared for her wrenching final scene by turning off all the lights in her dressing room and sitting in the dark, brooding over the tragedies in her life.

Her task was not made easier by last-minute script changes. "It was like getting trampled on every night." Mamet, she would recall for *Vanity Fair* years later, was "not interested in collaborating. I think he's interested in fascism." But Madonna deferred to the playwright. This was not, after all, the medium in which she was most comfortable. And Mamet, for all his "fascist" tendencies, had earned a Pulitzer Prize in 1984 for his previous Broadway effort, *Glengarry Glen Ross*.

Backstage, *Speed-the-Plow*, now more widely known as "the Madonna play," triggered an old-fashioned (if decidedly tongue-in-cheek) star feud. The play was at first scheduled to open at Lincoln Center's Mitzi Newhouse Theater. But Patti LuPone, who had won a Tony Award for her portrayal in *Evita*, was already appearing in another Lincoln Center theater, the Vivien Beaumont, in a revival of Cole Porter's *Anything Goes*. LuPone, who supposedly still resented being passed over in favor of Madonna for the film version of *Evita*, tacked up a notice on the theater's bulletin board. "Miss LuPone," it read mock-seriously, "wishes to inform the management that only one Sicilian diva at a time is allowed in this theater." Coincidentally, it was announced that *Speed-the-Plow* would move to a larger theater—to take advantage of record ticket sales.

Speed-the-Plow opened May 3 at the Royale Theatre. Sean, in Southeast Asia filming *Casualties of War* with Michael J. Fox, was not in the audience. Unhappily for Madonna, the critics were. "Her ineptitude is scandalously thorough," declared CBS's Dennis

Cunningham. "She moves . . . as if she were operated by a remote control unit several cities away." *The Washington Post*'s David Richards stated flatly of the play that "Madonna was the weakest thing in it," while John Simon of *New York* magazine allowed that "she can afford to pay for a few acting lessons." Clive Barnes of the *New York Post* struggled to be gallant: "There is a genuine reticent charm here, but it is not ready to light the lamps on Broadway." The headline for Howard Kissel's review in the New York *Daily News* spoke volumes: "No, She Can't Act."

Curiously, only *New York Times* reviewer Frank Rich, the most powerful of the nation's theater critics, praised Madonna's "intelligent, scrupulously disciplined comic acting"—a perception that enraged several of his colleagues. "I'm so ticked off," Cunningham said. "I think Frank should apologize for every actor he's ever given a bad review to. . . . Frank has taken leave of his senses."

Madonna, accustomed to the pyrotechnics that accompanied everything she did, took it all in stride: "I expected it. There are people who are violently opposed to the fact that I exist on this earth, so I was just thankful that there were people who liked it."

She certainly did not disappoint *Speed-the-Plow*'s backers. Advance ticket sales of over $1 million set a Broadway record for a serious play. Indeed, it was because of Madonna that many ticket buyers were seeing live theater for the first time. Nor did they seem to mind that the dark-haired, mousy creature they saw on stage bore scant resemblance to rock's brassy queen bee. At many performances, younger members of the audience stayed seated long after the curtain fell—just waiting, they would explain to the amusement of the ushers, to catch the second show.

Like all celebrities, Madonna lived in fear of those frightening moments when a fan crossed the line between devotion and obsession. Two weeks into the run of the play, a menacing-looking man in full punk regalia jumped onto the stage and lunged toward Madonna as she delivered her lines. She halted and stepped back, visibly shaken as costar Joe Mantegna quickly grabbed the disturbed-looking young man and led him offstage.

At about the same time, an overzealous fan known simply as Darlene began waiting for her idol outside the Royale Theatre and in front of her apartment building. Inexplicably, whenever Madonna changed her unlisted home telephone number, Darlene somehow managed to learn what it was and call. Madonna began losing sleep, plagued once again by the nightmare in which she is killed onstage by a crazed admirer. Darlene's activities were reported to the police.

Another, very different dream led Madonna to a new, complex, and ultimately much-debated friendship. She told friend Erica Bell that one night she dreamed that she and the comedienne Sandra Bernhard had survived some catastrophe together and were the last two people on earth. In fact, Madonna had met Bernhard and Warren Beatty briefly years earlier, on her first date with Penn.

Not long after telling Bell about her strange end-of-the-world dream, Madonna was sitting in the audience at Bernhard's hit one-woman Off-Broadway show, *Without You I'm Nothing*, when Bernhard described a favorite fantasy in which she and Madonna survive World War III "but Sean doesn't." "Madonna was floored when Sandra told that story," Bell said. "She had dreamed that *same* scenario, and she took it as an omen that this was a special person." After the show, Madonna raced backstage to introduce herself.

The pair hit it off instantly. "It was no surprise that they would become friends," said Madonna's former personal assistant Melinda Cooper. "Sandra is as wild as Madonna—in some ways, wilder. They are just two crazy girls out to raise some eyebrows and have some fun." For the first time, Madonna had encountered someone even more vulgar and out-on-a-limb tasteless than she was. She could laugh at Bernhard's coarse jokes—many of which were beyond even vulgarity and at least momentarily, feel free of the burden of stardom.

With Penn still off on location in the jungles of Thailand, the two women—"stuck" in New York for the summer, recalled Madonna—began "hanging out together, slagging everybody off together. She was just what I needed." Explained Bernhard: "Madonna likes my particular kind of insanity."

By mid-June Madonna, Bernhard, and *Dirty Dancing* star Jennifer Grey, the daughter of *Cabaret* Academy Award–winner Joel Grey, were hitting the town's trendiest spots on an almost nightly basis. Dubbed the Terrible Trio, they often wore tacky matching outfits (cutoffs with lingerie tops, diaphanous pajamas) and horrified other restaurant patrons by staging loud belching contests. If Sean Penn was a member of the Brat Pack, noted Bernhard, then they would have to come up with a name for their little group of hell-raisers. They called themselves the Snatch Batch.

The curious friendship between Madonna and the openly bisexual Bernhard soon evolved into something else. At such popular spots as The Odeon, M.K., the Canal Bar, and The World, the pair were spotted hugging, cradling, and kissing one another. They began visiting such lesbian bars as lower Manhattan's Cubby Hole, and as Madonna later confessed, "there was a flirtation going on."

Madonna had had sexual experiences with women, but she worried about what that revelation might do to her career, and— nearly as important—how her husband and her straitlaced Roman Catholic father might react. That question became academic when Bernhard asked Madonna to tag along with her to the NBC studios at Rockefeller Center, where she was to tape *Late Night with David Letterman.*

"Let's talk about you and your new good friend Madonna," said Letterman. "Is there any truth to this nonsense?"

"A hair, a tad," replied Bernhard.

"What do you do when you go out?" asked Letterman.

"We party and we get crazy. . . . We drink tequila, we talk about old times, and we get to know each other a little better. What do you think you do with a girlfriend? What do you do when you go out with *your* girlfriend?"

Madonna then appeared, wearing an outfit that matched Bernhard's (white T-shirt, cutoff jeans, white socks, black shoes). "Let's talk about me and Sandra," she insisted.

Letterman asked for Madonna's version of how they spent their time, and if he could be a part of it.

"If you got a sex change," Madonna shot back.

"We meet up," added Bernhard, "sometimes with Jennifer Grey, sometimes just the two of us. You usually find us at the Canal Bar or at M.K."

Madonna interjected: "En route to the Cubby . . ."

"Hole," finished Bernhard.

"I think it's time to fess up, get real," said Madonna. "She doesn't give a damn about me. . . . She loves Sean. She's using me to get to Sean."

Unwilling to be topped, Bernhard boasted facetiously that she had slept with both Madonna *and* Sean.

Madonna was delighted with the ensuing scandal. "Sandra and I were just fucking with people," she later insisted, "but then when I realized the reaction we had gotten, I of course couldn't leave that alone. So Sandra and I decided to tease everybody."

Penn, home in August after completing *Casualties of War*, failed to see the humor in his wife's latest antics. He not only disliked Bernhard (who returned the sentiment), but was appalled by the public debate over whether or not Madonna was bisexual. Worse, he now wondered if, given her longstanding links to the gay community, she might in fact be a lesbian. She brushed off the suggestion, assuring him that it was all a pose, that she and Bernhard were nothing more than buddies.

The Penns were once again on shaky ground, but they managed to pull things together enough to celebrate Madonna's thirtieth birthday with friends. Her fans were not so fortunate. Her bodyguards at the Royale Theatre did accept expensive birthday bouquets of roses on Madonna's behalf, but her fans then watched in dismay as she tossed them unceremoniously out her dressing room window.

One fourteen-year-old girl, who had taken the train from suburban White Plains every day for months just to watch Madonna enter and leave the theater, had purchased a ticket and planned to celebrate her idol's birthday by watching the show. But Madonna, claiming that she did not want "a disturbance" on the night of her birthday, had reportedly instructed the theater management to bar "groupies" from entering. Instead, their money was refunded. "I don't understand," sobbed the fourteen-year-old girl, "I'd never hurt Madonna."

Conceivably, Madonna was daunted by the notion of having to put on a happy public face for three milestone events—her thirtieth birthday and three days later, a belated joint celebration of her husband's twenty-eighth birthday and their third wedding anniversary. "Despite all the predictions," said Madonna's publicist Liz Rosenberg, beaming, "they're still together." Not for long. "My friendship with Sandra was just beginning," Madonna later observed, "as my relationship with Sean was dying."

18

"I've always been a romantic."

*"If the Pope wants to see me, he can
buy tickets like everybody else."*

Madonna left the cast of *Speed-the-Plow* in September,
and as expected, ticket sales promptly dropped 60 percent. Having
devoted the previous eight months to establishing herself as a legitimate stage actress (despite the critics), she now turned her
attention back to her music career. Although footage from the
emotion-filled Italian portion of her European tour was released
that month in a video called "Ciao Italia," Madonna had been
noticeably absent from the charts. Meeting in Los Angeles with
collaborators Patrick Leonard and Steve Bray, she began work on
her next album.

The new LP, which Madonna hoped would represent the
"adult" side of her, would deal with such weighty topics as Catholicism, relationships, and family. Madonna had written the lyrics
for several of the songs during the run of *Speed-the-Plow*, and they
reflected her somber state of mind.

There were technical differences as well. For the first time, Madonna was working with live musicians all in the studio at the same
time. Rather than going back and automatically "cleaning up" the

vocals by overdubbing, she was keeping many of the tracks just as they were recorded on the first take—hisses, strains, and all. The result, she reasoned, would be more spontaneous, emotional sound.

She was trying a new approach on the domestic front as well. Together in California and away from the influence of Sandra Bernhard and the other "Snatch Batchers," Mr. and Mrs. Penn seized the opportunity to rekindle the home fires. For his return to the theater in *Hurlyburly*, Penn insisted that the play be staged in Los Angeles so that he could be near his wife. Throughout rehearsals Madonna, now fully cognizant of how draining the process could be, phoned backstage to offer words of support.

Yet on *Hurlyburly*'s opening night Madonna trailed in late, clinging to her "date," Sandra Bernhard. Penn seethed. At the opening night party that followed, he cornered his wife in a private room at the Century City nightclub Twenty-20. "You *cunt*," he screamed. "How could you do this to me?" Sylvester Stallone was among the guests within earshot as their shouting match raged on. "The performance was good," a studio executive said of the play, "but *this* was even better."

"Sean's fragile male ego was badly bruised," said a friend of the couple's. "She was more famous than he was, made tons more money, and now she was rubbing his nose in the whole lesbian-affair controversy. It's bad enough when a man thinks his wife is leaving him for another man—but for another *woman?* Sean just couldn't handle it."

Nor could he accept the news that his wife had campaigned for and clinched the role of Breathless Mahoney in Warren Beatty's long-planned epic *Dick Tracy*. Before Madonna went after the part, her producer-friend David Geffen had tried to talk her into doing a film called *The Fabulous Baker Boys*. Madonna thought the script was "mushy"; Michelle Pfeiffer took the part and went on to win critical acclaim playing a nightclub singer in the hit film.

As determined as Madonna was to play Breathless Mahoney, she was not Beatty's first choice—far from it. Kathleen Turner, Kim Basinger, and a dozen other actresses were all ahead of her on the casting director's wish list. Still, she called him up. "Warren," Madonna told Beatty, "I really want this part." She later recalled of the conversation, "I saw the A list and I was on the Z list. I felt like a jerk." Finally, she told Beatty she was willing to do the one thing none of the other actresses would: work for union scale, $1,440 a week. By forgoing a multimillion-dollar salary, Madonna helped make it possible for Beatty to bring the film in under its $30-million budget.

Madonna went to Beatty behind Penn's back, violating her earlier vow to have a baby in 1989. She told him that they would have to postpone their plans for a family another year. Thus far, she was sticking to the pledge she had made to Erica Bell years earlier, that she had no intention of bearing Penn's children.

The stress of the holiday season once again served to magnify the Penns' marital woes. On December 23, Penn paid an unscheduled visit to Madonna at her Universal Studios bungalow to find out if she still intended to do *Dick Tracy*. The contracts, he was informed, had already been signed. Penn let loose with a volley of blistering obscenities and reportedly had to be led away by security guards. The embattled couple spent Christmas Eve separately— she with Bernhard, Penn with a stripper. Bernhard, meantime, actively counseled her friend to dump her headstrong husband. She sat her down and demanded, "What the fuck are you doing to yourself?" Madonna confessed to being in pain, but, she told Bernhard, "I still love Sean."

Christmas dawned like D-day at the Malibu house. After another shouting match, Penn moved in with his parents. From there, he allegedly made several abusive calls to Madonna. When she stopped answering the phone, he left obscenity-laced messages on her answering machine.

Three days later Penn, frustrated and drunk, staked out the Malibu house. Around four P.M., after Madonna had given her small household staff the rest of the day off to go to a party, he scaled the fence encircling the estate, broke into the house, and confronted a terrified Madonna. After slapping her around, he bound and gagged her, then strapped her to a chair with twine. He berated and beat her for two hours, then stormed out of the house.

Gagged, tied up, and trembling with fear, Madonna waited for hours for help to arrive. Incredibly, Penn returned, swigging tequila from a bottle, and began tormenting her all over again. This time, she managed to persuade him to untie her. Once free, she dashed out of the house, jumped into the coral-colored 1957 Thunderbird Penn had bought her for her twenty-eighth birthday, locked the doors, and called the police on her car phone. She then sped off to the Malibu sheriff's station to swear out a complaint against her husband. There, bruised and bleeding, she told the horrifying story of her nine-hour ordeal to dumbstruck officers.

As Madonna sought refuge at the home of her manager Freddy DeMann, sheriff's officers descended on the Malibu house. Heeding Madonna's warning that her husband might be armed, they circled the house. Guns drawn, they ordered Penn over a police bullhorn to surrender. Their command echoed off the Malibu canyon walls: "Sean Penn, come out with your hands up."

Handcuffed and carted unceremoniously off to the sheriff's station, Penn told police that Madonna had trumped up the charges to get even with him for dating a stripper. Not so, said friends in whom Madonna confided. They had seen plenty of evidence of Penn's abusive behavior over the years.

A week after the incident, Madonna filed for divorce on grounds of irreconcilable differences. The same day, she met with Deputy District Attorney Lauren Weiss and told her that she had decided to withdraw her complaint against her husband. "Madonna asked that there be no criminal charges pressed," explained DA's spokesman Al Albergate. "There is no other evidence with which to base a criminal charge, so there won't be a criminal charge filed."

Madonna's divorce petition once again asked that her full maiden name be reinstated, and she invoked the couple's prenuptial agreement concerning the division of property. Had it not been for that agreement, a legal battle royale might have taken place. Madonna, whose annual personal income had hovered around $30 million for each of the three years they were married, was believed by 1989 to be worth in the neighborhood of $70 million. Penn, with a per-picture salary of $1 million, could lay claim to a respectable net worth of $5 million. Under the terms of the prenuptial agreement, each got what they brought into the marriage and what money they had earned during it. Penn took the Malibu house, valued at $4 million, and Madonna held on to the Manhattan apartment.

Madonna wasted no time starting over. Within a week, she plunked down $2,950,000 for a ten-room sanctuary high in the Hollywood Hills and signed what at the time was considered the biggest endorsement deal in history. Christopher Ciccone, Madonna's brother and confidant, had looked at over twenty possibilities on his sister's behalf before taking her to see the hilltop aerie with its cool marble floors, glistening pool, and sweeping views of metropolitan Los Angeles below. Given an unfettered hand ("He has the best taste of anyone I know," commented Madonna), Christopher decorated the entire house in a head-spinning two weeks.

Outside, the contemporary hacienda was starkly white and unyieldingly angular. In sharp contrast, the interior fashioned by Christopher offered a beguilingly eclectic blend of the classic and the contemporary. A grand piano, overstuffed, tasseled chairs upholstered in gold brocade, Catholic candelabra, and eighteenth-century side chairs with their original needlepoint tapestry lent an Italianate aura to the living room. In the huge, mirrored bathroom/dressing room/gym, a pillow-strewn antique day bed contrasted sharply with gleaming black fitness equipment. Over the toilet: a David Salle drawing of a naked woman, legs akimbo.

Tasteful furnishings aside, the house was first and foremost a showcase for what was now considered to be one of the country's leading privately held collections of modern art. Beginning in 1989, the prestigious publication *Art & Antiques* listed Madonna as one of America's "Top 100 Collectors." She began collecting, Madonna once said, "as soon as I had the bread." Her first acquisition: an abstract by Robert Smithson that she called "her guardian angel." It hung over her bed.

By 1989, she employed her own art adviser. "She never said, 'Hey, here's cash, go buy me a collection,'" he insisted. "What she buys she likes and lives with." What she liked and owned were the works of Tamara de Lempicka, Picasso, Léger (whose abstract paintings hung over her fireplace and in her bedroom), her friend Keith Haring (a collage dedicated to her hung in her kitchen next to a wall-to-wall wooden periodical rack crammed with magazines featuring her on the cover), and Mexico's Diego Rivera and his wife, the fiery Frida Kahlo. Visitors to the house would glance up to see male genitals—a formidable Langlois rendering of the nude Hermes, Cupid, and Diana commissioned by a French king for the palace at Versailles, now covering Madonna's living room ceiling.

Although several of Madonna's paintings were nudes in various questionable poses, easily the most off-putting hung inside the front door—a test of each visitor's compatibility with the mistress of the house. The bloody *My Birth* by Kahlo shows the artist's head protruding from between her mother's widespread legs. "If somebody doesn't like this painting," Madonna would say, "then I know they can't be my friend."

To help pay for new acquisitions, Madonna signed to do her first-ever endorsement for an American product. Not only would Pepsi-Cola pay her $5 million, it would also make advertising history by becoming the first company to sponsor the debut of a new single—"Like a Prayer," the title track from her forthcoming album. Pepsi also agreed to sponsor her next tour.

Madonna's decision to join Michael Jackson, Tina Turner, David Bowie, Gloria Estefan, and other rock stars in the cola wars made good business sense. "I like the challenge of merging art and commerce," she explained to *Rolling Stone*. "As far as I'm concerned, making a video is also a commercial. The Pepsi spot is a great and different way to expose the record. Record companies just don't have the money to finance that kind of publicity." She pointed out that her music would be playing in the background and the product positioned "very subliminally" in the commercial. She made sure of that by refusing to drink the product on camera, and by agreeing to be shown holding the can no more than twice —and then only fleetingly.

Yet executives at BBDO, the New York advertising agency handling the account, were not aware of Madonna's hidden agenda.

Scandal was the lifeblood of her career. Her grand strategy—to focus attention on each new album by releasing its most titillating cut first—had worked brilliantly in the case of *Like a Virgin* and "Papa Don't Preach." She intended the video of "Like a Prayer" to top the others in shock value.

"Madonna did not want to compromise herself as an artist by becoming just another shill," said a former member of her staff. "She wanted there to be a big splash." The ex-staffer believes Madonna was actually pleased when Pepsi yanked the spot. "That way she got the headlines she felt she needed to sell the album, and she got to keep the five million dollars, too."

Before the contracts were signed, Madonna knew the "Like a Prayer" video as directed by Mary Lambert (who had also directed her "Like a Virgin" video) would be her most provocative ever. Originally, she had imagined the story of a Southern white girl in love with a black man who sings in a church choir. In this vision, they try to run away together but are shot in the back by the Ku Klux Klan.

Lambert's interpretation retained the interracial message, but also tossed in a plethora of religious images. In its final version Madonna, wearing her hair dark and long and looking like Anna Magnani, witnesses an assault on a young woman by a white gang. She sees a black man (played by Leon Robinson) rush to the victim's aid, only to be dragged away when the police arrive. Afraid to get involved, she runs to a church, where she comes upon the figure of a black saint who closely resembles the unjustly accused man. Lying on a pew, she dreams that the saint becomes a flesh-and-blood man. They kiss, and the music builds as their lovemaking reaches an orgasmic crescendo. Then, she awakens and rushes to the police station to tell them who really committed the rape, and the black man is freed as a full gospel choir joins in. For added effect, Madonna, clad in a clinging black slip, dances through a forest of burning crosses. Her hands are also inflicted with bleeding, stigmata-type wounds. The playlet ends with the entire cast taking a Broadway-style bow.

According to one crew member on the set of the video, "she was always saying things like 'Gee, I wonder what Nancy Reagan will think of this?' or 'Take that, [Moral Majority leader] Jerry Falwell.' She knew there was going to be an uproar." But even a few of her close friends felt uneasy with the theme. Niki Harris, a backup singer who would go on to her own successful solo career, turned down Madonna's invitation to work on the video. "Burning crosses," she explained, "meant something to me as a black woman."

For the Pepsi commercial that was to precede the video, the ad agency hired Joe Pytka, who had directed Michael Jackson's enormously successful Pepsi video. Apparently not satisfied that the video would cause enough of a stir, Madonna outlined her own concept for the soft-drink spot. She suggested that the agency hire a T-shirted James Dean look-alike to play her boyfriend. As Madonna saw the scene, the boyfriend comes up to her with a Pepsi can in his pants pocket. In a takeoff on the old Mae West line, Madonna would then sidle up to him and say, "Is that a Pepsi in your pocket, or are you just happy to see me?"

The agency, understandably, declined. Entitled "Make a Wish," the finished commercial showed Madonna holding a Pepsi in her hand and watching home movies of her own eighth birthday party. The child and the woman switch places, and as the little girl browses through the woman's apartment, Madonna sings "Like a Prayer" while she dances in the street, in the hallways of her old grade school, and in a church.

Innocent enough. But Pepsi officials were completely unaware of the nature of the "Like a Prayer" video—and Madonna kept it that way. One advertising executive intimately involved in making the commercial was Roger Mosconi, BBDO Worldwide advertising's senior creative director at the time. "One day," he remembered, "Madonna, who likes to joke with me, came up to me and said, 'Hey, Roger, are you going to have the burning cross reflecting in the Pepsi can?' And I said, 'What burning cross?' And she smiled and said, 'You'll see.' "

For her part, Madonna was an unflappable pro on the Pepsi set. She only came unglued when she lost her earrings, and justifiably so. Eighteenth-century French diamond drops set in platinum, she had bought them to cheer herself up.

CHRISTOPHER ANDERSEN

On the romantic front, cheering up is what she needed. On February 13, publicist Liz Rosenberg chauffeured her client through rain-swept streets to dinner at a venerable Hollywood restaurant, Musso & Frank. "It's Valentine's Day tomorrow, Liz," Madonna sighed. "It's the first time for years and years I haven't had a valentine on Valentine's Day." Liz answered reassuringly, "The night is young. You'll find one, Madonna. There'll be someone."

Within months, the ex–Mrs. Penn would indeed have a new valentine: a comic-book hero come to life whose attentions would leave Madonna, like scores of women before her . . . Breathless.

19

"Feeling regret is really destructive. I have learned a great deal from my marriage, so much. About everything —mostly about myself."

"I don't think you can ever love enough."

On March 2, 1989, Madonna's much-ballyhooed two-minute Pepsi commercial debuted during America's top-rated television series, "The Cosby Show." It aired simultaneously on prime time television in forty countries, before an estimated audience of 250 million. Hours later, the "Like a Prayer" single and video were released worldwide.

Reaction to the video was instantaneous—and ferocious. The American Family Association (AFA), a fundamentalist organization based in Tupelo, Mississippi, damned the video as "blatantly offensive." Even though the Pepsi spot itself—in contrast to the video airing on MTV—only showed Madonna singing and dancing with her eight-year-old alter ego, the connection was strong enough for AFA to call for a one-year nationwide boycott of all Pepsi products. "Madonna's new video," wrote AFA executive director Donald Wildmon in *USA Today*, was part "of a disturbing trend by some in the media, that of disrespect and disdain for the religious beliefs of millions of Americans." Soon after, the Roman Catholic bishop of Corpus Christi, Texas, also called for a boycott.

"Obviously I'm tapping into something in their subconscious," mused Madonna, "that they're very ashamed of. . . . It's like Hitler—they want to purify your thoughts."

In Rome, religious hard-liners had beaten Madonna to the punch. Following a press preview of the "Like a Prayer" video, a Catholic group threatened to file charges of blasphemy (a crime under Italian law) against Madonna's record company and the state television network. Fearing a public outcry, plans to air the video March 7 were suspended "to avoid further controversy." When the video finally did air two weeks later, Catholic leaders joined the chorus of condemnation.

Dazed and baffled by the public outrage, Pepsi executives publicly defended their association with Madonna; in the face of demands that the ad be withdrawn, they stood firm. In the boardroom, however, they scrambled for ways to cut their losses. Beyond the $5 million in cash they owed Madonna, the company had spent another $5 million producing and promoting the Pepsi-Madonna partnership. For the time being, they yanked the ad from the airwaves, replacing it with an ad featuring button-down British rocker Robert ("Addicted to Love," "Simply Irresistible") Palmer and his trademark bevy of expressionless, robotlike beauties. It may have been numbingly sexist, but the Palmer commercial contained none of the religious imagery or interracial overtones that raised the hackles of the devout.

Three weeks later, after airing the costly spot on "The Cosby Show" only twice, Pepsi canned the campaign just as the *Like a Prayer* album was released. Fueled by high-octane publicity, the single was already zooming up the charts. "We had expected the public would eventually separate the video from the ad," explained Pepsi spokesman Tod MacKenzie. But thousands of letters and telephone calls "have led us to conclude," he continued, "that, unfortunately, the confusion is greater than ever. And because we are a consumer products company, we must be responsive to the views of the consumers." There was considerable precedent for Pepsi's actions: Ralston Purina, Procter and Gamble, and several other sponsors had recently canceled ads or ordered advertising agencies not to buy more television time after consumers objected to a program's content. It was, however, the first time anyone had objected to the sponsorship of a video.

Liz Rosenberg had the honor of informing Madonna that Pepsi was pulling the plug and agreeing to pay Madonna her promised $5 million anyway. "Oh, goody," she said. "I hope I sell a lot of records."

She deserved to sell a lot of records. On that point the critics were in complete agreement. *Like a Prayer*, which she dedicated to "my mother, who taught me how to pray," was Madonna's most ambitious and keenly personal artistic statement to date. In another song, the anxiety-ridden "Till Death Do Us Part," she seems to be laying bare her soul when she tells of a woman's violent marriage to a drunken, self-loathing husband: "The bruises, they will fade away/You hit so hard with the things you say."

Steve Bray, Madonna's longtime collaborator and album coproducer, observed: "She is one of those people who work out their inner turmoil through mass acceptance and mass acknowledgment—that is the most fascinating thing about her. 'Till Death Do Us Part' was right in the moment—at the time they [she and Penn] decided to separate." Madonna was more blunt about her reasons for writing "Till Death Do Us Part." "I can't take a shit without reading about it," she said. "Everybody wants to know about everything I do, so I might as well confront it in my work."

Another strikingly autobiographical cut, "Oh Father," concerns a woman recalling the death of her mother at a young age and the anguished father who brutally vents his rage by abusing his little girl. "You can't hurt me now," she declares as the music swells majestically, "I got away from you, I never thought I would."

The song and the accompanying David Fincher–directed video *noire* in which she dances on her mother's grave begged comparisons with Madonna's own childhood, strongly implying that she, too, had been victimized. "I think it was an angry swipe at her father at a time when he thought things between them were okay," said a longtime family friend. "She knew that people would think she was talking about her own childhood whether the whole thing was true or not. That hurt Tony deeply."

During the filming of the "Oh Father" video, Madonna had trouble selecting a costume for the cemetery scene. She finally settled on a long frock coat and over the coat, a cross. Not willing to forsake the old Madonna entirely, she wore a G-string and a sheer negligee beneath the severe coat.

Continuing to exorcise her private demons in public, Madonna also summoned up the ghost of her mother for the poignant "Promise to Try." Here, she recalls the first Madonna Ciccone offering warm comfort and maternal advice. Playing off that same childhood theme is "Dear Jesse"—a wistfully psychedelic confection of carousels and pink elephants.

In the bouncy "Keep It Together," which would emerge as one of the several No. 1 singles from the album, Madonna proclaims her allegiance to the family in spite of all the turmoil and dissension. Ironically, there was no greater strain on the family than that exerted by the force of Madonna's own notoriety—and her insistence on serving up family secrets for public consumption.

Not all the cuts were soul-searing. To temper the anguish of "Like a Prayer, "Till Death Do Us Part," and "Oh Father," Madonna and old flame Prince collaborated by mail on the words and music for "Love Song." They then met in a studio to record the libidinous duet.

Proclaiming the album to be "as close to art as pop music gets," *Rolling Stone* critic J. D. Considine added that *Like a Prayer* is proof not only that Madonna should be taken seriously as an artist but that "hers is one of the most compelling voices of the eighties." *The New York Times*' Stephen Holden rhapsodized that "Madonna has never looked more beautiful or sung with more feeling" than in her "convincing bid for recognition as a serious rock artist." "Shareholders in Madonna Inc. should be delighted," chimed in Wayne Robins of *Newsday*. "The latest act from the one-woman conglomerate is an album that's finely crafted—and deeply personal."

Artistic excellence aside, Madonna was not above using a few gimmicks to add to the *Like a Prayer* experience. Determined that the record would even smell like a hit, she ordered that the incenselike fragrance patchouli be mixed into the packaging glue of the vinyl and cassette versions of *Like a Prayer*. All by way of giving the album "a church-type feel," explained Liz Rosenberg. Less pious was the garish ad wrapped around the trade publication *Billboard*: the patchouli-scented photo of Madonna's bare midriff with the slogans "It Shall Be Released" and "Lead Us Into Temptation."

An offhand comment to a *Rolling Stone* interviewer concerning a *Playboy* spread featuring Michael Jackson's sister LaToya stirred up some more valuable publicity. "She had a tit job for sure," Madonna had said when she saw the nude *Playboy* layout. "This is desperation. Well, maybe she'll get a job out of it." A wounded LaToya fired back: "Madonna is a no-talent. She slept with everybody on the way up. That's how she made it to the top. In 'Like a Prayer,' Madonna is the one who should have been crucified."

"Like a Prayer" was Madonna's fastest-rising hit, in the Top Ten after only three weeks. But could she count on rave reviews and publicity stunts to keep her records selling while she devoted the summer to working on *Dick Tracy?* Not one to leave such matters to chance, she filmed two videos from the album that spring. Each, to be released at carefully calculated intervals for maximum momentum, was carefully designed to keep her name in the papers —and her songs on the charts.

The first and most striking of these was the pounding, Motown-sounding "Express Yourself," in which she sheds her Material Girl mantle to argue for old-fashioned commitment. The song begins with Madonna shouting, "Come on, girls, do you believe in love?" and then advises, "You don't need diamond rings or 18 carat gold/ Fancy cars that go very fast you know they never last." The song's message, according to Madonna: "If you want something, don't be afraid to ask for it. Say what it is you want." But the message delivered by the video was very different. Against the advice of her manager, Freddy DeMann, Madonna sank $1 million of her own money into producing it.

Inspired by Fritz Lang's 1926 cinematic masterpiece, *Metropolis*, "Express Yourself" is ostensibly a futuristic tale with a strong sadomasochistic undercurrent. Set in a grim, soulless world of smoke, sweat, and steel, it depicts Madonna as a black-suited, monocle-wearing businesswoman atop an industrial pyramid. While shirtless laborers toil in the grimy world below, she grabs at her crotch, writhes atop a bed in slave collar and chains, and eventually summons one of the grimy workers (another oiled-up protégé-model simply named Cameron) to service her.

She bridled at the notion that "Express Yourself" once again cast the woman as victim. So long as *she* chose to wear the chains, Madonna argued, she controlled the situation. Victim? On the contrary, in this scenario she was decidedly The Boss. "No matter how in control you think you are about sexuality in a relationship," she explained, "there is always the power struggle . . . always a certain amount of compromise. Of being beholden, if you love them. You do it because you *choose* to. No one put the chain around this neck but me. I was chained to my desire." The theme of "Express Yourself": "Pussy rules the world," declared Madonna. "Okay, I said it."

Hyped by the video, "Express Yourself" would go to No. 1 in July of 1989, making it Madonna's fifteenth Top Five single in a row. She had surpassed the Beatles; only Elvis Presley has had more. The album itself would go on to sell an astonishing 11 million copies, pushing her total album sales past the 39 million mark.

Madonna continued her gender-bending ways with the video for "Cherish," a frothy song that borrowed heavily from the 1960s' Association hit of the same name. She hired her close friend photographer Herb Ritts to shoot a black-and-white fantasy in which she dances on the beach with a child while tail-wearing mermen cavort offshore like playful dolphins. Wisely, Ritts acquiesced to all his star's wishes during filming. "She is very ballsy," he said. "She knows exactly what she wants."

"I like to switch everything around," Madonna explained. "I like the idea of men with tails on. I like the idea of men being the objects of desire, the sirens that entrap women, instead of the other way around. Some people would say that I hate men and that I like to do things to take power away from them, but you don't have to get that analytical."

She would eventually take a serious interest in one of the brawny mermen on "Cherish," a male model named Tony Ward.

But at that moment, he was not making much of a splash with Madonna. She had her eye on bigger fish.

"Warren should have been a psychiatrist or a district attorney," said Madonna of Warren Beatty, with whom she was about to begin work on *Dick Tracy*. "When he wants to know somebody, he goes out of his way to investigate. You feel like you're under a microscope. You're not used to people spending that much time trying to get to know you. But it's admirable. Everybody ought to examine the people they're going to work with as intensely as he does."

To be sure, Beatty was famous for scrutinizing his female co-stars. Ever since bursting on the Hollywood scene in 1961's *Splendor in the Grass*, Shirley MacLaine's dashingly handsome little brother had reigned as the screen capital's leading lothario.

Actually, he was notorious for womanizing even before his first film's release, carrying on simultaneous affairs with *Splendor in the Grass* costar Natalie Wood (whose first marriage to Robert Wagner he thereby destroyed), Joan Collins, and French actress Leslie Caron ("He tends to maul you") during the shooting. Collins, who went on to star as Alexis Carrington in television's "Dynasty," was engaged to him in 1961. "He was insatiable," she has said. "Three, four, five times a day was not unusual for him, and he was also able to accept phone calls at the same time."

Beatty went on to more films—*Bonnie and Clyde, McCabe and Mrs. Miller, Shampoo, Heaven Can Wait, Reds* (for which he won an Academy Award as Best Director)—and more famous ladies: Julie Christie, Michelle Phillips, Carly Simon, Joni Mitchell, Diane Keaton, Britt Ekland, Barbra Streisand, and Isabelle Adjani. The only passion that could compete was politics: Beatty, an outspoken liberal Democrat, was intimately involved in the failed presidential bids of George McGovern in 1972 and Gary Hart in 1988.

Now at fifty-two, he was nearly twenty-two years Madonna's senior when they set out to bring Chester Gould's jut-jawed comic-strip hero to the screen. She was in high school when he first became attached to the project in 1975. The film was set to go into production with Walter (*48 Hours*) Hill directing, but faltered when director and star clashed over the general approach. Beatty wanted *Dick Tracy* to be a splashy Technicolor romp that conjured up the magic of the comic strip itself. Hill pushed for realism. Beatty finally bought the rights himself in 1985.

Then came the 1987 comedy *Ishtar*, which soon ranked alongside *Heaven's Gate* and *Howard the Duck* as one of the biggest bombs in film history. The following year, Beatty managed to secure the backing of Walt Disney Studios—with the caveat that he keep the budget to $25 million. The Coldwater Canyon Casanova needed a blockbuster as much as Madonna did. Together, they were hell-bent on conceiving one.

But first, Disney Studios chairman Jeffrey Katzenberg had to be convinced that Madonna was right for the part of Breathless Mahoney, the brassy blond nightclub singer who schemes to lure Dick Tracy from his pure-as-the-driven-snow lady love, Tess Trueheart (played by Glenne Headley). There was a downside to casting Madonna. Her notoriety could distract from the story and actually turn more conservative moviegoers away. But her appeal was also strongest among that segment of the audience where Beatty and Tracy had little recognition value. Her enormous following among preteens, teenagers, and young adults, Beatty and Katzenberg reasoned, could offset the fact that most Americans under thirty were essentially unaware of either Beatty or the comic strip on which the movie was based. In this, *Dick Tracy* differed greatly from the stupendously successful *Batman*, based on a superhero who was instantly recognizable because of the continued success of the Batman comic books and the campy hit television series. Besides, Madonna had essentially agreed to work for free. She was hired.

Madonna later admitted that Beatty's decades of experience ("Warren understands the bullshit. He's been an icon for years") and protectiveness toward her made him a father figure of sorts. That, however, did not stop them from becoming lovers even before the cameras rolled. At first, Madonna found the affair daunting. "Sometimes I think, he's been with the world's most beautiful, most glamorous women. I go, 'Oh, my God! Oh, my God!' . . . Then there is the side of me that says I'm better than all of them."

As for Beatty, he was in awe of Madonna's discipline, of her willingness to work eighteen hours with little complaint. At one point in the story, Breathless is forced by archvillain Big Boy Caprice (played by Al Pacino) to rehearse a dance number over and over until she nearly collapses from exhaustion. To make the scene utterly convincing, Beatty had Madonna do forty takes.

All was not peace and harmony during filming. Madonna's self-avowed lack of patience and Beatty's penchant for taking his time guaranteed there would be some friction on the set. "Come *onnnn*," she would whine during long waits between takes. "Hurry up, *Warren!*" In the face of such tantrums, Beatty remained the unflappable, indulgent parent. Typically, he would grin and roll his eyes heavenward, then put his arm around her shoulders reassuringly. This did not always work; more than once she responded by yelling, "Don't *touch* me!" at her director and storming off the set.

He was more than willing to put up with Madonna's frequent fits of petulance. What she offered him both as a movie star and as a man transcended her box office appeal and her undeniable professionalism. He was not inured to the thrill of making love to the world's leading sex symbol. It was nothing less than a reaffirmation of his virility and perhaps equally important, his own sex appeal at the box office. They necked openly on the set, snuggled at the most high-visibility Hollywood nightspots, and even concocted pet names for each other. She called him Old Man. He called her Buzzbomb.

During filming a dancer on the set of *Dick Tracy* paid a visit to Madonna's dressing room and found the two stars in a highly compromising position. "They were a little embarrassed," she said, "but nowhere near as much as I was. They just kind of pulled themselves together, and it was business as usual."

Madonna was grateful that, in contrast to Sean Penn, Beatty did not appear to be threatened by her intimate friendship with Sandra Bernhard. "Warren," said a friend, "is open to everything sexual. If anything, the hint of bisexuality probably aroused him."

On June 11, Madonna and her friend artist Kenny Scharf, hosted a Don't Bungle the Jungle benefit at the Brooklyn Academy of Music. The event, aimed at saving the world's endangered rain forests, raised $750,000 and millions of eyebrows. The concert, attended by such luminaries as Meryl Streep, Calvin Klein, Billy Joel, and Glenn Close, featured the B-52's, the Grateful Dead's Bob Weir, the Del Fuegos, and a display of the dance craze vogue-ing. Bernhard did a solo number, wrapped in an American flag and waving incense as she sang "Woodstock."

But the show's most memorable moments came when Bernhard and Madonna took to the stage together in matching sequined bras and graffiti-splashed cutoffs. As the couple performed a raun-chy rendition of "I Got You Babe"—complete with bumps and grinds, crotch-tugging, and off-color asides—the audience gasped audibly. Undeterred, Madonna and Bernhard hugged and rubbed up against each other while the audience sat in shock. Bernhard then sidled up behind Madonna suggestively and wrapped her hands around her hips. As they swayed to the beat, Madonna told the crowd, "Don't believe those stories." Leering back, Bernhard countered, "*Believe* those stories!" They then walked off stage holding hands.

A postconcert party was held at the chic Vietnamese restaurant Indochine, and many of the celebrities showed up to see if Bern-hard and Madonna were as tender a couple away from the foot-lights. They were not disappointed. "Madonna and I have a heart-and-soul friendship," Bernhard said. "Beyond that, it's nobody's business. The way we act together is a political statement. It's to say to the world, 'Get past the judgments. Accept people for what they are.' The rain forest is dying. What do you care more about, the rain forest or our sexuality?" Judging by the uproar over the couple's suggestive behavior, the state of the rain forest ranked a distant second in the national consciousness.

Beatty did not ask Madonna for an explanation, and she prof-fered none. Yet he found it more difficult to accept her interest in other men—namely his longtime friend and neighbor Jack Ni-cholson. During the filming of *Dick Tracy*, Nicholson, a respected collector of impressionist and modern art who regularly prowled the New York auction houses, got together with Madonna to chat about their mutual passion for the work of painter Tamara de Lempicka.

"*Batman* was out and Jack was the biggest movie star around," said a friend of both Beatty and Nicholson's. "He was intrigued by Madonna and Madonna was flattered by his attention, but Warren wasn't happy at all when he heard they were dating. The bottom line was she wasn't going to do anything to jeopardize *Dick Tracy*."

For her thirty-first birthday, Beatty gave Madonna an Ilse Bing photograph of a group of dancers, one of whom is tossing back her head in a flagrant effort to upstage the others. "She," said Beatty, pointing to the would-be soloist, "reminds me of you."

"Gee, Warren," she said, striking the same histrionic Isadora Duncan pose, "I can't imagine why."

After nineteen weeks working on *Dick Tracy*, Madonna billed the producers for $27,360. Her real payoff would come much later. Now she confronted the prospect of planning another world tour —this time for mid-1990. She had told her brother Christopher and her manager Freddy DeMann after the Who's That Girl? roadshow she would never tour again. "And I meant it," she said. "It is too fucking *hard*."

Yet there were millions to be made and once again, a movie to promote. Having transformed herself from the demure brunette of "Like a Prayer" back into the peroxided spitfire of "Express Yourself" and *Dick Tracy*, Madonna minced no words in describing her motives. This, she told her brother as she puffed on one of her ever-present Marlboro Lights, would be her "Blond Ambition tour."

In September, Madonna began the arduous task of assembling the army of designers, artists, craftsmen, musicians, backup singers, dancers, and technicians that would be needed to bring her concepts to life on the concert stage. Over the next seven months she would, as she put it, "hire and fire, hire and fire" with gleeful impunity. Her most notable victim: avant-garde choreographer Karole Armitage. After moving from New York to Los Angeles to work on the tour, Armitage was summarily dismissed when her ideas failed to satisfy the boss.

Armitage was replaced by Vince Paterson, who had directed Michael Jackson's *Bad* tour. When they met, Madonna asked him point-blank, "Are you the one who had Michael Jackson grab his balls [in the "Bad" video]?"

"No," replied Paterson, "he was grabbing his balls before I got on the 'Bad' video."

"Well, maybe I should do it," she mused.

"Well," replied Paterson, "you should, because you have more balls than most of the men I know."

Her marching orders to Paterson: "Let's break every rule we can." Said Paterson: "She wanted to make statements about sexuality, cross-sexuality, the Church, and the like. But the biggest thing we tried to do is change the shape of concerts. Instead of just presenting songs, we wanted to combine fashion, Broadway, rock, and performance art."

A formidable undertaking, and one for which Madonna enlisted the support of her brother Christopher. It was Christopher who had urged her to go ahead with the tour, and in return she hired him to create some of the most imaginative sets in rock concert history. French fashion designer Jean-Paul Gaultier, whose platinum flat-top haircut delighted Madonna, was tapped to create the most outré outfits imaginable.

The world Madonna and her minions worked feverishly to create was months from completion. And with Beatty immersed in editing *Dick Tracy*, Madonna returned to New York alone. Life imitated art when, away from Beatty and the prying eye of the Hollywood press and left to her own devices, she visited a sex club.

Located in a penthouse in the West Fifties, Club Nine was so named because of its one requirement for admission—that male members boast sexual equipment measuring up to that number. According to eyewitness Jasmine Boyd, Madonna arrived at a so-called "specialty party" wearing a slinky black dress and a gold tinsel wig. With her were three young Latin men, all shirtless and wearing slave collars.

"She called them her 'toy boys,' " Boyd said, "and she conducted this measuring contest. One of the boys produced a tape measure, handed it to her, and they all unzipped their pants. Then she would measure each one with great ceremony and write down the results in a little black book. She was very flamboyant, there was lots of banter—it was a performance, really. Then she put a leash around the biggest guy—and I do not mean around his neck —and led him off to a bedroom." Boyd added that "Madonna bragged that she could tell how well endowed a man was by looking at the bulge in his pants."

"It's no joke," said a former friend, "size counts to her. She's not interested in somebody who's not . . . above average." Although she denied in one magazine interview that this was a consideration of particular importance to her, Madonna often took aside girlfriends to debate the relative genital merits of men. "Yeah, we'd go to the ladies' room after meeting some cute guy, and she'd say, 'I wonder how big his penis is.' Of course, she said it loud to shock as many people as possible."

On another occasion, Madonna complained to a secretary at Warner about the sad quality of the men she had been meeting recently. The secretary asked what she meant. "They're all," she said, holding her thumb and index finger one inch apart, "like this."

The nights spent prowling New York's hottest clubs also yielded a professional payoff. Still searching for ideas to spice up the Blond Ambition tour, Madonna and her makeup artist–friend Debi M. paid a nocturnal visit to an establishment called the Sound Factory. There she saw two men, Jose Guitierez and Luis Camacho, doing the vogue, a dance style that had taken hold in the gay community two years before but never caught on with the general public. Madonna claimed she was too intimidated to approach them.

The next afternoon, she arranged for a club to be specially opened for her, and a vogueing group called the House of Xtravaganza showed up to do an entire vogueing show for her. "They were all free-styling," recalled Madonna. "I didn't know where to look. I was blown away." She invited Guitierez and Camacho to come to auditions for her show, and both were ultimately hired.

Open auditions—"cattle calls"—for the seven male dancers (no women) were held in January of 1990 in New York and Los Angeles under the unforgiving eye of Madonna herself. Ads placed in

Daily Variety asked for a few "fierce" men to dance behind the Material Girl. "Must know the meaning of troop style, beat boy and vogue. WIMPS AND WANNA-BE'S," the ad shouted, "NEED NOT APPLY!"

Wearing black stretch pants, a black tank-top, and a black bowler, Madonna sat on the floor of the rehearsal hall as the men paraded, ten at a time, in forty-five-minute sessions. In each case, dancers were asked to do three dances: the Cabbage Patch, Roger Rabbit, and Running Man. If an auditioner passed the first round, he was then asked to stick around for elimination rounds.

Once hired, the dancers, like all other employees of Madonna, were required to sign a confidentiality agreement, vowing not to talk to anyone about the boss without her explicit approval. This pledge of secrecy was to remain in force until after her death.

On February 16, Madonna received the devastating news that her old friend Keith Haring had died of AIDS. Haring had waged his life-and-death battle with his disease in the open and even met with youngsters to discuss the myths and the realities of AIDS. Eight months earlier, he had been a part of Madonna's headline-making Don't Bungle the Jungle concert. Two weeks prior to his death, he was still painting and sculpting.

A grief-stricken Madonna, who had known Haring before either was famous, issued a statement. "Even with his massive success," said Madonna, who had visited her friend in the hospital, "Keith still came out and said, 'I have AIDS, I'm gay.' He didn't worry if it was going to jeopardize his career, he just went with it. He gave all people courage to be strong and to stare death in the face." Erica Bell, also one of Haring's friends, said that his death left Madonna feeling "particularly vulnerable. Like her, he was strong, very disciplined, a real workhorse. If Keith could be defeated, it must have made her feel a little less invincible—for a minute at least."

By this time Madonna had known many gay men who had succumbed to AIDS. But Haring's death hit her particularly hard. Next to Martin Burgoyne, he was perhaps her closest male friend from those lean early times in New York. Haring's death also signaled the loss of another cherished link to New York's downtown art scene. Andy Warhol had died suddenly in 1987 following gall bladder surgery. Jean-Michel Basquiat, in 1989 after a heroin overdose.

Madonna's personal AIDS nightmare was far from over. Her early dance teacher and mentor Christopher Flynn, the figure most responsible for putting her on the road to stardom, was also sick with AIDS. He had moved from Michigan to Los Angeles to be closer to "my girl" as he affectionately called her. One by one they vanished, leaving Madonna to grieve—and to ponder her own mortality.

20

"My movie company is Siren Films. You
know what a Siren is, don't you? A woman
who leads men to their deaths."

"As much as people complain and criticize
me, I've touched a nerve in
them somehow."

In the Hollywood Hills house—to the right of her Picasso and
her Kahlo and the black-and-white portraits of nude women by
the world's leading photographers, Madonna sat at her desk surrounded by shiny metal filing cabinets and whirring fax machines.
This was the epicenter of Madonna Incorporated, a one-woman
empire that in five short years had earned nearly $150 million. At
the age of thirty-one, she was already the highest-grossing woman
in the entertainment business, with an average yearly income of
nearly $40 million.

Madonna had proven herself to be one of the savviest business-
women in the country, yet it was one side of her many-faceted
personality that she tried desperately to conceal from the public.
It was a topic about which she had become obsessively secretive.
"The public shouldn't think about this," she snapped at one inquiring journalist. "Part of the reason I'm successful is because I'm
a good businesswoman, but I don't think it's necessary for people
to know that." The vision of Madonna as a multimillionaire tycoon
might not be easily reconciled with the trampy image she had so
finely honed. It would not, in a word, sell.

The general public remained largely unaware of Madonna's business acumen, but inside the industry it was already well known that she rivaled the entertainment moguls of yore. Piloting her affairs through a handful of companies, most notably her wryly named Siren Films, Slutco, and Boy Toy Inc., she employed hundreds of people on both coasts. Her brain trust included the biggest names in the business: personal manager Freddy DeMann (whose commission was 15 percent of Madonna's gross earnings), business manager Bert Padell (5 percent), and lawyer Paul Schindler of New York's Grubman, Indursky & Schindler (another 5 percent).

Yet every deal bore Madonna's imprimatur. Disney Studios chief Jeffrey Katzenberg, expecting to deal with Madonna's representatives, was surprised at the degree to which she "runs the show. She is personally involved in every decision." Having grossed over a billion dollars for several conglomerates—over half that going to her record company, a subsidiary of Time Warner—few corporate bigwigs were complaining.

Pepsi was an obvious exception. After it pulled the plug on her soft-drink spots following the "Like a Prayer" brouhaha, Madonna had begun to cast about for another product to endorse—and another corporation to underwrite her upcoming tour. With rival pop songstress Paula Abdul lending her name to Reeboks, Madonna agreed to endorse a new dance shoe for Nike. Her fee: $4.25 million. When she refused to be shown actually wearing the shoes in the Nike commercial, however, the deal was nixed. Madonna's attorneys then insisted that a deal was a deal and demanded she be paid the full $4.25 million—television spot or no television spot. Eventually, they reached a settlement.

Between deals, Madonna and Beatty pursued their romance—and milked it for all its considerable publicity value. Nearly every night in Los Angeles, the couple could be seen on the town—in the front booth at Adriano's in Bel Air, at the glitzy Louis XIV restaurant and the fashionable nouvelle cuisine eatery Citrus on Melrose Avenue. Between courses, other diners would gape as Madonna sat on the taciturn Beatty's lap.

She also dragged him to hip dance spots like Club Louis. There

Madonna, usually clad in something black, lacy, and revealing, danced—sometimes with another woman—while Beatty watched from the sidelines. Then they moved on to another spot, and more space in the next morning's gossip columns. But it was never reported that, wherever Beatty and Madonna went, Sandra Bernhard often lingered in the shadows. A favorite pastime was for the two women to disappear into a rest room while Beatty waited and emerge wearing each other's clothes.

To dispel lingering doubts that her affair with Beatty was strictly a publicity stunt, Madonna devoted a significant amount of her interview for a cover story in *Vanity Fair* to the subject. "Sometimes I'm cynical and pragmatic and think it will last as long as it lasts," she told writer Kevin Sessums. "Then I have moments when I'm really romantic and I think, 'We're just perfect together.'" Beatty was less forthcoming, although he broke precedent by talking at all. His final assessment of their affair: "She's no accident."

Madonna's uncanny ability to fan the flames of controversy without getting burned was evident in the photographs that accompanied the *Vanity Fair* article. She decided to go partially nude for the first time since the unauthorized *Playboy* and *Penthouse* spreads. One of the photographs, taken by the celebrated Helmut Newton, shows Madonna dancing atop a bar with men at her feet. She wears a bowler hat, fishnet stockings, and a vest that she is pulling open to reveal her right breast. Rather than being overtly sexy, the photograph has an unsettling, androgynous quality. This was only a fleeting glimpse of the spectacle Madonna would soon be taking to her fans around the world on her Blond Ambition tour.

First, she would release a video designed to neither outrage nor provoke. Aimed at reviving the long-dormant dance craze, "Vogue" was Madonna's black-and-white paean to the glamour of Old Hollywood—a Horst photograph come to life. Madonna, backed by the slick male dancers she had handpicked for the tour, vamped, posed, and ordered her fans to "strike a pose" as she sang the praises of her idols: "Greta Garbo and Monroe, Dietrich and DiMaggio/They had style, they had grace/Rita Hayworth gave good face." MTV had only one reservation. They wanted her to cut the one shot where her breasts are clearly visible through her transparent blouse. She refused, and MTV backed down.

Propelled by the stylish video, "Vogue" shot to the top of the singles chart—the eighth No. 1 single of Madonna's career. It would wind up selling more than 2 million copies, making it the biggest-selling single of 1990.

Dick Tracy was still months away from release, but Madonna was already mapping out plans for her next theatrical film—a concert video of her world tour. Months earlier, her agents at Creative Artists had sent her an imaginative video done by a new client when he was still a student at Harvard. A pop opera version of *Wuthering Heights*, at one stage it utilized Madonna's songs to convey the character of Cathy.

Twenty-five-year-old Alec Keshishian was hunched over his home computer working on concepts for his next project when the call came. "Hi, Alec, it's Madonna," said the voice on the other end of the line. "I don't know if you've heard, but I'm about to go on a world tour, and I was wondering if you'd like to film it."

It was the proverbial opportunity of a lifetime for the handsome, long-haired director whose previous credits included music videos for Elton John and pop-rap star Bobby Brown. Within two hours, Keshishian was at the Disney Studios watching Madonna rehearse. She told him that she wanted the film to focus on the performances, with only a few glimpses behind the scenes. Days later, Keshishian, who instructed his camera crew to always wear black and say nothing so as not to be obtrusive, was aboard a Tokyo-bound plane with Madonna and her entourage.

On Friday, April 13, Madonna kicked off her Blond Ambition tour before 35,000 screaming fans in the Tokyo suburb of Chiba—a much-heralded event that also marked the official opening of Chiba's futuristic-looking outdoor Marine Stadium. Despite the months of painstaking preparation, no one had considered the simple fact that this was Japan's rainy season.

In the hours before the nighttime concert, Madonna grew panicky as storm clouds gathered. During rehearsals in Los Angeles, there had been a number of near-fatal technical glitches; in several instances, a stagehand had tripped a trapdoor at the wrong moment, nearly sending Madonna plummeting into the abyss below. That problem and others had been fixed, but there were no contingency plans for a rain-slicked stage.

Madonna's advisers pressed her to cancel the performance, and tempers grew short as Madonna weighed her options. "Stop, stop, *stop!* Mother*fucker!*" she shouted in a typical display of temper when she encountered earsplitting feedback during rehearsals. "If we can't get it to sound better than this, then I'm not doing the show. So someone better get up here *now*." When a sound man appeared to make excuses, she abruptly ended the debate. "Everyone's entitled," she said, "to *my* opinion."

Looking out at the fans' eager faces and remembering the riots that resulted when she canceled a Who's That Girl? performance in Tokyo, Madonna refused to call off the show. As if on cue, the rain began just as the hydraulic stage designed by tour artistic director Christopher Ciccone lifted the $2-million high-tech "Express Yourself" setup into view of the audience. Madonna, wearing a Barbie doll ponytail, an ivory-colored bullet bra corset with free-dangling garter belts, and a control-tower headset, tugged at her crotch and shouted, *"Genki desu ka?"*—which she then loosely translated as "How ya doin'?"—to the thundering throng.

"You didn't know you were here for an ice-skating show," she said to her blank-faced audience as she slid across the slippery stage. "Well, I'm Dorothy Hamill." The joking stopped when one of the dancers slipped and fell. "It was scary out there," Madonna said, "but we had to do it."

Certainly economic factors played a part in that decision. for the first three concerts in Tokyo alone, fans were paying around $4.5 million. They were not disappointed. Aimed at shattering sexual, social, and religious taboos, the garish 18-song, 105-minute spectacle served up heavy doses of androgyny, homosexuality, sadomasochism, and down-and-dirty heterosexual sex. The vignettes wrapped around each song were designed, said Madonna, to create an "emotional arc."

In her slowed-down "Like a Virgin" number, two topless men caressed the jutting conical "breasts" strapped to their chests while Madonna, legs splayed, thrashed about in masturbatory ecstasy atop a crimson velvet bed as music pounded and strobe lights flashed. Temporarily sated, suddenly she looked skyward and cried out, "God?"—her segue into "Like a Prayer." The boudoir scene dissolved, replaced by soaring Corinthian columns, votive candles, and an enormous cross lit with orange and purple light. As a priest watched this "confession," she partially disrobed, straddled an altar, made highly suggestive gestures with an incense burner, and smashed a crucifix to the ground.

"I was exorcising myself of the guilt of the Catholic Church over sex and masturbation," she would later explain. The shift from the bordello-red bed to church meant that "now I'm going to have to deal with male authority figures, whether it's my father or a priest or the Pope."

There were several relatively tame numbers: fish-tailed mermen flopped around at her feet in "Cherish" while Madonna plucked a harp; she bopped around like a sixties go-go dancer in "Holiday." But the act's highlights were designed to shock. At one point, Madonna pretended to sodomize one male dancer, then straddled and heaved atop another in an overt act of simulated intercourse. For her S&M-tinged "Keep It Together" number—described by one critic as "A Clockwork Orange meets the Weimar Republic"— Madonna and her dancers wore black bowler hats with chin straps, black boots, fingerless gloves, and knee pads.

Indeed, violence—or at least a parody of it—was one of the show's recurrent themes. At various moments Madonna feigned slapping, punching, shoving, and conversely, fondling her two female backup singer-dancers. "When I hurt people," she teased, "I feel better. You know what I mean?" Pretending to kick her singers, she added, "I know people say I'm ruthless, violent, and manipulative. But you love that, right? When people get in your face, when they stab you in the back, you got to show them who's boss, right? In America, people really dig a little senseless violence, what about you? Everybody feels like a little bit of pain!"

The big production number, however, revolved around the

Dick Tracy numbers from her new *I'm Breathless* album. As she sang "Sooner or Later" and "Now I'm Following You" (her duet with Beatty, with his part provided on tape), Madonna cavorted with her yellow-trench-coated dancers, then knocked them over like so many bowling pins.

Not even Dick Tracy was immune to Madonna's convention-warping ways. On stage she performed her first single from the new album, "Hanky Panky," her frank endorsement of at least a mild form of masochism ("I'll settle for the back of your hand"). The idea for the song had grown out of her earlier visit to New York's S&M Club Nine and, it was rumored, other sex clubs on both coasts. Thrusting up her derriere for a spanking, she told her audience: "You all know the pleasures of a good spanky."

By way of a further plug for *Dick Tracy*, previews were flashed on huge screens. The double entendres were less than subtle. In the middle of "Now I'm Following You," the music shifts gears and Madonna's Breathless Mahoney delivers the following line: "Dick. That's an interesting name. My bottom hurts just thinking about it." But even that paled in comparison to her monologue concerning a favorite Anglo-Saxonism: "Fuck is not a bad word! Fuck is a good word! Fuck is the reason I am here! Fuck is the reason you are here! If your mother and father did not fuck, you would not be here tonight. . . . So fuck you!"

Her requisite safe sex message may, in fact, have been under-mined by her presentation. At one point Madonna and her backup singers stood stage left, whispering among themselves and leering at the male dancers, who milled together a few yards away. "Hey, guys," Madonna called out in a parody of a New Jersey accent, "wanna fuck us? You never get to know a guy until you ask him to wear a rubber. Hey, you," she then added, singling out one of the sheepish-looking men, "don't be silly, put a rubber on your willy."

That first night, the soaked crowd roared its approval. His sister, Christopher Ciccone told the press, was "delighted" with the re-sults. "She overcame rain, a full moon, and Friday the thirteenth, and put on a terrific show." Privately, she was not so satisfied. "The only thing that kept me from slashing my wrists," she con-fessed, "was coming back to America."

Alec Keshishian, on the other hand, was extremely excited about the film he shot in Japan and eager to show it to the boss. She had battled him ferociously in Japan. "I had to fight her and continue filming despite her screaming at me to stop," he recalled. "I shot thirty hours of behind-the-scenes stuff, and I did all these interviews with all the individual dancers and Madonna, and I would capture them all in bed when they were waking up, so the interviews had an incredibly intimate tone to them, and I was able to capture a lot of other little stories that took place in Japan."

He showed Madonna the dailies and waited for her reaction. "I couldn't give a shit about the live show," she told him. "This is life! This is what I want to document." Rather than a concert documentary, they now agreed to make a feature film focusing on the backstage drama as it unfolded during the course of the entire three-month tour. For contrast, behind-the-scenes footage would be shot in black and white, the concert scenes in color. She agreed to finance the film herself, at a cost of $4 million.

Before they launched the thirty-two-date North American leg of the tour in Houston on May 4, Madonna urged Keshishian to stand his ground. "You have to know that I'm going to want to throw you out of the room," she warned him. "You have to be willing to say no." She later marveled that Keshishian "had the balls to stand up to me, which is fairly difficult . . . that requires fairly large balls."

Keshishian was given carte blanche, with one major caveat. To shield her public from the knowledge that she was a first-rate businesswoman, Madonna barred him from all her serious dealings with managers, promoters, agents, and lawyers. "Get out!" she ordered him when his cameras tried to invade a conference. "I'm having a business talk." She also barred him from a touching reunion with her ailing grandmother.

The American tour got off to an uncertain start when Warren Beatty inexplicably failed to come to the opening show at Houston's Summit arena—even though she had dispatched a private jet to fly him in from Los Angeles. Madonna postponed the show a half hour in hopes that Beatty would show. He did not.

Beatty phoned after the show to explain that he was swamped

handling a million details for the upcoming release of *Dick Tracy*. So much was riding on this film for both of them, he was sure she understood. She did not. Bitterly disappointed—and noticeably angry—she slammed down the receiver, made only a brief appearance at her own opening night party, canceled the rest of her plans for the night, and locked herself in her hotel room.

As the tour careened from city to city (she claimed she hated Chicago for no other reason than "Oprah Winfrey lives there"), Madonna threw one foot-stamping tantrum after another. During her opening show in Los Angeles, her headset kept cutting out midsong, although her background singers experienced no difficulties with their equipment. Backstage after the show, Warren Beatty ("Uncle Warren" or "Dad" to Madonna's young entourage) lurked quietly in the background as she demanded an explanation from a hapless crew member. "I'm singing a cappella and my fucking headset goes out and everybody thinks the fucking show is over with. How come it doesn't happen with the girls?"

"Because you're all on separate frequencies."

"Then put me on their fucking frequency. Mother*fuck!*"

She then aimed her invective at manager Freddy DeMann, complaining about the dour industry types who had somehow managed to monopolize the first several rows. "Somebody sits a big fat man up in front and he's been giving me dirty looks all night long, I swear to God," she said. "Freddy, you lied to me—there's nothing but industry in the first row. They totally bummed me out —they sat there with their arms folded and dirty looks on their face—I swear to God. That's so distracting and so depressing to me. . . . There were three rows of assholes and a space . . . Everyone looks like a goddamn William Morris agent!"

To diffuse the situation, DeMann and the others doused their diva with sycophantic praise. "By the way," he gushed, "you were particularly awesome tonight?"

"See how good I am"—she smiled—"when I'm pissed off?"

Beatty was not spared for long. "Don't hide back there, Warren," she commanded. "Get over here. You stink. You pussy man, what's with you? Can you believe I have to do this every night? Are you going to be nicer to me now, Warren?"

Later, celebrities flocked backstage to meet the star. Among them was actor-director Kevin Costner, whose then-current film *Dances With Wolves* made him Hollywood's hottest property. He thanked her for inviting him to the show, described her show as "neat," but said he would not be able to attend the opening night party because he had to get his children home to bed.

"Not 'neat' enough for you?" she asked. As he left, she stuck her finger down her throat as if to gag. "*Neat?* Anybody who says my show is 'neat,' " she said before Keshishian's rolling cameras, "*has* to go."

That night, she dreamed that Mikhail Gorbachev had attended her show, and the first thing she could think of was "that Warren is going to be so jealous because I got to meet him first." The next morning in her hotel room, she sat plucking the petals from a flower. "He loves me, he loves me not," she said. "He loves me, he loves me not. . . . He just wants to fuck me . . . he really cares about me. . . . He loves me, oh-oh."

The final two nights in Los Angeles, the good-natured bantering between Beatty and Madonna turned to bitter quarreling. In a fit of petulance, she revoked the free tickets that had been set aside for Beatty's buddies; mortified, he had to call his friends and withdraw his invitation.

In Toronto, Madonna scored a major coup when police threatened to close down the show and arrest the cast for public indecency. At question: the scene where she imitates masturbation to the strains of "Like a Virgin." During her regular preconcert prayer session with her dancers and backup singers, Madonna condemned "the fascist state of Toronto" and solemnly promised to "kick ass." (Normally, she would merely have asked the Almighty to grant her a great show). The authorities in Toronto backed down, falsely denying that they had ever made such threats. But not before Madonna had reaped a publicity windfall that helped spur ticket and album sales.

While Madonna was locked in a test of wills with the Toronto police, *I'm Breathless: Music from and Inspired by the Film Dick Tracy* was released to strong sales and glowing reviews. The album —although technically not the movie sound track—did include the three main Stephen Sondheim tunes from the movie, as well as "Vogue" and "Hanky Panky."

Sondheim, the Broadway composer whose ground-breaking hits included *Follies*, *Sweeney Todd*, and the Pulitzer Prize–winning *Sunday in the Park with George*, had been friendly with Beatty ever since he was hired to write the theme for *Reds*. He bridled at the suggestion that the *Dick Tracy* assignment now meant he had gone Hollywood. "I just wrote three songs for *Dick Tracy*," he said. "That's not writing for the movies. That's writing songs for movie performances, and that's the same as writing for a stage show." Yet the composer could hardly ignore what Madonna could do for him—introduce an entire generation of MTV addicts to the work of the man many regarded as the American musical theater's most talented composer.

Madonna had been taken aback when she first heard the songs during the making of the film. "What is this shit? I can't sing this. It isn't me," she said at the time. Madonna was unaccustomed to what she called the "chromatic wildness" of the tunes, one of which is written with five sharps. "They're brilliant," she allowed, "but really complex." Working with Sondheim, she managed to overcome her own fears—and the doubts of critics who heretofore had hardly viewed Madonna as a serious vocal stylist.

"*I'm Breathless* is easily the best record Madonna has made," wrote David Hinckley of the New York *Daily News*. In *USA Today*, Anne Ayers called it "sophisticated pop, as compelling as the scenes unfolding in a Broadway hit. Good show!" *Rolling Stone*'s Mark Coleman was not surprised: "She pulls it off with brass and panache, but then everybody knows Madonna doesn't mess around."

The album once again proved that Madonna was every inch a businesswoman. Part of the deal she struck with Disney's Katzenberg called for her to release *I'm Breathless* on her own Time Warner label. That alone stood to earn her a staggering $14 million. In addition, she had negotiated a percentage of the gross box office receipts, merchandise, and video sales. If the movie took off at the box office as expected, she would clear at least another $5 million. Madonna's salary may have been a paltry $1,440 per week, but she stood to collect around $20 million in *Dick Tracy* proceeds once the dust had settled.

She certainly felt she deserved it. "Disney didn't come to me and ask me to help market the movie," she told *Newsweek*. "Let's just say I'm killing twelve birds with one stone. It's a two-way street. . . . Most people don't associate me with movies. But I have a much bigger following than Warren does, and a lot of my audience isn't even aware of who he is."

Always on the lookout for another publicity gimmick, Madonna got the idea of insuring her breasts à la Marlene Dietrich's legs after she was literally glued into the low-cut gowns she wore as Breathless. "I was terrified she'd have an allergic reaction," said makeup man John Caglione. "If I'd discolored a breast or inflicted permanent damage, she could've sued me for a fortune." However, the plan was jettisoned after insurers balked at the size of the policy being considered. Madonna wanted her ample frontal assets insured for $6 million—each.

Madonna could hardly be faulted for failing to draw attention to herself and to *Dick Tracy*. In early May she made one of her rare TV talk show appearances, on the hip and highly rated "Arsenio Hall" show. That evening, the tailored white suit she wore was the only thing conservative about Madonna. In an interview riddled with deleted expletives, she hinted that host Arsenio Hall and his movie star friend Eddie Murphy were lovers. She also took another swipe at LaToya Jackson's breasts, cheered on by Hall. "Neither of us believe LaToya's breasts are real," he said. "But," he added, citing Madonna's exposed breast in *Vanity Fair*, "*yours* are real."

"If you've got it, flaunt it," she said, shrugging.

Hall wanted to know about the genesis of "Hanky Panky" and Madonna allowed that the controversial ode to the glories of spanking was drawn from her own experience. "I don't like it really hard, though. Just a little stinging and it's good."

"What does Warren Beatty have that we don't have," Hall asked coyly.

"About a billion dollars."

"Joan Collins once called Warren sexually insatiable," he continued.

"He was twenty at the time," Madonna replied in an unexpected swipe at her lover. "Aren't all twenty-year-olds insatiable?"

"Does the mention of the name Joan Collins make you jealous?"

"No. I mean," Madonna said, "have you *seen* her lately?"

Turning the tables on her prying host, Madonna slyly commented about Hall's relationship with singer Paula Abdul. At the MTV Awards, which Hall hosted, Madonna had noticed that Abdul's "tights weren't pulled up as far as they could have been. I was wondering if you had anything to do with that, Arsenio?" Then she sexily stroked his left hand and slipped a large gold ring on his finger.

Hall was offended, not only by Madonna's comments about Eddie Murphy and Paula Abdul, but by her on-air comment that his hairstyle was "tired." She told him that if he were one of her dancers, she wouldn't allow him to wear his hair like that. Hall said nothing to defend himself on camera. "It would not have been good television," he explained. Later, however, he addressed Madonna directly in the pages of *Ebony* magazine: "First, Madonna, I will never have to work for you because I have as much money as you have. Number two, I've seen your dancers and . . . I'm nothing like them. They work *for* you. I work *with* you. Point number three is that you wanted to be Black when you were little but you are not Black, so don't try to understand Blackness. It is not your place to dictate Black hair care or fashion. You have borrowed our sound but not our sensibilities, so don't make an attempt to tell me how I should look."

Before the viewing public had a chance to recover from Madonna's performance on "Arsenio," she was back on the road in Blond Ambition. Since the grueling schedule required a tremendous amount of stamina, trainer Rob Parr accompanied her to each city, getting up at six A.M. every day to scout out the day's running course—usually seven miles of varied terrain, near the hotel but away from fans, winding up with thirty flights of hotel stairs. The regimen worked. The five-foot-four-inch-tall Madonna kept her weight below 115 pounds, and her measurements at 32-23-33. Her cup size remained a C.

The nonstop demands of the tour schedule still took a toll, and by the time she reached Detroit for a reunion with her father and stepmother, Madonna was physically and emotionally drained. "This is my hometown," she told the Almighty during her preperformance prayer circle, "so I'm extra nervous, and even though it's not supposed to matter, it does matter what they think. So I ask you to give me that little extra something special to show everybody here that I did make something out of my life. Amen."

She betrayed none of her apprehension, however, when she invited her father onstage and led the crowd in a rendition of "Happy Birthday." Bowing down to him, she declared, "I worship the ground he walks on." But during the show, she had actually felt "strange" about some of the more explicit parts of her performance. She had promised her father that she would not disrobe that night, and she felt awkward enough about the "Like a Virgin" masturbation scene to rush through it. Yet even as she expressed some of these misgivings to her assistant, she pulled off her bra, gleefully shaking her breasts for Keshishian's ever-present cameras —all while her father and stepmother sipped cocktails in an adjacent room.

The tensions between Tony Ciccone and his famous daughter had never entirely abated, but they were brought together on this night by the troubles of Madonna's brother Martin. The previous day "Marti" had been released after twenty-one days at an alcohol rehabilitation center. He was supposed to attend his sister's concert, then visit her at her hotel room. Instead, he reportedly went out on a drinking binge and failed to show.

That night after the show Madonna and Christopher Ciccone waited for their brother to come to her hotel. "My brother is *crazy*," she told her bodyguards, and warned them that he might bring a crowd of rowdy friends along. In the event that happened, only Martin was to be allowed up to her floor. Martin eventually did arrive, but only after Madonna had gone to bed. He knocked on her door, but the Material Girl refused to materialize. Dejected, he left. (Martin, who worked for a time as a disc jockey in Detroit, would later try without success to sell himself as rapper "M.C. Ciccone.")

The Ciccones were, in fact, a family beset by troubles. Paula, unable to get her own show business career airborne, was said to be intensely envious of her sister's success. Half brother Mario, a full decade younger than Madonna, battled a long-standing drug problem and numerous run-ins with the law—including two assault convictions. To her credit, Madonna tried to intercede on her brother's behalf, offering to pay for counseling and treatment. Beyond the obvious pressures her fame exerted on all family members, Madonna had other reasons to feel at least partially responsible for Mario's woes. He had idolized Sean Penn, and it appeared at times as if he was emulating Penn's violent ways.

By the time the tour reached Boston, a viral infection that had plagued Madonna since Chicago now forced her to cancel the last of her three shows in nearby Worcester—only the third time in her career that she had ever called off a performance. By way of a little therapy, she, brother Christopher, and two bodyguards went shopping. At a Newberry Street perfumery named Essence, she chose a $112.50 erotic "love oil" and reached into her purse for the cash. She managed to scrape up the $112 in small bills, but she had no change. Madonna did, however, dig further into her purse and pull out a packet of Japanese condoms. "Will you take these?" she asked the storeowner. He did, then displayed them in the window of his shop with her autograph.

With the tour in full swing, Madonna had much more than just her biological family to worry about. Increasingly, she found herself mothering the dancers and support troops who surrounded her—her surreal "family" on the tour. "I've chosen people who are emotionally crippled in some way," she conceded, "and need mothering from me. They're innocent, not jaded. I wanted to give them the thrill of a lifetime." Toward that end, she took them to the finest stores in the cities they visited and lavished gifts on them.

It was not enough to ease serious tensions between her sole heterosexual dancer Oliver Crumes, then twenty-one, and the gay dancers who made up the rest of Madonna's troupe. He felt isolated and at times, threatened. "It was scary," he said, "it really was. 'Cause they wanted me. They said, 'On this tour we're gonna get him.' That's what they told me." Madonna responded by mothering Crumes the most. "I was carrying on an oedipal relationship, a mother and son," she confessed. "It wasn't fully realized. . . . He got attached." Someone leaked news of this "attachment" to the tabloid press, which then reported that Crumes had supplanted Beatty as her lover.

Madonna shrugged off the rumors, but Crumes's gay colleagues were amused. "Oliver was a toy for Madonna," said Salim "Slam" Gauwloos. "He was dumped and he gagged, and we laughed because we knew it would happen."

This dissension angered and concerned Madonna, for it threatened to sabotage the precise teamwork necessary to keep the Blond Ambition tour humming efficiently. "There was so much tension," she recalled. "I blamed myself. I felt like a mother who deserted her kids, and then comes back home to realize how much trouble they've all gotten themselves into." She ordered her gay dancers, whom she described as behaving like "queens on the rag," to "be nice" to their straight colleague.

The timing of this internecine turmoil could not have been worse for Madonna, who was about to dedicate her concert at New Jersey's Meadowlands Arena to the memory of Keith Haring. She wondered how she could walk onstage and inspire thousands to unite in the fight against AIDS when she "couldn't even inspire seven dancers." At the prayer session that night, she choked back tears at the mention of Haring's name. It marked the first time the dancers had seen Madonna cry, and it was enough, for the time being at least, to convince them to overlook their differences in the interests of the show.

One AIDS charity was less than impressed with Madonna's commitment to the cause. The House of Sweet Charity was holding a fund-raising vogueing event, and they asked Madonna to make a brief public service announcement via satellite feed from her Nassau Coliseum concert on Long Island. The Event's organizers, some of whom were among Madonna's friends from her early days in New York, had waited for an answer for nearly two months before she finally turned them down.

"She gives nothing back," said singer Johnny Dynell, her old friend from the early struggling days in New York. "These kids invented vogueing. They *gave* Madonna the number one record in the world. She was in town. All she had to do was sit down for two minutes in front of a TV camera and say two sentences."

Citing her statement in *Vanity Fair* that she wanted "to do anything I can to promote AIDS education, awareness, prevention —whatever," House of Sweet Charity organizers publicly accused Madonna of hypocrisy. "I don't want to start a war with these people," Madonna's publicist Liz Rosenberg told the *New York Post.* "I'm sure Madonna wishes them well, but it's the prerogative of the artist to choose the charities she wants to support. Madonna is involved with AMFAR [the organization headed by Elizabeth Taylor] and many AIDS-related charities."

Madonna "went through the roof" when she read the story in the newspaper, according to one of her dancers. "Why do these people hate me?" she demanded. "*Why does everyone hate me?*" She then sat down and wrote out a check for $50,000 and handed it to her dancers Jose Guitierez and Luis Camacho to give to the House of Sweet Charity. The next day, she had a change of heart and canceled the check.

Warren Beatty appreciated just how fickle Madonna could be. When he and Jack Nicholson tried to visit her dressing room backstage in New York, she refused to let them in despite Beatty's pleadings. "She told them she had a headache," said a witness to the incident, "but she was really just pissed off in general at both of them." Yet she still harbored strong feelings for Beatty. When a female crew member paid too much attention to him, says one insider, she was fired on the spot.

Following her last concert date in the New York area before taking the Blond Ambition tour to Europe, Madonna and Beatty hosted a glittering wrap party at Broadway's Palace de Beauté. She dutifully watched a drag artist named Coco lip-synch to "Vogue" and hugged him gratefully. When a busboy who had seen her show twice shyly approached her for a hug, she pulled back. "I don't hug people," she sniffed, "I don't know."

Madonna was not always so warm and nurturing toward her employees, either. When her makeup girl was sexually assaulted during the tour's New York stopover, Madonna expressed more astonishment than concern. In an extraordinary display of ego-centrism, she theorized the attack only occurred after the young woman had told strangers at a nightclub that she worked for Ma-donna.

She was even less generous in her dealings with those who were not part of her retinue. Throughout the tour, she went under the alias Kit Moresby, after the heroine of *The Sheltering Sky*. When-ever Madonna entered or exited a hotel, she did nothing to dis-courage her bodyguards from elbowing bystanders out of the way, which they did with alacrity. In each city on the tour, hotel em-ployees were forbidden to speak her name, talk to or even look directly at her. Autographs or even pleasantries were verboten. Each hotel kitchen was given a special vegetarian menu to pre-pare, and she frequently complained when hotel kitchens took more than fifteen minutes to deliver it to her room.

Madonna's attempts at exerting control over her environment were exhaustive. They were not, however, completely effective. A long-standing foe of hard drugs she was nonetheless incapable of enforcing total abstinence among others on the tour. On the road, drug use was rampant—up to and including cocaine and heroin. For her part, she confined her substance intake to champagne, cigarettes, and the occasional sleeping pill.

If Madonna increasingly viewed herself as a maternal figure in the lives of her troupe, that contrasted sharply with her public image. To some, such as Boston University president and onetime gubernatorial candidate John R. Silber, she was nothing less than a symbol of evil. "Nobody on God's green earth has the right to do whatever he or she pleases," he said at a university fund-raiser. "Madonna has no more right to set this example for our kids than Adolf Hitler did or than Saddam Hussein does."

Madonna was unshaken. "In our society," she observed, "a woman who is overtly sexual is considered a venomous bitch, or someone to be feared." Being feared, she decided, wasn't "all that bad."

Given the comparatively laissez-faire attitude of most Europeans when it comes to matters of sex, Madonna's sojourn across the

Atlantic provided a welcome respite from criticism. She delighted in showing her "children" the glories of London and Paris and even took them on a sky's-the-limit shopping spree at Chanel.

During her stopover in Paris, Madonna was the guest of honor at a glittering dinner thrown by *Vogue*. The dining room was so packed that in order to get to her seat at the head table, she hiked up her Gaultier gown, climbed on top of the table, and in her spiked heels, walked across it. "I wish," sighed none other than Marilyn Monroe's former lover Yves Montand, "I had known her thirty years ago." He sent Madonna a dozen roses.

The tour's Paris stop also offered Christopher Ciccone an opportunity to exhibit his own artwork—primarily large, boldly colored religious paintings. At the opening, Madonna held court. When asked for her autograph, she would snap, "Give me a break! I'm tired of giving my autograph!" or "Oh, will you cut it out with the camera; I don't want my picture taken again!" According to one guest, Madonna "wasn't gracious at all."

That night, the party moved to a nightclub called Scheherezade. Madonna insisted that only men be invited. "There was Madonna with a club full of boys, and the designer Gaultier with all his gay boys," says an associate of Gaultier's. "Madonna likes to think she's the most desired woman in the world. . . . I always liked her because she is strong. The day I met her I realized she *was* strong, but she was also mean."

Controversy soon reared its head, however, when she arrived at Rome Airport. A week earlier, Italy's Catholic establishment had condemned Madonna's show as blasphemous and demanded that her concerts in Rome and Turin be canceled.

Stepping off the plane wearing a severe black suit and pearls, Madonna read a statement to the jostling press: "If you are sure I am a sinner, let whoever is without sin cast the first stone. I ask you, fair-minded men and women of the Catholic Church—come and see my show and judge it for yourselves. My show is not a conventional rock concert but a theatrical presentation of my music, and like the theater, it poses questions, provokes thought, and takes you on an emotional journey."

Madonna believed that the Pope was behind efforts to ban her show. "The Vatican was putting out all this propaganda about how blasphemous my show was," she observed, "and I was amazed—completely enraged. How dare they judge it without seeing it?" The controversy followed her through Italy; ultimately she was forced to cancel two concerts.

Intent on ending Blond Ambition with a bang, Madonna had negotiated behind closed doors with Home Box Office to broadcast her final concert in Nice, France, live to the United States. The corporate hookup was already in place: HBO, like Warner Records, was a subsidiary of Time Warner. HBO paid Madonna $1 million for rights to broadcast the one live performance.

Using sixteen cameras—some shooting from helicopters—to capture the outdoor spectacle, HBO cable-cast Madonna into millions of American homes. It would be the most-watched nonsporting event in cable TV history. Standing on the stage in her ponytail and *bustier*, Madonna ran over to her dancers and pretended to slap them around. It was a scene she had repeated dozens of times on the tour, but tonight the line she was to deliver had a special resonance. "I," she shouted as the throng roared, "am the boss around here!"

21

"It's a great feeling to be powerful. I've been striving for it all my life. I think that's just the quest of every human being: *power.*"

"Warren *is* a pussy. . . . He's a *wimp.*"

More than any other entertainer, Madonna ruled the summer of 1990. She dominated the video and record charts (by now her albums had sold a total of 48 million copies), had just been seen by more than 2 million people in ten countries during a headline-grabbing world tour, and was now starring in the most ballyhooed feature film of the season. One survey for the movie industry showed that an amazing 100 percent of moviegoers were aware of *Dick Tracy* prior to its opening. Coinciding with a $10-million advertising blitz and the marketing of everything from coffee mugs and T-shirts to expensive silk pajamas, the movie and/ or its stars were splashed across the covers of *Newsweek*, *People*, *Entertainment Weekly*, and *Rolling Stone*—to name a few.

For all the hoopla, one person never saw the film in its entirety: Madonna. She was so upset about the way in which her big musical numbers were hacked up in the editing process, she could not bring herself to sit through an entire screening.

Did the film live up to its exquisitely orchestrated hype? Shot in ravishing primary colors by Vittorio Storaro against Dick Sylbert's striking production design, *Dick Tracy* succeeded in bringing the comic book hero and his supporting cast of grotesques—Pruneface, Mumbles, Flattop, Big Boy Caprice—vividly to life. *Newsweek* heralded the arrival of "Tracymania," and critic David Ansen raved: "*Dick Tracy* is a class act: simple, stylish, sophisticated, sweet. This comic strip come to life is not like any other movie Warren Beatty has made, and yet his personality is stamped on every carefully considered frame." As for Madonna: "Quivering with lust, double entendres, and bad intentions, Madonna is smashingly unsubtle as the *femme fatale*."

Dick Tracy was Madonna's first big screen success since her debut in *Desperately Seeking Susan* and Beatty's first outing as a director since *Reds*. They were more visible than ever as a couple, but the public was beginning to wonder if their romance had been nothing more than a publicity scam. "Oh, she definitely screwed his brains out," said a member of Madonna's inner circle. "Of that I am absolutely certain. But that doesn't mean that they were ever in love. Madonna doesn't want *maturity* in a man. She likes them young. That whole time, Madonna carried a torch for Sean."

It had become clear to both principals by midsummer that the Madonna-Beatty pairing had served its purpose. *Dick Tracy* was a hit. Madonna's Blond Ambition tour had benefited from all the publicity generated by the romance. Neither had even feigned fidelity, so it came as no surprise that ego, not jealousy, would sever the final thread that held them together.

Madonna discovered in mid-July that Beatty had told *Newsweek* editors he would give them full cooperation only if he appeared on the magazine's cover alone. *Newsweek* editor in chief Rick Smith telephoned Disney Studios president Jeffrey Katzenberg and made it clear that without Madonna there would be no *Dick Tracy* cover story. Disney provided a still from the picture.

In a heated telephone exchange, Madonna blasted Beatty for his lack of loyalty and his dalliances with other women. Weeks from turning thirty-two, Madonna now seemed a little old for Beatty; he was already involved with an aspiring actress who had just turned twenty-two.

Beatty now also seemed a little too old for her. At a birthday party thrown for her in Malibu, Madonna puffed on a Marlboro Light and scanned the beach guests until she came upon a shirtless young man talking to her brother Mario. She walked over and put her cigarette out on his back. Mario Ciccone then introduced her to twenty-seven-year-old Tony Ward—his "birthday present" to his big sister.

Tony Ward had actually been one of the mermen who splashed around in Madonna's "Cherish" video, but back then she had not given him so much as a second glance. The night of the party, however, she took Ward home.

Two weeks later, Madonna took Ward to another birthday party in Malibu, this time for photographer Herb Ritts. She had ordered him to wear jeans only, but he insisted on wearing a black leather vest over his bare chest. Dressed head to toe in black—including black boots—Madonna sat on Ward's lap all evening while he remained mute. She ordered him in front of Ritts's guests to shave off his mustache. He obeyed.

By Labor Day, Beatty had heard about Madonna's new boyfriend. Stretching credulity, he denied chasing other women during their affair and demanded that Madonna date him exclusively. Madonna did what she had always done when faced with an ultimatum. She told Beatty, said a friend, "to go to hell."

At five feet seven inches and 170 pounds, the muscular, darkly handsome Ward nonetheless bore a passing resemblance to Sean Penn. "Madonna was essentially holding casting calls for a boyfriend," said Erica Bell, "and this is the guy she chose. Physically, he was *perfect* for her. If you had a computer dating service, and you fed all her preferences into the computer, Tony Ward is what would come out. In terms of looks, he was everything she likes in a man."

And everything, apparently, that some gay men look for in a man. Ward, who also worked under the names Anthony Borden Ward and Nick Neal, was a favorite nude pinup of the homosexual community. In a 1985 issue of the Los Angeles–based gay magazine *In Touch for Men*, Ward was shown on the cover and in a six-page layout wearing nothing but an ankle bracelet. Herb Ritts, who had cast him in the "Cherish" video, also shot Ward nude for his 1989 book *Men and Women*. At about the same time he met Madonna, Ward also appeared in a series of full-page frontal nude shots for a book by photographer Greg Gorman.

Madonna did not mind when she learned of Ward's past as a gay model. As someone who had been pilloried in the press for posing nude early in her own career, she sympathized with him. The fact that gay men admired Ward's body, and that he was not shy about exposing himself for this purpose, simply added to his allure.

She also discovered that Ward, who was now represented by the respectable Ice Modeling Agency, had a fondness for leather and for cross-dressing. For fun, Madonna was soon dressing her new lover in stockings, bra, panties, high heels, and dangling jewelry, then making him up with red lipstick, eye shadow, face powder, and beauty spot to look like her. Then she would go out on the town with her new "girlfriend." There were also trips to sex toy shops; Ward expressed a particular fondness for leather chaps and shiny black jackboots. "As far as 'Herself' is concerned," Erica Bell said, "the kinkier the better."

Madonna, who by now insisted that the men she slept with wore condoms, did not trouble herself with doubts concerning Ward's sexual history. He had frequented gay bars for years—often in the company of another man and a woman—but so had Madonna, and many of her closest friends. He also refused to be tested for AIDS—preferring to be spared the truth if indeed he had contracted the incurable disease.

Ward's heterosexual past was more nettlesome. He had neglected to inform Madonna in their first weeks together that he was still engaged to twenty-three-year-old fashion designer Jayme Harris. Ward and Harris had met a year earlier at a bar called Club Rubber and had moved in together a week later. In April of 1990, Harris reportedly told Ward she was pregnant, and the two celebrated by getting engaged.

Incredibly, Ward took his fiancée to a Santa Monica sex store where each had a nipple pierced and gold "engagement" rings inserted. Even after Harris miscarried in mid-May, the couple remained together, living out what she called his "love slave" fantasy in which he did all the household chores and catered to her sexual demands. One of Ward's recurrent fantasies even before he met her was to sleep with Madonna, then have her look on as he made love to Harris.

Madonna had fantasies of her own. She was dissatisfied with the way her lips showed up on-screen in *Dick Tracy*. Despite layers of generously applied scarlet lipstick, Madonna's naturally thin lips paled in comparison to the bee-stung pucker of Kim Basinger, the femme fatale in the previous year's summer comic-book blockbuster *Batman*. Neither was Madonna ever completely satisfied with the way photographs of her impersonating Marilyn Monroe turned out. There, too, she felt deficient in the mouth department.

A number of actresses had already turned to collagen implants for more voluptuous lips. *Pretty Woman*'s Julia Roberts was rumored to be one of those, and Barbara Hershey, Bette Midler's pal in *Beaches*, confessed to having her lips surgically augmented. In early September, Madonna went to one of Beverly Hills' leading plastic surgeons for the collagen injections, which took ten minutes and cost her $500. Since the collagen is absorbed into the body, causing the tissue to deflate, she was told to come in every four months for refills.

Madonna showed off her new lips in an MTV spot urging people to register and vote in the 1990 elections. Yet even her public service announcements could be counted on to ruffle feathers. Flanked by two of her male dancers, wearing skimpy red lingerie and draped in the American flag, Madonna urged American voters to do their duty and show up at the polls or risk a "spanking."

The spot infuriated some who felt her winking, naughty-stripper approach with mild S&M overtones was inappropriate, particularly since it was aimed at getting younger viewers to register. Ironically, after the dust had settled, it appeared that Madonna herself deserved to be sent to the woodshed. Hers may have been the most-talked-about public service ad in recent memory, but that November Madonna herself ignored her own advice and did not even bother to vote.

That month Madonna also caused a commotion at the internationally televised MTV Awards show at the Universal Amphitheater in Los Angeles. The evening's grand finale was a live performance of the year's No. 1 hit, "Vogue." But instead of conveying the mannequins-come-to-life feel of her hit video, Madonna served up something unexpected—an elaborate recreation of an eighteenth-century French court, with Madonna and her dancers outfitted in satins, powdered wigs, and buckled shoes.

Those who expected Madonna to once again push the boundaries of taste were not disappointed. At one point, she lifted up the hoop skirt of her elegant Madame de Pompadour costume and invited a male dancer to explore underneath. Later, she pressed another dancer's nose into her cleavage. She was then carried off on a sedan chair, her face coyly hidden behind a fan.

Her naughty image very much intact, Madonna flew to New York with Ward in tow and showed off her new boyfriend at a screening of Martin Scorsese's *Goodfellas* at the Museum of Modern Art. She introduced him to everyone as "Nick Neal." He stayed at her Central Park West apartment, and the following morning they were photographed jogging together in Central Park. The message she was sending to Warren Beatty was unmistakable. For the first time since their affair began fifteen months earlier, "Buzzbomb" was announcing to the world that the "Old Man" had been officially replaced.

On September 24, *Forbes* magazine hit the newsstand with its annual issue listing the world's highest-paid entertainers. Billed as "America's Smartest Businesswoman," Madonna was splashed across the cover in her pink satin Material Girl outfit with the fur trim and dollar-sign buttons. The story inside inverted a famous line from the then-popular film *Working Girl*, praising Madonna for having "a brain for sin and a bod for business." The magazine conservatively estimated her 1989 income at $39 million, making her that year's highest-paid female entertainer.

Madonna was enraged by the *Forbes* article. She had refused to cooperate with the magazine and had ordered her employees and friends to stonewall the venerable publication. One insider who did talk to the writers of the piece called back and begged the magazine not to use his name. "I could get into a lot of trouble," he said. "I have a family."

Forbes made much of the fact that, unlike most of those on its annual highest-paid list, Madonna had staying power. She had remained near the top for five years because, the magazine speculated, she "restyled" herself every year. The magazine provided its own proof of that: the Madonna issue was one of the highest-selling issues in *Forbes*'s history.

Beyond her talent and intuition, a prime element in Madonna's success as a businesswoman was her obsessive self-discipline. Every project was mapped out step by step, months in advance. A compulsive organizer and list-maker, every night before she went to bed Madonna wrote down the things that had to be accomplished the next day—breaking the day into thirty-minute increments that allowed no time for relaxation. "I never take any time off," she said, "if I can help it."

Throughout the fall of 1990, Madonna feverishly pursued the film projects that had been held in abeyance during work on *Dick Tracy* and the Blond Ambition tour. By way of research on Mexican artist Frida Kahlo, whose life story she now wanted to bring to the screen, she donned combat boots and a military coat to catch a Mexican art exhibit with brother Christopher at the Metropolitan Museum. She also met with ninety-six-year-old Martha Graham and persuaded the dance legend to sell her the movie rights to her memoirs for a reported $100,000 (Graham died six months later).

As she had with her dancers during her world tour, Madonna now enjoyed introducing Tony Ward to la dolce vita. Nowhere did she feel more appreciated than in Paris, where she was worshiped by the world of haute couture as a trend-setting fashion deity. Chanel's Karl Lagerfeld proclaimed Madonna to be "the single greatest fashion influence in the world. We all watch her to see what she will do next." *Vogue* editor Andre Leon Talley concurred: "I think Madonna is a goddess of fashion, especially high fashion in Paris. The force of her fantasy is accessible to everyone from eighteen to eighty."

In Paris, Madonna made a point of showing up at Jean-Paul

Gaultier's show to lend support to her favorite designer. As *Glamour* magazine trumpeted her on its cover as its Woman of the Year and *Ladies' Home Journal* listed her alongside First Lady Barbara Bush and Supreme Court justice Sandra Day O'Connor as one of America's most powerful women, Madonna sat in the front row at Gaultier's show waiting for Tony Ward to model a suit. When her boyfriend walked down the runway, she lifted up her dress to show Ward—and other male and female models parading down the runway—that she was not wearing underwear. Madonna plunked down more than $35,000 for several outfits, then put on an R-rated fashion show of her own for Tony Ward and a few friends that night in her hotel room.

The Parisian escapade was actually more of a busman's holiday for Madonna. Record producer Shep Pettibone had already mixed a "greatest hits" package for Madonna using QSound, a revolutionary advance in recording technology that effectively turned ordinary stereo speakers into a sort of 3-D sound system. Madonna, excited about the process—hers was to be the very first QSound album released—had also recorded two new songs for the album. The first to be released, which she cowrote with Lenny Kravitz, was titled "Justify My Love." For the album title, Madonna drew on her recent battles with the Vatican for inspiration. It would be called, simply, *The Immaculate Collection*.

Madonna, as always, was planning far ahead. With so much riding on the upcoming release of *Truth or Dare*, the feature-length documentary of the Blond Ambition tour, it was obvious she would need another smash video not only to drive album sales but to enable her to maintain career momentum. Every time she had gone too far, the payoff was spectacular: witness the enormous success of *Like a Prayer* in the wake of the Pepsi imbroglio.

What was left to excite and exasperate the public? Madonna had recently been asked by a reporter if MTV had ever banned one of her videos, and she felt slightly embarrassed at having to say no. Not only were all of her videos aired, but they aired at all times of the day and night. Even Madonna's archrival Cher had one video restricted to late-night viewing because of the flamboyant star's risqué costume.

Keeping these facts in mind, Madonna hired director Jean-Baptiste Mondino to bring his erotic touch to the "Justify My Love" video. "It was the title that created the images," said Mondino, who listened to the record until "the saturation point" before deciding what approach to take. "When you listen to it, you hear an incredible sensuality in it. It exudes very adult fantasies."

Still in Paris, Madonna, Ward, Mondino, and thirty others occupied an entire floor of the exclusive Royal Monceau hotel for two weeks. Using the corridors and rooms as their set, they shot the five-minute black-and white vignette entirely on the premises. "Madonna was fantastic," Mondino said. "She did what she came to do. She and her partner [Ward] kissed, and they weren't fake kisses."

The video begins with Madonna lugging a briefcase down a hotel corridor, then dissolves into fantasies that include bisexuality, transvestism, voyeurism, mild sadomasochism, and of course, nudity. "It's the interior of a human being's mind," Madonna explained. "These fantasies and thoughts exist in every person."

While familiar storm clouds gathered on the horizon, Madonna received word that Christopher Flynn had died of AIDS in Los Angeles on October 27. Flynn was sixty and had been battling the disease for three years, but news of his death still came as a blow to Madonna.

Flynn had been a pivotal figure in her life. Her former ballet teacher back in Michigan was the first adult to take a serious interest in her when she was only fourteen years old, the first to introduce her to the worlds of art and theater, dance and nightlife, the first to tell her she was beautiful, and special. Madonna owed everything to Flynn, and she had described him as "my mentor, my father, my imaginative lover, my brother, everything, because he understood me." Yet when he had tried to see her at a party in Los Angeles only a few months earlier, he could not get past the phalanx of bodyguards and hangers-on that separated her from her adoring public.

So many of Madonna's friends in the arts had succumbed to

AIDS that it sometimes seemed as if life was little more than a succession of openings and funerals. Flynn's death left Madonna shaken, but when friends in Los Angeles put together a memorial service for him on December 2, once again Madonna did not show. Perhaps she was afraid her presence might cause a riot, or that the experience might prove too emotionally taxing. Still, Madonna's decision not to attend any of her friends' memorial services left other friends scratching their heads. "It was amazing to me that she didn't go to the service for Martin [Burgoyne]," one said. "But when she didn't attend Christopher Flynn's either, I got the impression she just didn't want to be bothered."

At the end of November, Madonna was once again the calm eye of a media hurricane. MTV had plans for a forty-eight-hour "Madonnathon" beginning December 1, to be kicked off with the world premier of the "Justify My Love" video. But after getting its first look at the video on November 26, MTV canceled its plans to air it. "We respect her work as an artist," read a statement explaining MTV's decision, "and we think she makes great videos. This one is not for us." Plans went ahead for the remainder of the Madonnathon, however, which featured interviews, concert footage, and film clips as well as videos representing each phase of her career.

Madonna contacted MTV executives and asked if there was a specific scene that could be cut to meet their standards. No, they objected to the "whole tone" of the video; there was nothing that could be done to earn MTV's stamp of approval.

Was Madonna genuinely surprised by MTV's ban? How could she have been? Nudity had never been seen on MTV, much less the kind of kinky fare served up hot in "Justify My Love." Or was Madonna, surrounded by her largely gay entourage and exposed to the worlds of bisexuality and sadomasochism, so shielded from the world at large that she no longer grasped what was and was not considered permissible? On the contrary. Madonna knew precisely what she was doing, insiders said. By producing a video that would be banned even by MTV, she launched a public debate over censorship that once again kept her in the limelight.

Accordingly, Madonna's first reaction was to express dismay over the MTV ban. "Why is it that people are willing to go to a movie and watch someone get blown to bits for no reason," she asked, "and nobody wants to see two girls kissing or two men snuggling? I think the video is romantic and loving and has humor in it." As an artist whose career hinged on her exposure through music videos, however, she stopped well short of declaring war. "MTV has been good to me," she allowed, "and they know their audience. If it's too strong for them, I understand that."

For another singer, having MTV refuse to air her video would have proved catastrophic. In Madonna's case, it meant that she had another blockbuster on her hands. Rushed onto the market as the first-ever five-minute-long video "single," "Justify My Love" sold a hefty 250,000 copies at $9.95 apiece—a $2.5 million windfall. The song itself would eventually go to No. 1.

MTV was not the only organization that found "Justify My Love" objectionable. The Simon Wiesenthal Center charged that the remix of "Justify My Love," titled "The Beast Within," contained blatantly anti-Semitic lyrics—an allegation that Madonna found baffling and that her representatives dismissed out of hand. The furor reached its apex on the night of December 3, 1990, when Madonna appeared on the ABC news program "Nightline" to defend herself and her work in a wide-ranging interview with Forrest Sawyer. Wearing a high-collared suit and her platinum hair pulled back in a severe-looking bun, Madonna, on satellite feed from Los Angeles, looked every inch the no-nonsense career woman.

The uniform did not disguise the fact that Madonna was terrified about her appearance on a hard news program, and that the terror made her, in the words of *New York Times* writer Caryn James, "shockingly inarticulate." To be sure, Madonna's comments were liberally sprinkled with enough "you know"'s, "okay?"'s and "I mean"'s to make a high school English teacher cringe. Yet grammar aside, she did manage to get her points across.

After ABC aired "Justify My Love" in its entirety, Sawyer waded into the fray. Had Madonna expected to get nudity past the MTV standards board? Pointing out that her breasts were visible through the blouse she wore in her "Vogue" video, Madonna told Sawyer she thought MTV would allow her to again "bend the rules."

Madonna: "I guess half of me thought that I was going to get away with it . . . and the other half thought, 'Well, with . . . the conservatism that is sort of sweeping over the nation . . . there was going to be a problem.' "

Sawyer: "But in the end you're going to wind up making even more money than you would have."

Madonna: "Yeah, so lucky me."

She went on to tell the "Nightline" audience that she drew her line of what is permissible on television at "violence and humiliation and degradation." She then sarcastically suggested that MTV should schedule a "violence hour and a degradation to women hour" rather than air such videos as they do twenty-four hours a day.

Sawyer then asked if feminists weren't justifiably riled by her "Express Yourself" video in which she appeared in chains, crawling under a table.

"I have chained myself," she replied. "There wasn't a man that put that chain on me. I did it myself. I was chained to my desires. I crawled under my own table, you know? There wasn't a man standing there making me do it. I do everything of my own volition. I'm in charge."

Sawyer pressed the feminists' case, dredging up her previous Boy Toy and Material Girl incarnations, but Madonna stood firm. "I may be dressing like the traditional bimbo, whatever, but I'm in charge," she insisted. "And isn't that what feminism is all about, you know, equality for men and women? And aren't I in charge of my life, doing the things I want to do?"

That a ten-year-old watching "Justify My Love" might walk away confused about sex did not seem to bother Madonna at all. "Good," she shot back. "Then let them get confused and let them go ask their parents about it."

Her obvious nervousness aside, Madonna declared herself to be the cynosure of feminism in the nineties—the woman who chooses to be sexy, so long as that choice is solely hers. "The feminist message of 'Justify My Love,' " wrote Caryn James in *The*

New York Times, "is that Madonna can control a career as shrewdly as any man." Millions had tuned in to hear that message. Ratings for "Nightline" were the second highest in the program's decade-long history, surpassed only by the appearance of Jim and Tammy Faye Bakker at the height of their televangelist scandal.

Three days later, Madonna was brought down to earth by more mundane matters: a court instructed her to trim the shrubbery on her Hollywood Hills property. Her neighbor, Donald Robinson, had sued Madonna for $1 million claiming that she had allowed a pine tree and hedge on her property to grow so that they obstructed his view.

Madonna refused even to meet with Robinson and in a move that may have reflected her growing paranoia, charged in turn that her privacy had been violated by neighbors spying on her through the trees. The aptly named Superior Court judge Sally Disco found no evidence of this and dismissed Madonna's countersuit. She did not award Robinson $1 million, but Judge Disco did order Madonna to do the one thing no one else had been able to make her do: cut back—her shrubbery.

If she had appeared even more anxious than usual in mid-December, there may have been medical reasons. On December 10, Ward drove Madonna to Cedars-Sinai Medical Center in Los Angeles for tests. Reportedly, obstetrician Randy Harris, a specialist in high-risk pregnancies, informed her that she was pregnant. Ward and Madonna were jubilant, but their hopes were soon dashed when Dr. Harris informed them there were potentially life-threatening complications. Four days later, she underwent a dilation and curettage (D&C) that ended the pregnancy.

Asked if Madonna had suffered a miscarriage (as opposed to an abortion), her publicist Liz Rosenberg issued a denial. Yet to confirm that Madonna was pregnant, a reporter masquerading as Dr. Harris's nurse phoned Madonna under the pretext of discussing the test results. "Yeah, I knew I was pregnant," Madonna told the "nurse," adding that her breasts had been "swollen" and "tender" and she "knew what that meant."

Becoming a mother was still part of Madonna's life plan. But a long-term relationship with a man came first. "A father who's around—that's essential," she said. "I'm not interested in raising an emotional cripple."

Madonna celebrated New Year's Eve as best she could by throwing a party for forty of her closest friends. The setting was her eight-room Manhattan apartment, complete with its own steam shower, state-of-the-art gym, and streamlined kitchen. After gobbling up one adjacent apartment, Madonna had offered to buy out her remaining elderly neighbors so that she could own the entire floor. No way, said the holdout couple. They also complained that Madonna was a noisy neighbor who played loud rock until four in the morning.

As 1990 drew to a close, partygoers mingled amidst Madonna's carefully chosen art deco furnishings and paintings by Picasso, Dalí, Léger, and Tamara de Lempicka. A palmist had been hired to entertain, and after some prodding by the host she reluctantly agreed to read Madonna's palm.

The fortune-teller informed Madonna that she had been heartsick once and would be again, that her current affair with Tony Ward was fleeting, that she would be a washout in her career, and that she would never have children. Madonna responded by getting herself drunk on martinis. Then she went into the bathroom and threw up before passing out on the floor. She was in bed when she came to the next morning. The palm reader had made Madonna believe her predictions. "And I kept thinking," said Madonna, "what a way to start the New Year."

22

"I wish I had slept with [Marlene Dietrich]. She had a very masculine thing about her, but she maintained a sexual allure."

What a way to start the New Year, indeed. While the "Justify My Love" debate raged on, the notoriously press-shy Woody Allen offered Madonna a small part playing a circus acrobat in his next film, *Shadows and Fog*. She accepted, and this time on the set, the atmosphere was very different. Increasingly isolated by her fame, she could no longer banter with the crew. "I can feel all the grips and electricians looking at me," she said. "I'm painfully aware of it. They don't see me as an actress, they see me as an icon, and it makes me extremely exhausted."

It did not help that Allen offered little guidance on the set. Initially Madonna found the experience of working with him "unnerving," until she realized that his approach was to let each actor be himself and bring his own unique qualities to the role. "I was uncomfortable at first," she conceded. "There was not a lot of guidance, and that kind of freedom is daunting. But Woody casts you perfectly. He gets people to exude what they already exude."

Newsday would later report that Allen cut Madonna's part because of a shoddy performance—a story Allen vehemently denied.

"It is a total fabrication," he said. "Not a frame of hers has been cut nor has that ever been contemplated. She's first-rate in the film."

This was high praise from the reclusive master of the medium, but little compensation for the personal anguish Madonna would experience not long after Valentine's Day. On February 18, a tabloid reported that Tony Ward had sneaked off behind Madonna's back to secretly marry another woman.

Ward had been dating fashion stylist Amalia Papadimos for a year when Madonna put her cigarette out on his back at her thirty-second birthday party. Unbeknownst to his pregnant fiancée, Jayme Harris, Ward had been seeing Papadimos whenever he flew to New York on modeling assignments. Rather than have Papadimos, an Australian citizen of Greek origin, visit him in Los Angeles where she might encounter Madonna, Ward had arranged for the couple to rendezvous in Las Vegas for a few days of fun. Their tryst quickly mushroomed into matrimony.

Ward and Papadimos had become man and wife at the Las Vegas Wedding Gardens on August 21—just five days after he began his affair with Madonna. He then sent Papadimos back to New York while he returned to Los Angeles, presumably to tie up a few loose ends. But once Madonna welcomed him home from his "business trip," Ward realized he had made "a hideous mistake" in marrying Papadimos. He could hide his bride from Madonna, but hiding his affair with Madonna from Papadimos was not so easy. Ward assured her that his relationship with the world's most famous woman was purely platonic, but as the months dragged on, it became obvious to even the gullible Papadimos that Ward and Madonna were locked in a passionate affair.

"I married him," Papadimos said, "because I loved him. It's as simple as that—and I didn't do it to get a green card to be able to stay and work in America. What you've got to remember is that I had been going out with Tony for twelve months, and we were very much in love. I even planned to take him back to Australia on our honeymoon and introduce him to my parents." That never happened.

The tabloid story revealing Ward's marriage promised that once Madonna read of Ward's marriage she would "blow her little blonde top!" And she did. It seemed utterly incomprehensible to her that, practically from the moment they met, Ward had deceived her so completely. On the few occasions when she had mentioned marriage to Ward, he had abruptly changed the subject. Now she understood why. Ward's frantic calls to Madonna went unanswered, As a friend once observed, "cross her, and you're dead." Madonna's model boyfriend, unable to justify his love for another woman, now seemed a thing of the past.

It was hard to put Sean Penn in the past. Madonna still teared up whenever his name was mentioned, and to a *Vanity Fair* reporter she said that she liked "folding Sean's underwear, I like mating socks. You know what I love? I love taking the lint out of the lint screen." When she went to see *State of Grace*, in which Penn starred with his new girlfriend Robin Wright, Madonna admitted that she felt "territorial" during the love scenes. "It's like, 'Hands off, bitch! I was married to him!' "

By this time, Wright was expecting Penn's child. Yet there were signs that he was feeling a bit territorial about the ex–Mrs. Penn, as well. After a tribute to Robert De Niro by New York's Museum of the Moving Image, Penn joined Jeremy Irons, Matt Dillon, Penny Marshall, Liza Minnelli, and other celebrities at a party in De Niro's honor at the Tribeca Grill. John F. Kennedy, Jr., was also there, and when he spotted Penn chatting with a friend, Kennedy extended his hand and introduced himself.

"I know who you are," Penn replied stonily. "You owe me an apology." Kennedy said nothing and walked away. Apparently, Penn was still seething over reports linking Kennedy to Madonna during their marriage. The next morning, Kennedy received a funeral wreath of white roses with a black-and-gold ribbon bearing the inscription "My Deepest Sympathy." The card read simply, "Johnny, I heard about last night." It was signed, "M."

The Penn-Kennedy incident coincided with yet another *Vanity Fair* Madonna cover story. Again, Madonna conjured up the ghost of Kennedy's father's legendary paramour. To illustrate a story titled "The Misfit," Madonna struck two nude poses as part of her "Homage to Norma Jean" pinup portfolio.

· · ·

With Blond Ambition, "Justify My Love," and Tony Ward behind her, Madonna could again focus on her film career. The week of her traumatic breakup with Ward, she presented Andrew Lloyd Webber with an award at a star-filled Los Angeles Music Center gala in the composer's honor. Now that her main competition for the lead in *Evita*, Meryl Streep, was out of the picture, Madonna once again had the inside track. By flattering Lloyd Webber with her presence, she hoped to hold on to that advantage.

While freshening her makeup in the ladies' room that night, Madonna remarked, "Too bad Andy got married again already. I could've been a contender for wife number three."

"You're not missing anything," said the woman standing behind her. "You can do better." It was then that Madonna recognized the woman, Lloyd Webber's recently divorced second wife and *Phantom of the Opera* star Sarah Brightman.

Barbra Streisand, out of the running herself, was actually reported to have backed Brightman for the role of Evita, praising her formidable skills as a singer. Madonna hardly felt threatened; Brightman had never acted in films before and was a box office cipher. Yet Streisand's enthusiasm for the British stage star hardly endeared her to Madonna, who phoned Streisand and told her in no uncertain terms to "butt out."

In the eyes of the Hollywood establishment, Madonna remained a largely unproven commodity as an actress. *Dick Tracy* had certainly helped, but even that victory was undermined when Disney's Jeffrey Katzenberg set Hollywood abuzz with his famous "confidential" memo decrying spiraling costs within the industry. In the leaked document, which found its way into *The New York Times*, Katzenberg wondered if all the time, energy, and money invested in making and promoting *Dick Tracy* was actually worth it in the end.

Madonna had something to prove when she agreed to perform Stephen Sondheim's Oscar-nominated "Sooner or Later (I Always Get My Man)" at the Academy Awards ceremony March 25. But first she faced the classic movie star dilemma: who was famous enough to escort her to the show? The field quickly narrowed down to the one star whose megawattage matched her own: Michael Jackson.

A week beforehand, Madonna and Jackson met at a trendy Los Angeles restaurant called The Ivy to plan their impending Big Date. Jackson wore his trademark dark glasses, and the moment they sat down at their table, Madonna leaned over, yanked off the glasses, and nonchalantly tossed them across the room. "You're with me now," she said. "I want to see your eyes." When Jackson kept eyeing her cleavage, Madonna grabbed his hand, placed it on her breast, and held it there for several seconds.

Madonna and Jackson had been fascinated by each other for some time. They were, after all, pop icons nonpareil and as such could empathize with each other in ways that few others could. Jackson was intrigued by Madonna's uncanny ability to continually refashion her image, and by her own shrewd handling of the "suits" who run the entertainment industry. He was also jealous of her success. "She isn't that good," he had complained to an associate after she was named Artist of the Decade in 1989 (at the award ceremonies, Madonna had expressed her gratitude by licking her trophy). "Let's face it: she can't sing. She's just an okay dancer. What does she do best? She knows how to market herself. That's about it."

Jackson had reportedly phoned Warner executives to complain that Madonna didn't deserve her award, pointing out that it made him "look bad." It was then suggested that he ask MTV to name him Video Vanguard Artist of the Decade—a notion that appealed to him. "That'll teach that heifer," he was quoted as saying. Madonna harbored no such resentment of Jackson. She was in awe of his talent, his legendary weirdness, and most of all his business acumen.

Madonna had much to learn from the master. Just five days before the Oscar telecast, Jackson made headlines by signing the most lucrative record contract ever—a pact with Sony, the Japanese conglomerate that had gobbled up CBS Records. The deal, which could net Jackson a cool $1 billion, included six albums, films, TV projects, and his own record label. The announcement was timed to eclipse Jackson's younger sister Janet, whose $50-million deal with Virgin Records was for several days the biggest package in music history.

At the Shrine Auditorium the night of the Academy Awards

ceremony, the biggest names in Hollywood strained to get a good look at Madonna and Jackson as they took their front-row seats on the aisle. They had made certain to coordinate their outfits. Jackson wore gold-tipped cowboy boots, a white sequined jacket, a huge diamond brooch, and for this special occasion, not one but two gloves. Madonna wore a glittering, white, strapless Bob Mackie gown, an ermine wrap, and $20 million worth of diamonds on loan from Harry Winston, courtesy of the late jeweler's son Ron.

Host Billy Crystal introduced Madonna. Referring to the new motion picture ratings category to replace the old X rating, he told the audience, "Here's the NC-17 portion of our program." In her most obvious Marilyn Monroe parody to date, Madonna stood alone in the spotlight, vamping her way through Sondheim's "Sooner or Later." There was a slight glitch; at one point, one of her million-dollar earrings fell off and got hooked on her pearl-encrusted dress. Madonna did not break stride, although she later said she "felt like a retard." (Madonna professed to be "in shock" when her normally uncommunicative father left a message on her answering machine describing her Oscar show performance as "great.")

Madonna appeared jubilant when "Sooner or Later" went on to win the Academy Award as Best Song. There was another surprise in store. When Jeremy Irons won his Best Actor Oscar for playing Claus Von Bulow in *Reversal of Fortune*, he jumped down to the row in front of his and bypassed all the other stars to kiss Madonna. The very-married Irons had a motive for cozying up to Madonna. Behind the scenes, he had already been approached by Disney to play Argentine dictator Juan Perón opposite Madonna in *Evita*.

"I can't believe all this," Madonna whispered to Jackson. "It's so unbelievable. What a night! I'm having such a good time." They were, of course, the focus of everyone's attention. "They almost looked like caricatures," Barbara Walters said of Madonna's two-on-the-aisle act with Jackson. "They seemed untouchable, larger than life."

The new oddest couple moved on after the awards to literary agent Irving "Swifty" Lazar's annual Oscar bash at Spago. Columnist Army Archerd asked Madonna how she got Jackson to attend the party. "Michael's coming out more," she said, smiling. But once inside Spago and away from the cameras, they split up—Madonna to flirt with old flame Warren Beatty (whose date, model Stephanie Seymour, had stood him up), and Jackson to cuddle with Diana Ross. They reunited for one more photo op when the Material Girl and the Gloved One bid their host adieu.

Madonna invited Jackson to a bizarre pajama party at her candlelit Hollywood Hills home. At three A.M., their bodyguards were banished from the premises and according to published reports, they then disrobed in the dim candlelight, each inspecting the other's body with the curiosity of two beings from different planets. Afterward, still nude, they snacked on popcorn and watched old movies on her VCR until daylight.

When asked what two superstars did when they got together, Madonna cracked, "We exchange powder puffs, powder our noses, and compare bank accounts." The pair actually had business to discuss—they were planning a duet for Jackson's next album, *Dangerous*. But Madonna had stipulations. Arguing that "nobody's going to buy a stupid ballad or love duet," she told him, "Look, Michael, if you want to do something with me, you have to be willing to go all the way or I'm not going to do it."

And what did she mean by "all the way"? To begin with, she was determined to change Jackson's look. "I would like to completely redo his whole image," she said, "give him a Caesar—you know, a really short haircut—and I want to get him out of those buckly boots and all that stuff." She told Jackson, "I'd love to turn Jose and Luis [the two gay dancers who taught her to vogue] loose on you for a week." To all this, she claimed, Michael "keeps saying yes."

Before she could begin Jackson's makeover, Madonna faced another public crisis. One week after the Oscar telecast, the Motion Picture Association of America declared that the preview trailer for her R-rated documentary, *Truth or Dare: On the Road, Behind the Scenes and in Bed with Madonna*, was too explicit for even a

PG-13 rating. Director Keshishian reedited the trailer three times to win approval for at least a PG-13, but the MPAA stood firm: the previews could only be shown to audiences attending R-rated and NC-17-rated movies.

Executives at Miramax, the film's distributors, were confident that the film would not alienate most ticket buyers. By way of some innovative market research, they had gone to record stores in the New York area and asked people what they thought of Madonna. "If they said they hated her guts," explained Miramax's Harvey Weinstein, "we said, 'Good, if you'll come to this movie and fill out a card, we'll give you two free tickets to the next Miramax premiere.'"

Surrounded by 150 self-avowed Madonna-haters, Madonna slipped quietly into a screening room at Manhattan's Tribeca Film Center to watch *Truth or Dare*. It was the first time she had seen the film with an audience, and she was prepared for them to hate it. "We knew that Madonna fans would love the movie," Weinstein said. "What we wanted to know before we started marketing was whether anyone else would like it." But an impressive 65 percent of the Madonna-haters in the preview audience had to admit they liked the movie—enough to convince Miramax that it had a potential hit.

For those in search of a thrill, *Truth or Dare* (the title is taken from a game played by Madonna's dancers) was, as one wag put it, a "voyeur's jamboree." It certainly brimmed with delicious detail. In addition to showing some very provocative performance footage, Madonna's backstage tantrums, her cutting comments about Costner and Zsa Zsa Gabor ("She's a *cochon*"), her chats with Beatty, and her stripping for the camera with her father in the next room, *Truth or Dare* also contained footage of Madonna demonstrating oral sex on a bottle of Evian. She orders a dancer to expose himself, watches two men French kiss ("Oh, God. I'm getting a hard-on," she says), cavorts with her naked dancers in bed, recites a "fart poem," describes her sexual games with childhood friend Moira McPharlin (Madonna angered Moira by misspelling her name "McFarland" in the credits), coldly dismisses McPharlin after she begs Madonna to be the godmother of her child ("You little shit," McPharlin fires back once Madonna's back is turned), and exposes her brother Martin as a "crazy" alcoholic. In one scene, as she eats breakfast in her Paris hotel after a sleepless night, crowds cheer outside her window. "Even when I feel like shit," she says matter-of-factly, "they still love me."

The film did not show dancer Luis Camacho complying with Madonna's order to simulate making love to a wall, or Madonna passionately kissing backup singer Niki Harris. Throughout the tour, her little Blond Ambition "family" found it hard to deny Madonna anything. "She radiates power and authority," said Camacho. "She smiles, and those eyes just pierce right through you."

Even the more tender moments in the film had an air of calculated exhibitionism about them. While brother Christopher Ciccone leans against a tree in the background like some minor prop in Madonna's big scene, she lies on her mother's grave and wonders about "what she looks like now. Just a bunch of dust." On screen, much is made of Madonna's benevolent maternalism toward her dancers, but that, too, rings hollow. During one segment, moviegoers were treated to close-ups of Madonna's tonsils as she has her throat examined. "She doesn't want to *live* off-camera," observes Beatty from the sidelines, "much less talk."

Manager Freddy DeMann had pleaded with Madonna to tone down the film; he worried that scenes highlighting the cold, demanding, and temperamental sides of her personality could trigger a backlash. She refused. There were a few last-minute cuts in the film, however, and those were made at Beatty's insistence. He demanded that phone conversations that had been taped without his knowledge be deleted. In these romantic chats, Beatty told Madonna he loved her and called her "honey." Said Madonna: "I thought [the conversations] were really moving and touching and revealing. . . . Ultimately I don't think he respected what I was doing or took it seriously. He just thought I was fucking around, making a home movie."

Madonna's "home movie" gave little insight into the star's true character, but it was juicy enough to become a hit with critics and audiences alike. *Time*'s Richard Corliss called it "epically entertaining—a spectacular dare," while David Ansen of *Newsweek* declared the film to be "fascinating . . . no-holds barred, and provocative! The questions Madonna poses about sexuality, power, and persona make her the most stimulating pop icon around, and the most fun to follow!" *"Truth or Dare,"* concurred Janet Maslin in *The New York Times,* "can be seen as a clever, brazen, spirited self-portrait, an ingeniously contrived extension of Madonna's public personality."

A little more of that public personality was divulged in the pages of the Los Angeles-based gay magazine *The Advocate.* In a two-part interview that tied up what little the film seemed to leave to the imagination, Madonna said that her earliest sexual experiences had been with girls and that she had a strong attraction to the masculine-looking country western songstress k.d. lang. She called Catholicism a "really mean religion," suggested that Jesus and Mary Magdalene "probably got it on," and that straight men needed to be "slapped around. Every straight guy should have a man's tongue in his mouth at least once."

Was she kinky, writer Don Shewey wanted to know. "I am aroused by two men kissing," answered Madonna. "Is that kinky? I am aroused by the idea of a woman making love to me while either a man or another woman watches. Is that kinky?" The *New York Post* thought so. On the newspaper's front page, Madonna was depicted in leather, a cigarette dangling from her mouth. "What a Tramp!" screamed the headline. "Vulgar Madonna is the degenerate Queen of Sleaze."

In two areas at least, Madonna discovered too late that she had gone too far. Michael Jackson was livid about her stated plans to remold him. And when her brother Christopher found out that she had discussed his homosexuality, he exploded. Last-minute calls to *The Advocate* from Madonna's lawyers to remove the sensitive remarks concerning Jackson and Christopher Ciccone arrived after the magazine had gone to press.

In the interview Madonna had cited her special relationship with Christopher—"my brother Christopher's gay, and he and I have always been the closest members of my family"—as one reflection of her affinity for gays. "I'm always working with gay men. . . . To me they're whole human beings, more so than most of the straight men that I know."

She said that she had first realized Christopher was gay when she brought him to ballet class and he met her dance teacher

Christopher Flynn. "I just saw something between them. I can't even tell you exactly what," she said. "But then I thought, 'Oh, I get it. Oh, okay. He likes men, too.' It was this incredible revelation."

The disclosure rocked Christopher, if for no other reason than for the first time it forced their father to confront his son's homosexuality. Relations between father and son were delicate at best, and this issue was far too sensitive ever to have been raised. Most significantly, Christopher now felt bitter and hurt; he accused Madonna of betraying him. It was the first serious rift between the two, and it left Madonna chastened. She apologized, but there was nothing she could do to rectify the situation.

Meanwhile, she and her film continued to reap the benefits of a publicity whirlwind. The whirlwind gained momentum as it spun across the Atlantic to France, where Madonna would preside over a May 13, 1991, showing of *Truth or Dare* at the forty-fourth Cannes International Film Festival. Even her arrival at the Nice airport was tumultuous. Acting on a tip that there were drugs aboard Madonna's flight, authorities conducted a strip search; even her barbells were taken apart to make sure they contained no contraband. Needless to say, they found nothing.

Madonna's mere presence at the festival created an unprecedented frenzy. Hundreds of fans gathered outside various hotels and public buildings solely because of a rumor that she was somewhere in the vicinity. The special midnight out-of-competition screening at the Palais du Festival caused a minor riot as thousands crowded outside just to get a glimpse of Madonna. When she finally climbed out of her limousine behind Alec Keshishian, the throng cheered.

Madonna chose this occasion to unveil a striking new hairstyle —jet black hair piled high atop her head in curls like rolls of celluloid. But plenty of the familiar model remained to thrill the assembled multitude. At first declining to remove her floor-length red satin cape for the clamoring photographers, Madonna waited for precisely the right moment to throw open her wrap, revealing nothing but underwear beneath: a white satin cone bra and a see-through girdle. Turning around, she wiggled her very-visible backside as strobes flashed and cameras clicked.

Police managed to hold back the crowd, but in the process they also barred two hundred legitimate ticket holders in evening dress from getting into the theater. Ironically, by the time *Truth or Dare* began, the star and her entourage were surrounded by empty seats. Yet the most sought-after ticket was not to the screening, but to the lavish party thrown in Madonna's honor. Established stars competed frantically for invitations, now considered to be the definitive indication of who did and did not qualify for the A list at Cannes.

Whoopi Goldberg, a member of the festival jury, was not amused. When food service at a party was delayed for Madonna's arrival, Goldberg blew up. "Madonna, Madonna, Madonna! I am sick of hearing about Madonna," she told the waiter. "I'm hungry and I want to eat *now!*"

Still, *The New York Time*'s Vincent Canby credited Madonna with adding "redeeming lunacy" to the proceedings, pairing her with Japanese director Akira Kurosawa as the real stars at Cannes. "Often lugubrious," Canby wrote, "this year's festival definitely needed the pop star's pizazz and Akira Kurosawa's prestige." Pizazz did not come cheap. In the end, Madonna spent over $1 million for two floors in the Hôtel du Cap, a fleet of limousines, a helicopter, a yacht, and several extravagant parties.

Veteran actor Anthony Quinn was bemused by all the fuss surrounding Madonna, but once the festival was over, he could not wait to leave. He was told that the first-class section was sold out on the next day's flight out of Cannes, but after some finagling, Quinn and his wife managed to secure a pair of tickets.

When the Quinns boarded the flight, however, the rest of the first-class section was empty with the exception of two women sitting a few rows forward and across the aisle. One of the women wore dark glasses and a hood that nearly concealed her face. The Quinns recognized Madonna. She said nothing during the flight, and when she got up to go to the lavatory, she kept her head down and turned away despite the fact that only the Quinns were there to see her. Quinn's wife urged her husband to introduce himself to her, but he declined. "Why should I?" he said. "She'd just say, 'So you're Anthony Quinn? Who the hell cares?' "

As the flight taxied to the terminal, Madonna was given the news that there had been a mixup and no limousine was waiting for her. "What?" she demanded, panicking. "There's no limo? What do you mean there's no *limo?*"

Minutes later, Madonna, still trying to shield her face, was crammed onto a shuttle bus bound for the terminal with the Quinns and half the passengers from coach and business class. One made the mistake of politely asking Madonna for her autograph. "Go fuck yourself!" was her automatic reply.

Upon her triumphant return from Cannes, Madonna was greeted by news that *Truth or Dare* was a box office smash—and that Disney chief Jeffrey Katzenberg had dashed her plans to star in *Evita*. Heeding the call for austerity he had issued in his famous leaked memo, Katzenberg refused to spend more than $25.7 million to bring *Evita* to the screen. That fell nearly $4 million short of what producer Robert Stigwood had budgeted for the film with Madonna as its star. "It's very frustrating," she sighed. "Jeffery Katzenberg is squabbling over pennies. We're all paying for that crazy memo he wrote. If they don't want to spend the money, that's fine. But I don't want to be in a low-budget version of *Evita.*"

Director Penny Marshall (*Awakenings*) and Columbia Pictures felt differently, inviting Madonna to star as Debra Winger's younger sister in the $30-million film *A League of Their Own*, the story of an all-women's baseball team set in the 1940s. Rounding out the cast was Tom Hanks, whom Marshall had directed in *Big*. Madonna plunged into research for the project by making private closed-door visits to several of the game's top players. The inevitable rumors flew after photographers, tipped off by Madonna's own staff, showed up outside her apartment building in New York to shoot Oakland A's outfielder Jose Canseco leaving at five A.M. When a fan heckled Canseco with references to Madonna, the star player, estranged from his wife at the time, raced into the stands and started a fight. Madonna called Canseco the next day to confer on ways to handle the press, and to tell him he deserved a "spanking" for his behavior during their night together.

Faced with Madonna's scene-stealing antics even before shooting began, Debra Winger pulled out of the picture. Winger might have stayed on if Madonna had not publicly slammed her performance in the film version of *The Sheltering Sky*. "Debra was so wrong," she said of Winger's portrayal of Kit Moresby. "Oh, it was so wrong, so wrong. It was so unsexy. It was horrible."

A month before shooting was to begin in Chicago and parts of Indiana, Academy Award–winner Geena Davis stepped in to take Winger's place. Madonna was also signed to star in another female buddy picture, *Leda and Swan*, but it was put on the back burner due to the arrival of costar Demi Moore's second baby by actor Bruce Willis. Still Madonna was not surprised that Winger viewed her as something other than a gifted actress. Calling her own career so far "a failure," Madonna only blamed herself. "I haven't honored or respected a movie career the way I should have. I didn't approach it the way I approached my music career."

In June of 1991, another pop diva who had successfully made the transition to film did not mince words when it came to Madonna. "No one knows how to work this business like she does," Cher conceded to a television interviewer, "but there's something about her that I don't like . . . She came to my house a couple of times and she was so mean to everybody. She could afford to be a little more magnanimous and a little less of a cunt." Determined to keep stoking the fires of controversy, Madonna phoned in to the nationally televised talk show "Geraldo" and offered to appear on the program if host Geraldo Rivera would "make out" with one of the show's male guests, rock journalist Kurt Loder. The two men respectfully declined.

Irrefutably, Madonna was the single most powerful woman in the multibillion-dollar music industry. Now that Michael Jackson had sealed a $1 billion deal with Sony, she wondered what she was worth to her employers. That was the question Madonna and her high council of advisers put directly to Time Warner chairman Steven Ross and Warner Brothers Records head Mo Austin. In private meetings with Ross and Austin, Madonna outlined a plan for her own media company that would embrace not only records but also movies, television, video, and concerts. Her eventual slice of the revenue pie: a rumored $700 million.

328

Her private life, by comparison, was in shambles. She still wanted to be a mother, but there was no serious candidate for fatherhood on the immediate horizon ("As a mother, I'd be a stern taskmaster—a real disciplinarian"). Obsessed with the birth of a baby girl to the unmarried Sean Penn and Robin Wright in April, Madonna showered the couple with enough baby and nursery gifts to unnerve Wright. Her note of congratulations to Penn read, "Silly boy, if you'd given me a baby, we'd still be together."

Madonna's public declarations of affection for her ex-husband were now frequent and impassioned. When asked in *Truth or Dare* to name the love of her life, she did not hesitate to answer: "Sean." It was even suggested that Madonna's spectacular invasion of Cannes was merely intended to impress Penn, who was at the festival with Wright and their daughter Dylan promoting his new film, *Indian Runner.*

At the behest of her friend, record mogul David Geffen, Madonna had begun seeing a woman psychiatrist. "Everything I do is measured by what I think her reaction will be," she told fellow patient Carrie Fisher. "I'm so worried about impressing her . . . And so far she's disapproved of everything I've done since I've started seeing her. That's why I haven't gone lately."

Madonna had reason to return to her analyst's couch, however, when actress Annette Bening announced she was bowing out of the coveted Cat Woman role in the much-anticipated *Batman* sequel to give birth to Warren Beatty's baby. "First Sean went off and fathered another woman's child, and now Warren," observed a friend. "It left her feeling hurt and confused." By August of 1991, Madonna had forgiven Tony Ward and accepted him back into the fold. Yet, as she was negotiating to buy an $8-million, ten-thousand-square-foot, twenty-one-room villa near Ronald Reagan's estate in Bel Air, she did not appear ready to commit herself wholly to one man.

More obsessed than ever with her career, Madonna spent sleepless nights analyzing the mistakes of the day and plotting every minute of tomorrow's schedule. "I'm anal retentive," she said. "I'm a workaholic. I have insomnia. And I'm a control freak. That's why I'm not married. Who could stand me?"

Epilogue

"I grew up saying I wanted to be
somebody. I tried to look different,
tried to be different. You get what
you've been searching for all those
years, and then you spend the rest of
your life trying to hide."

There has never been anyone like her. On top of the show business Everest since 1984, Madonna is, quite simply, the most famous woman in the world today. She is not just the planet's number one female pop star with over 50 million albums sold and more consecutive top hit singles than The Beatles, but more: a self-made icon. She has held the public's attention by repeatedly shocking and offending it. "Hate this!" seems to be her credo, as she smashes one taboo after another. Like a stinging slap in the face from an angry lover, Madonna is often painful to take but also impossible to ignore.

As crassly transparent as she often seems, Madonna and simplicity are antithetical. She is, in truth, a Gordian knot of contradictions: the straight-A student from an affluent Midwestern suburb who explodes on the music scene as streetwise urban vixen; the high school cheerleader who ridicules traditional American values; the thrift-shop reject who becomes the single greatest influence on fashion; the feminist who flaunts her body outrageously, publicly declares she likes to be spanked during sex, chains herself to a bed, and appears to defend teenage motherhood; the party animal who calls herself "a certifiable workaholic"; the product of a devout Catholic upbringing who says she respects the rituals and sacraments of her religion while blatantly exploiting them; the self-described daddy's girl who respects her father yet does everything she can to embarrass him; the outspoken rebel whose financial acumen is so acute that "NBC Nightly News" deemed her a "growth industry" and no less an authority than *Forbes* magazine proclaimed her "the smartest businesswoman in America." (There is ample evidence to support this. In 1991, it was estimated that she would earn over $65 million.) Most disturbingly, she is the safe sex proponent whose own promiscuous lifestyle and erotically charged image conveys a message to impressionable wannabes that can be charitably described as "mixed."

She is the very apotheosis of unabashed self-promotion, over-exposed to the hilt. Yet the public craves more. So Madonna shamelessly packages and repackages herself as we wait eagerly for the next incarnation. From Boy Toy to Material Girl to negligee-clad Catholic penitent to platinum bombshell, she has kept us wondering who's that girl—or at least who will she be next.

Madonna is among those who wonder why we care so much. She experiences momentary flashes of self-doubt, but quickly banishes them lest the world at large catch on. The empress may indeed have no clothes, but in the past Madonna has managed to turn even that into an asset.

Judging by the number of respected colleges and universities that now offer classes on Madonna, her impact on our culture is irrefutable. At Harvard, a course on Madonna is offered as part of the university's Women in Popular Culture series. She is also the subject of serious study at the University of Massachusetts, the University of California, Loyola University, the State University of New York, Florida State University, and dozens of other institutions of higher learning.

Certainly, Madonna's influence far transcends her music and her MTV persona. By exploiting crucifixes, rosaries, stigmata, votive candles, and other fragments of Catholic imagery, she has provoked rage but also questions regarding the impact of religion on our lives. Her tongue-in-cheek "hey, sailor" vixen act incorporates elements of every flirt from Betty Boop and Mae West to Monroe and Bardot—a throwback to the days when the main power women exerted over men was sexual. It infuriates hard-line feminists, but makes the valid point that if a woman chose to be a tease, it was, after all, *her* choice.

Equally controversial are Madonna's ceaseless efforts at obliterating sexual stereotypes. By flirting with bisexuality, multiple partners, cross-dressing, and even sadomasochism, she blurs the line between male and female. She calls it "gender-free sex," because "gender-free sex doesn't limit you. Whether you're a man or a woman, it gives you freedom to dominate or be submissive. It permits a man to dress feminine, a woman masculine. It's important to express different sides of yourself."

The psychological motivations for Madonna's hell-raising antics and chameleonlike changes are deeply rooted in the tragic early death of her mother and the subsequent competition with her stepmother and siblings for her father's attention. This is the pivotal relationship in Madonna's life. She is what Tony Ciccone made her. She concedes, "I still have my father's philosophies ingrained in my brain." After she broke away to find success on her own terms, their relationship seesawed between love and resentment. As recently as the summer of 1991, Madonna claimed that her father has never acknowledged her phenomenal accomplishments, for fear of angering her envious sisters and brothers. When she visits home for the holidays, no special preparations are made: the superstar still sleeps in a sleeping bag on the living room floor.

As for the man she still described in 1991 as "the love of my life," Sean Penn, much remains unexplained about their near-fatal attraction for one another. She claimed that his mind and his talent were what first drew her to Penn. But it is more likely that she was lured by the sense of danger that swirled around the volatile young actor. In her public and her private lives, she has always made the conscious choice to live on the edge—and suffer the consequences.

Where is all this likely to take Madonna? What she has done so far has been completely overshadowed by who she is, and therein lies a major problem for her future. She has focused not on her work, but on herself. Personality and image are important, of course. But in terms of longevity, the public often stays true to creative artists but falls out of love with caricatures. Unlike Katharine Hepburn, Bette Davis, or even the more contemporary likes of Barbra Streisand, Bette Midler, and Meryl Streep, Madonna has built her career almost entirely on her own evolving persona, not on her versatility or creativity as an actress. How long she remains on top depends on how quickly she can establish a film career and make the transition from curiosity to craftsman.

Years after she began parodying Monroe in her "Material Girl" video, Madonna still finds new ways to pay homage to the ill-fated sex goddess. She spends almost as much time protesting too much about the similarities. I'm not Marilyn, she has said again and again. I love my life, I'm in control, I'm not a victim. And so far at least, that seems to be true—she is Marilyn without martyrdom.

Still, there are disturbing parallels between history's two most famous women. Like Monroe, Madonna has known tragedy and personal heartache—including the early death of her mother, several messy affairs, abortions, a hellish marriage to a man she still claims to love, and the loss of many of her closest friends to AIDS. Also like Monroe, she has begun to show serious signs of strain from what amounts to constant hounding by fans and the press.

By the time she reached her thirties—the age Madonna is now —Monroe had come to the realization that, in trading solely on her smoldering sexuality, she had made a grievous error. At thirty-five, she tried to rectify her mistake, and there was an endearing sweetness and true acting talent that shone through her last film performances. But it was too little too late. Time may be running out for Madonna, too, unless she can admit to herself that what she does onstage in her thirties might seem grotesquely inappropriate for a woman in her fifties.

Madonna once disingenuously described losing her virginity as "a career move." But for icons such as Monroe, James Dean, and Elvis Presley, untimely death has been the ultimate career move. It is not a move Madonna plans to make, although unsubstantiated rumors abound. One of the more intriguing reports is that she has bought the crypt next to Monroe's so that they can spend eternity side by side.

Today, however, she is very much alive and millions pray at the altar of Madonna, Our Lady of Perpetual Promotion. She is ubiquitous, part of the furniture of our lives. More than merely reflecting her times, Madonna is a virtual fun-house hall of mirrors, casting back distorted and fragmented images that both dazzle and disturb. In her film *Truth or Dare*, she says, "I know I'm not the best singer. I know I'm not the best dancer. But I'm not interested in that. I'm interested in pushing people's buttons."

Believe it.

Sources and Chapter Notes

THE FOLLOWING CHAPTER NOTES are designed to give a general view of the sources drawn upon in preparing the book, but are by no means all-inclusive. The author has respected the wishes of many interview subjects not to be named here and accordingly has not listed them here or elsewhere in the text.

CHAPTER 1

Interviews include Erica Bell, Melinda Cooper, Christopher Flynn, Susan Seidelman, Marcus Leatherdale, Maripol, Tony Brenna, Johnny Dynell, and Camille Barbone. Accounts of the wedding also appeared in numerous newspapers and magazines, including *Time*, *Newsweek*, and *People*, the *Los Angeles Times*, *New York Times*, *Washington Post*, *New York Post*, the New York *Daily News*, the *Miami Herald*, and the *Boston Globe*.

"It was the right mixture": Andy Warhol, *The Andy Warhol Diaries*, edited by Pat Hackett, p. 670.

CHAPTER 2

Interviews include Nancy Ryan Mitchell, Moira McPharlin Messana, Elsie Fortin, Wanda McPharlin, Sarah Tarkas, Ann Sauve, Walter Pugni.

Accounts of Madonna's Italian stop on her Who's That Girl tour appear in the Rome *Republica*, *The New York Times*, the *Washington Post*, the New York *Daily News*, the *Bay City Times*, *People*, *Time*, *New York Post*, the *Boston Herald*, the *Miami Herald*, 30 *Giorni*, *Il Tempo*.

Articles include "Madonna" by Harry Dean Stanton, *Interview* magazine, December 1985; "Madonna Rocks the Land" by John Skow and "Madonna on Madonna" by Denise Worrell, *Time*, May 27, 1985; "Totally Outrageous" by Richard Price, *USA Weekend*, June 8–10, 1990; "Spanking New Madonna" by Brian D. Johnson, *Maclean's*, June 18, 1990.

CHAPTERS 3–5

Interviews include Christopher Flynn, Lori Jahns, Nancy Ryan Mitchell, Carol Belanger, Mary Conley Belote, Karen Craven, Beverly Gibson, Susan Crimp, Erica Bell, Dr. Abbie Salmi, Janice Galloway, Elsie Fortin.

Among the articles consulted: "Maybe She's Good" by Laura Fissinger, *Record*, March 1985; "Madonna" by Carl Arrington, *People*, March 11, 1985; "True Confessions" by Carrie Fisher, *Rolling Stone*, June 27, 1991; "I Was Her First Lover" by Russell Long, the *Sunday Mirror*, July 22, 1990; "An Affair to Remember" by Robert Hofler, *Life*, December 1986; *The New Republic*, August 26, 1985; "Madonna" by G. Carpozi, Jr., *Oui*, January 1988. "Madonna Confesses," *Spin*, May 1985.

CHAPTERS 6–8

Interviews include Pearl Lang, Martha Graham, Martin Schreiber, Stephen Lewicki, Camille Barbone, Futura 2000, Ed Steinberg, Cranston Jones, Erica Bell, Patrick Hernandez, Roberta Fineberg, Gregory Camillucci, Christopher Flynn, Steve Newman, Michael Musto.

Articles include "Madonna" by Glenn Albin, *Interview*, April 1984; "Madonna Goes All the Way" by Christopher Connelly, *Rolling Stone*, November 22, 1984; "Madonna" by M. Stanley, *Genesis*, June 1985; "Madonna Crosses the Borderline to Stardom" by Martin Porter and Steven Schwartz, the *New York Post*, March 2, 1985; "Madonna," the *Village Voice*, June 18, 1985; "Madonna: Her New Era" by Will Slattery, *Mc*-

Call's, September 1988; "Madonna's Men" by Olivier Cachin, *Le Matin*, August 28, 1987; "A Madonna Complex" by Bobbie Stein, New York *Daily News Magazine*, September 29, 1985; "Madonna, the Power and the Glory" by Nick Tosches, *Penthouse*, September 1985.

CHAPTERS 9 AND 10

For these chapters, the author drew on conversations with Erica Bell, Johnny Dynell, ChiChi Valente, Mark Kamins, Ed Steinberg, Michael Rosenblatt, Howie Montaug, Lenny McGurr, Bobby Martinez, David Switzer, Marcus Leatherdale, Patricia Lawford, Lee Wohlfert, Karen Bahari.

For biographical material on Jean-Michel Basquiat, the author consulted "SAMO is Dead" by Phoebe Hoban, *New York* magazine, September 26, 1988. Books include *Lucky Star* by Michael McKenzie, Contemporary Books, 1985, and *Hit Men* by Frederick Dannen, Vintage Press.

CHAPTERS 11 AND 12

Interviews include Susan Seidelman, Philippe Manoeuvre, Mark Kamins, Erica Bell, Mark Franceschini, Guy Andressano, Jay Cashman, Johnny Dynell, Steve Newman, Melinda Cooper, Patrick McMullen, Bobby Martinez, Bruno Bayon, Philippe Ox.

Articles include "Lucky Stars" by Fred Schruers, *Rolling Stone*, May 9, 1985; "Rock's New Women" by Jim Miller, *Newsweek*, March 4, 1985; "Madonna Weds Sean" by Roger Wolmuth, *People*, September 2, 1985; "Madonna" by Chris Chase, *Cosmopolitan*, July 1987; "Hollywood Sizzle" by James McBride, *People*, May 13, 1985; "She Works Hard for the Money" by Christopher Connelly, *Chicago Sun-Times*, April 28, 1985; "Material Rewards" by Fred Schruers, *Daily News Magazine*, June 2, 1985; "The Virgin and the Dynamo" by Barry Walters, the *Village Voice*, June 18, 1985; reviews of *Desperately Seeking Susan* by Pauline Kael (*The New Yorker*, April 22, 1985), David Denby in *New York* magazine (April 22, 1985), also reviews of the film from *The New York Times*, *Washington Post*, *Los Angeles Times*, *Boston Globe*, *Chicago Tribune*, and other publications.

CHAPTERS 13 AND 14

Among those interviewed: Anthony Savignano, Mark Kamins, Erica Bell, Susan Crimp, Russell Turiak, Johnny Dynell, Stephen Lewicki, Valerie, Ed Steinberg, Melinda Cooper, Yoshiro Nakamura, David McNamara, Karen Bahari.

Articles include "Virgin Territory" by Joel D. Schwartz, *The New Republic*, August 26, 1985; "Madonna" by Harry Dean Stanton, *Interview*, December 1985; "Madonna Confesses," *Spin*, May 1985; "Madonna: The X-Rated Interview" by Don Shewey, *The Advocate*, May 7, 1991; "Madonna" by Chris Chase, *Cosmopolitan*, July 1987; "Can't Stop the Girl" by Fred Schruers, *Rolling Stone*, June 5, 1986. "Covering Sean and Madonna in Macao Leaves One Reporter with a Penn in the Neck," *People*, February 10, 1986; "How Madonna Dealt with a Hostile Press" by John Peel, *The Observer*, March 9, 1986; "It's Her Party" by Vince Aletti, the *Village Voice*, July 22, 1986; "Madonna's New Beat Is a Hit, But the Message Rankles" by Georgia Dullea, *The New York Times*, September 18, 1986.

CHAPTERS 15 AND 16

Interviews include Christopher Flynn, Johnny Dynell, ChiChi Valente, Erica Bell, Camille Barbone, Monica Stevens, Melinda Cooper, Lee Wohlfert, Karen Bahari, Sanae Yamazake, Elsie Fortin, N. Ryan, Yoshiro Nakamura, Russell Turiak.

Articles include "Madonna Goes Heavy on Heart" by Stephen Holden, *The New York Times*, June 29, 1986; "Madonna in the Missionary Position" by Harry Dean Stanton, *Le Matin*, October 29, 1986; "Classic Madonna" by Michael Gross, *Vanity Fair*, December 1986; "Madonna in Japan, Rock Capital of Asia" by Stephen Williams, *Newsday*, June 17, 1987; "Hotter than Ever" by Leslie Van Buskirk, *Us*, August 10, 1987; "Madonna and Me" by Nick Kamen, the London *Daily Mirror*, 1987; "How's That Girl?" by Fred Schruers, *Us*, September 7, 1987; "Madonna" by Lynn Phillips, *American Film*, July/August 1987; "That Fabulous Couple: Madonna and the Camera" by Robert Hofler, *Life*, December 1986; "Sean Penn Talks About Life with Madonna," *Bunte*, October 1, 1987; "In Search of Madonna's Persona" by Vincent Canby, *The New York Times*, August 23, 1987; "Don't Fence Me In" by Gene Siskel," the *Chicago Tribune*, August 5, 1987; "Madonna's Triumph" by François Deletraz, *Figaro*, September 5, 1987; "Madonna: An American in Paris" by Marie Guichoux, *Liberation*, August 30, 1987; "Jacques

Chirac Is Charmed by Madonna," *Figaro*, August 29, 1987; "Chirac Says 'Oui' to Madonna and Angers a Local Mayor" by Steven Greenhouse, *The New York Times*, August 29, 1989; "Madonna Paris Gig Saved by Chirac," *Variety*, September 2, 1987.

BBC interview with Simon Bates, December 9, 1986.

CHAPTERS 17 AND 18

Interviews include Erica Bell, Melinda Cooper, John Marion, Robert Mosconi, Anthony Savignano, Stephanie Mansfield.

Articles include "A Director's Race with AIDS Ends Before His Movie Opens" by Aljean Harmetz, *The New York Times*, November 1, 1989; "*Speed-the-Plow* Stars Talk Things Over" by Mervyn Rothstein, *The New York Times*, May 16, 1988; "Just Whose Play Is It, Anyway?" by Patricia O'Haire, New York *Daily News*, April 24, 1988; "White Heat" by Kevin Sessums, *Vanity Fair*, April 1990; "Tracymania" by David Ansen, *Newsweek*, June 25, 1990; "Madonna Drops Assault Charges Against Sean" by Jack Schermerhorn, *New York Post*; "Madonna Holds Court" by Vicki Woods, *Vogue*, May 1989; "The Top 100 Collectors," *Art & Antiques* magazine, March 1991.

Appearance with Sandra Bernhard on "Late Night with David Letterman," NBC, July 2, 1988.

CHAPTERS 19 AND 20.

Interviews include Christopher Flynn, Bobby Martinez, ChiChi Valente, Sam Frank, Roberta Fineberg, Philippe Ox, Jasmine Boyd, Chuck Garrelick, Erica Bell, Peter Newcomb, John Caglione.

Among the articles consulted: "Without a Prayer," Associated Press, April 5, 1989; "Madonna's True Confessions" by J. D. Considine, *Rolling Stone*, April 6, 1989; "The Power of Prayer" by Wayne Robins, *Newsday*, March 19, 1989; "Madonna!" by Glenn O'Brien, *Interview*, June 1990; "White Heat" by Kevin Sessums, *Vanity Fair*, April 1990; "Arsenio Hall Talks" by Laura B. Randolph, *Ebony*, December 1990; " 'If You're Going to Reveal Yourself, REVEAL YOURSELF!' " by Adrian Deevoy, June 13, 1991.

SOURCES AND CHAPTER NOTES

CHAPTERS 21 AND 22

Interviews include Mark Kamins, Melinda Cooper, James Randall, Erica Bell, Tony Brenna, Jeanette Peterson, Emily Schneider, Peter Newcomb, Rosemary McClure.

Among the articles consulted: "America's Smartest Businesswoman?" by Matthew Schifrin with Peter Newcomb, *Forbes*, October 1, 1990; "The Saint, the Slut, the Sensation" by Don Shewey, *The Advocate*, May 7, 1991; "The Misfit" by Lynn Hirschberg, April 1990; "Notorious" by Patrick Goldstein, *Los Angeles Times*, May 5, 1991.

"Nightline" interview with Forrest Sawyer, December 3, 1990.

Acknowledgments

IN THE COURSE OF PREPARING any comprehensive biography, a tremendous amount of research is necessary, and this was especially true in the case of *Madonna—Unauthorized*. Even more time was spent interviewing friends, family members, former teachers, classmates, coworkers, neighbors, acquaintances, employers, employees, mentors, protégés and lovers. Some sources asked not to be named in the book, and others who went on the record on certain matters asked not to be identified as the source for others. I respected their wishes.

On several occasions I telephoned Madonna and faxed letters to her requesting an interview. Through her ubiquitous publicist, Liz Rosenberg, she declined. Many months later, Rosenberg told New York *Daily News* columnist Richard Johnson that Madonna had ordered her friends not to speak to me. By that time, many of them already had, while others were eager to talk, orders or no.

More than any single individual, my editor, Fred Hills, was responsible for this book. It was Fred who conceived the idea for the first serious biography of Madonna, and without his passionate commitment and editorial vision *Madonna—Unauthorized* would not have been possible. I owe an additional debt of gratitude to Fred's associate, Burton Beals, for helping to fine-tune the manuscript, and to Fred's assistant, Daphne Bien.

I am also grateful to my agent Ellen Levine, and to her associates Diana Finch and Anne Dubboison in New York, and to Lisa Eveleigh of AP Watt Ltd. in London, as well as to my British editor, Louise Haines. For their unflagging support to *Madonna—Unauthorized*, my thanks to the entire Simon & Schuster family —particularly Jack McKeown, Frank Metz, Eve Metz, Marcella Berger, Emily Remes, Leslie Ellen, Victoria Mayer, Lisa Petrusky, and my old friend Sandy Bodner.

My wife, Valerie, who gave birth to our daughter Kelly midway through the gestation of this book, buoyed my spirits with her patience and humor—as did Kelly's big sister, Kate.

Hundreds of people cooperated in the writing of this book. For many, this was the first time they had agreed to talk for publication. While all my sources are not listed here, I am deeply grateful to each and every person who took the time to assist me. My special thanks to: Jeanette Andersen, Nancy Ryan Mitchell, Erica Bell, Mark Kamins, Camille Barbone, Susan Seidelman, the late Christopher Flynn, Elsie Fortin, Stephen Jon Lewicki, Melinda Cooper, Pearl Lang, Ed Steinberg, Johnny Dynell, ChiChi Valente, Steve Newman, Lori Sargent Jahns, Moira McPharlin, Marcus Leatherdale, Martin Schreiber, Karen Bahari, Patrick Hernandez, Bobby Martinez, Carol Belanger, Mary Conley Belote, Karen Craven, David Switzer, Beverly Gibson, Gregory Camillucci, Maripol, Roberta Fineberg, Sam Frank, Futura 2000, Wendy Leigh, Janice Galloway, Rosemary McClure, Russell Turiak, Patrick McMullen, Patricia Lawford, Philippe Ox, Anthony Savignano, Steven Karten, Susan Crimp, Guy Andressano, Patricia Burstein, Dr. Emily Schneider, Tony Brenna, Mary Vespa, Philippe Manoeuvre, Michael Musto, Joyce Wansley, Stephanie Mansfield, Dr. Abbie Salmi, Lee Wohlfert, Ann Sauve, Sharon Dargay, Sharon Churcher, Cyndie Finkle, Laurie Putnam, Sarah Takas, Peter Newcomb, Cathy Cesario Tardosky, Andie Miller; the staffs of the Bay City *Times*, the Rochester *Eccentric*, West Middle School, Rochester Adams High School; the Bay City, Detroit, Pontiac, and Rochester, Michigan, public libraries; the Lincoln Center Library for the Performing Arts; the New York Public Library; the Hartford, Woodbury, Watertown, Southbury, New Milford, Middlebury, and Danbury, Connecticut public libraries; the Silas Bronson Library; the Los Angeles Public Library; Ralph DeBlasio, Warner, the Academy of Motion Picture Arts and Sciences, Harvard University, Loyola University, ASCAP, MTV, Time Warner, Gita Mehta, Miramax, AMFAR, the organizers of the Cannes Film Festival, the Alvin Ailey American Dance Theater, Sarah Takas, the *Village Voice*, Graphictype, Sygma, the Gamma Liaison Network, Pictorial Parade, Sharon Dargay, the Bettmann Archives, Ron Galella, Wide World, the Associated Press, the Memory Shop, Movie Star News, Photoreporters, DMI, and John Caglione.

Index

343

INDEX

INDEX

INDEX

INDEX

INDEX

Photo Credits